D0437736

THE
UNIVERSITY

THE UNIVERSITY

The
Anatomy of Academe

MURRAY G. ROSS

McGRAW-HILL BOOK COMPANY
New York   St. Louis   San Francisco
Düsseldorf   London   Mexico   Montreal   New Delhi
Panama   Paris   São Paulo
Singapore   Sydney   Tokyo   Toronto

Library of Congress Cataloging in Publication Data
Ross, Murray G
  The university.
  Bibliography: p.
  Includes index.
    1. Universities and colleges—United States—History.
    2. Universities and colleges—Great Britain—History.
    3. Universities and colleges—Canada—History. I. Title.
LA227.3.R66   378.1'009   75-43957
ISBN 0-07-053876-x

 234567890 BPBP 709876

**The editors for this book were Nancy Frank, Cheryl Love, and
Michael Hennelly, the designer was Elaine Gongora, and the
production supervisor was Milton Heiberg. It was set in Times
Roman with display lines in Old English by Rumford Press, Inc.**

Printed and bound by Book Press.

To
Janet and Jennifer,
two staunch supporters

CONTENTS

PREFACE

This is a book for those who have a general interest in the growth and development of the university, the problems and issues it faces, the future it confronts.

There have been many books written about the university. Most of these have tended to focus on and analyze one problem (e.g., academic freedom) or one group (e.g., professors) or one period of time (e.g., the medieval years) or one system (e.g., California). The reader looks in vain for a single volume that will inform him about how the university evolved, its customs and traditions, its recent difficulties, its current dilemmas. I have tried in this book to present a brief but comprehensive picture of the university as a whole, but at the same time to highlight those critical issues that emerged in 1975 and on the resolution of which the future of the university depends.

This is not a history of the university, although, of course, historical materials are used. Nor is it strictly a sociological study of the university, although we draw upon some sociological insights to sharpen our analysis. The aim is less pretentious. It is simply to give an account of the development of the university in the terms suggested above.

Except for brief references to the medieval university, my analysis is concerned with developments in Canada, England, and the United States. Apart from the fact that these are the universities I know best, there is some value, I believe, in selecting three English-speaking countries with many similar roots and traditions but with differences sufficiently great to make comparisons interesting and illuminating. What is perhaps as remarkable as the different systems that evolved in these countries is the gradual reduction of these differences as all universities reacted to similar forces in the postwar world and faced similar problems in respect of goals, governance, academic freedom, and state control. There is one small problem in this respect: I deal descriptively with the universities in England, but some of the data I use apply to Great Britain and in some cases to the United Kingdom as a whole. I have indicated when this is the case.

I have used quotations and notes perhaps more frequently than is the general practice in a book of this kind. There are reasons why this is so. I assume that this may be the only book on universities with which many readers will have contact, and I would like them to have some direct knowledge of the great people who have done original studies and written about the universities: historians like Hastings Rashdall, H. C. Maxwell Lyte, C. E. Mallett, W. H. G. Armytage, Laurence R. Veysey, Richard Hofstadter, and Walter P. Metzger; social scientists like Daniel Bell, Joseph Ben-David, A. H. Halsey, Seymour Lipset, Richard Nisbet, David Riesman, Edward Shils, and Martin Trow; and analysts such as Sir Eric Ashby, Clark Kerr, Bruce Truscot, to name but a few. Further, it is important in some cases that readers see the precise words of a student, a university president, or a historic statement made by a faculty group rather than the author's interpretation of them. In one sense this book is close to being "a reader" on the university but there is far too much of the author's own words and analysis to permit such a designation.

The book is divided into four parts. The first deals with the major thrust of the universities over an 800 year period: the continuity, adjustments, and changes over the centuries; the interaction of society and the university. This is provided as background for the examination of more specific issues—an attempt to show the whole before its parts are examined.

The second part deals with students and teachers, their changing roles, and their changing relationship to each other through the years and the revolt of the sixties, which affected their roles and the university profoundly. The third part of the book deals with four critical issues: goals, governance, academic freedom, the university and the state. There are other current issues but none as important as these in the modern university. The fourth part summarizes briefly the character of the university as it emerged in the 1970's, and attempts to identify the forces that will shape the university in the future.

In each chapter, topics are placed in some historical perspective, which makes for some repetition. I have, however, done this deliberately, believing that some readers, using the book as a reference for a particular topic, will consult only one or two chapters for that purpose. I am deeply prejudiced about the importance of understanding the background of our current problems and thus err on the side of describing the context in which these problems arose.

As is inevitable in a work of this kind, I am indebted to many people. I have tried to indicate throughout the authors whose work stimulated my own. I am especially grateful to Professor Robin Harris, who permitted me to read his substantial manuscript on the history of Canadian universities. My manuscript was read by Dr. Thomas O'Connell, Professor John Conway, Professor John O'Neill, Dr. McCormack Smyth, and by Dr. R. E. G. Davis, all of whom made useful comments. Finally I am appreciative of the patience and skill of Mrs. Linda Fudge and Mrs. Carol Pratap, who built up large files of relevant material and who typed the draft and final edition of my manuscript.

THE
UNIVERSITY

part one

THE
BACKGROUND

chapter one

THE
BEGINNING

"Tradition without revolution is empty; but revolution without tradition is blind." [1] This is to say that the institution which continues to live on its past successes and practices without regard to the changing social situation of which it is a part will probably find itself without a relevant purpose, without vitality, and without usefulness to any but its most devoted members. On the other hand, to force change in an institution without regard to past experiences—both its successes and its failures—without recognition of the subtleties of past adjustments, without sensitivity to tradition, is to ignore the need for internal coherence and orderly creative growth. [2]

How to go forward between these two extremes is indeed the central issue of the university today. On the one hand there are traditions that over the centuries have proven to be useful and effective and are supported by those who find them both sensible and comfortable. On the other hand there are growing pressures from various constituencies for radical changes which can be made only by ignoring or eliminating many traditional university practices. To follow either course exclusively is dangerous: one leads to gradual decay, the other to chaos. If the university is to survive, a means must be found of accommodating these divergent views.

This is no simple task, for it is not to be resolved by having rational man meet to develop a variety of easy compromises. Great social forces have profoundly affected the role, the

3

status, the interests of those in the universities—students, professors, administrators. A vast shift in social values and concerns has altered society's expectations of what the university must do if it is to merit support. The need is to retain some continuity in a period when radical change seems inevitable.

The university has survived because it has provided for (1) man's insatiable desire to know and (2) society's need for advanced knowledge and skilled manpower. These are and will continue to be valid services. But within this framework who is to be served, what is to be taught, how the university is to be governed and financed, what meaning and relevance there is and will be for such hallowed university terms as "community," "freedom," "objectivity," "neutrality," and "autonomy," are all questions now vigorously debated. The traditional versus revolutionary forces focus on them. This book will seek to put these issues into context with the hope that they may perhaps be better understood and thereby more readily resolved.

A study of the university is inevitably a study of change and resistance to change, of the structures and forms that facilitate each, of the interaction of the institution and society in ways that facilitate or that inhibit new developments. Presented in brief is a sweeping analysis of the growth of the university since its beginning. Four stages in its evolution emerge as focal: (1) the medieval university, (2) the university from 1500 to 1850, (3) the 1850-to-1950 period of growth, and (4) the university from 1950 to 1975. This overview of the historical and sociological aspects of university growth is essential as background for any sound understanding of the modern university and the problems it confronts.

Medieval Universities

The university, as we know it, evolved in the Middle Ages in Europe. There were other, more ancient forms of higher learning in China, in India, and in the Islamic world. But of the various types that emerged, only the university grew, adapted itself to new conditions, survived, and flourished.[3] The university is now among the oldest of institutions in

Western society. Its durability and its success relate, in part at least, to the mission, the organization, the ethos that evolved in the early European universities some eight hundred years ago.

In some respects the Middle Ages did not provide the most fertile soil for the growth of universities. Elements of the Dark Ages—violence, superstition, license, barbarism—remained deeply embedded in European society.

But there were other conditions that favored the growth of higher learning. One was economic development; all material indexes moved upward from the eleventh century on. Economic development was accompanied by the growth of cities, the spread of commerce, the creation of a new social class of men involved in trade and commerce, increased wealth and increased leisure.[4] A new society was emerging which required trained administrators, lawyers, physicians, theologians. These needs called for a higher learning than was provided by the many cathedral schools which flourished in the eleventh century. A form of postsecondary education was required, and the universities emerged to meet this need. In these early centuries something occurred which approximated an explosion of knowledge—not as dramatic as in the modern day but withal of great import in medieval times—the transmission of medical knowledge from Arabia, the rediscovery of Roman law, and the translation of Aristotelian logic. This new knowledge was to stimulate and nourish men's natural interest in learning and to provide new content and purpose for the early universities. The changing economic, social, and intellectual climate made the creation of universities possible and indeed necessary.

The medieval university did not emerge full-blown as a university; rather it began with little groups of students gathered around a man of learning, grew, and became a formal organization only gradually, even as the society in which it evolved and developed became richer and more complex.

For the earliest Universities of Europe there are no single founders, no certain dates to be assigned. As the darker ages passed away and men's thoughts turned to learning once again, searching for a rule of right even in days of violent wrongdoing, searching for reasons to satisfy the doubter even in days when authority and dogma were supreme, the power of the teacher, never altogether lost, revived. Students gathered with strange enthusiasm, and if the records may be trusted in surprising numbers, wherever famous teachers made a school, travelling up from lonely districts, voyaging from distant countries, amid the daily perils of medieval life. The chief of these resorts sprang into European fame. A *Studium Generale,* where students from all parts assembled, began to be something more than a vague term. The *Universitas,* the whole body of Masters or students there collected, began to have something like a corporate existence, to adopt customs, to claim privileges, to form an organization of its own.[5]

The early universities were relatively informal, unstructured, and spontaneous organizations. Individual teachers and students associated, joined forces, and read and studied together. Only gradually did these "gatherings" become structured and grow into formal organizations which at some uncertain date were incorporated and recognized as universities.[6] The first universities were probably those of Bologna, Paris, Salerno, Oxford, and Cambridge, formally organized in that order[7] and all begun in the late eleventh or early twelfth century. By the year 1500 there were seventy such institutions in Europe.[8] These are the universities from which the modern university derives its most important heritage.

It is often said that these early universities were centers of pure scholarship and humanistic study, by which it is usually meant that they were concerned with what is now called the "liberal arts." But the great university historian Rashdall says:

The rapid multiplication of universities during the fourteenth and fifteenth centuries was largely due to a direct demand for highly educated lawyers and administrators. In a sense the academic discipline of the Middle Ages was too practical. It trained pure intellect, encouraged habits of laborious subtlety, heroic industry, and intense application, while it left uncultivated the imagination, the taste, the sense of beauty— in a word, all the amenities and refinements of the civilized intellect. . . . From a more practical point of view their greatest service to mankind was simply this, that they placed the administration of human affairs—in short, the government of the world—in the hands of educated men.[9]

The early universities were indeed vocationally oriented, created to provide leaders for the state and the church and practitioners in law and medicine. But as the institutions evolved, marked differences appeared. The Italian universities tended to emphasize the practical: the professions of law, medicine, theology, and administration; whereas Paris, Oxford, and Cambridge were soon dominated by doctors of theology who taught what became known as the seven liberal arts: grammar, dialectic, rhetoric, geometry, arithmetic, astronomy, and music. It is this latter form and tradition which took root in England and later spread to the United States and Canada.

One of the reasons these differences developed may well relate to the role of students in the university. Bologna was organized on the initiative of students—students who tended to be mature, wealthy men—who hired masters to teach subjects in which they (the students) were interested. At Paris and Oxford, on the other hand, the masters took the initiative in organizing the classes and later the university. Their view of what should be taught and what should be done in the university soon dominated.

But in most universities there was "for a few glorious years" intellectual discovery and excitement. Within the boundaries of knowledge and imagination feasible in that day, the university was a place of adventure. Unorthodox topics, ideas, theories were investigated and discussed. The whole world of knowledge as it was then known was to be explored—no facet of it was to be forbidden. Hyde reports on the teacher Irnerius and his students at Bologna discovering documentation of the old imperial system of law:

What he and his pupils found must have been quite unlike anything they had ever known. . . . That the text was in places difficult to understand only added to the excitement of the discovery. The contrast between the brave old world of Justinian and the tattered society in which they lived was sufficient to inspire generation after generation of students at Bologna and elsewhere to study, explain, and comment, until at last . . . in about the middle of the fourteenth century, the game of reconciling the contemporary world and its institutions to the ideal of Justinian began to lose some of its fascination.[10]

The first chancellor of Oxford was Robert Grosseteste, who wrote on the magnifying properties of lenses, the teachings of the Salerno school of medicine, and the calendar. His wide-ranging interests in mathematical, physical, astronomical, and philosophical problems[11] undoubtedly influenced many of his students. One of these was Roger Bacon, whose creative and restless mind gave vitality to the university and of whose work it is said:

. . . he was nearer not merely to the physical conception of measurable force but to the wider conception of general laws harmoniously combining to form a general system, than any thinker who lived before the seventeenth century, and this is a greater intellectual achievement than any real or supposed "anticipations." [12]

One of the important developments in the medieval period was the beginning of colleges within larger university complexes. At Bologna, Paris, and Oxford students came to study from many parts of Europe. They were often organized into "nations," the members from a particular nation sometimes dining together in a hostel owned or rented by a tutor.[13] These became, as is sometimes said, "part manor, part monastery." [14] A natural outgrowth of this was the college, an endowed or privately supported building in which members of the college—tutors and students—lived and studied together. The first such was Merton College at Oxford, founded in 1274 by Walter de Merton, of whom it was said, "[He] not only founded a community. He gave shape and purpose to a new idea." [15] This was the idea of molding thought and character in a small, shared domestic situation in a large center of learning—an ideal which had profound influence on the shape of higher education in the future.

There was a buoyance and zestfulness in the early medieval university. The main impression is one of dynamic institutions exploring new fields of intellectual thought with stimulating teachers and enthusiastic students. Both students and teachers traveled back and forth to various universities, carrying with them fresh ideas and views that stimulated intellectual debate and nourished university growth.[16] It was, apparently, an attractive life. Ideas of austerity, chastity, and religious devotion were, of course, prevalent,[17] but there is much to suggest that these were fairly consistently disregarded, for it was clear that scholars of the day "loved strong drink, good food, and buxom women in their rooms." [18]

As the university gradually became more formalized and institutionalized, some of its vitality was to diminish. But while it prevailed, the range of subjects, the intensity of study, and the passion of debate were such that the true mission of the university was established in the minds of scholars for centuries thereafter as being the enthusiastic, uninhibited, unfettered search for knowledge in all forms and in every manner.

The status of the university, the rights and privileges it achieved for itself, and its influence and prestige were seldom to be surpassed in the centuries to follow.

> The Universities of Europe stand beside the Empire and the Papacy among the most illustrious institutions which the genius of the Middle Ages shaped. They became powerful and privileged communities. They built up a great tradition. They made themselves the mouthpiece of medieval thought. But originally they were only guilds of teachers or of students, drawn together by the instinct of association which played so large a part in a disordered age.[19]

This very considerable achievement did not come without courage, sagacity, and skill. There was, of course, a growing need and respect for learning in society, and the university developed its own mystique to exploit these to the full. The university also took advantage of the desire by the church and by many small states to acquire legitimation and prestige. In the absence of monolithic power, the universities maneuvered for special privileges and a large degree of freedom and autonomy. "They appealed to king or council against pope, to pope against king or bishop, and to kings and popes alike against truculent town governments." [20] In a time of struggle for power and status, neither rulers of church or of state were anxious to tangle with established universities.

Two other techniques used by the universities to achieve autonomy and to secure privileges were "cessation" and "migration." The former was in effect a strike—the cessation of all university activities until the matter in dispute was settled. When difficulties in a particular community were too great or the privileges provided were insufficient, the university would move to a more favorable environment—migration. At a time when the universities did not have large buildings but were merely a group of masters and students learning together, this was quite possible and constituted a continuing threat to local officials, who were aware that the university brought both prestige and income to their community. By these means the universities were able to secure unusual privileges—exemption from local laws and taxes, for example—and make legal their separation from the daily life of society.[21]

The university took full advantage of its position to experiment and teach with a degree of freedom seldom enjoyed since that time. The teaching of Aristotle in the universities is a case in point. In 1210 the reading or teaching of Aristotle on natural philosophy at the University of Paris was forbidden by the church. In the ensuing years various popes warned the university of the consequences of using the forbidden books, but with little effect. In 1240, Roger Bacon openly flouted the prohibition by lecturing on these very books and,

> . . . by 1255 Aristotle was not only studied but was prescribed reading in the faculty of arts at Paris, even though no expurgation had been made. Thus within a period of thirty years, thanks to the stubbornness of the masters and the laxity of the authorities, his natural philosophy had run the entire range from unqualified proscription to general use.[22]

Of course, this must be seen in context. Medieval scholars did not dispute the dogma of the church. Indeed, the effort was to use Aristotelian logic and some of Aristotle's conclusions to rationalize papal ideology. And much that was new was simply the discovery of old texts.[23] Nonetheless the medieval university tested the limits of free thought in its society, and as Haskins reports of these universities, "experiment and research were much freer than has been supposed." [24]

The privileged position of the university was not without challenge. Cessation, the right to strike—called by royal prosecutors "a license for disobedience"—was particularly bothersome to both church and state. The university dealt with these difficulties with diplomacy and resourcefulness. For example:

> The university men . . . faced such attacks with flexibility. They refrained from invoking the supranational origin of their privileges and were content to consider them as royal concessions, while stressing that these privileges, necessary to the normal organization of studies, were by no means a threat to the king's sovereignty but were part and parcel—along with the privileges of all the other corporate bodies of the realm—of the common law invoked by his prosecutors. Now, if the king was not a tyrant, he was in duty bound to respect the privileges he had himself granted.[25]

But the great days of the medieval university were few. As nations grew and became stable states, rulers sought to expand control over all institutions within their jurisdiction. The freedoms of the university were attacked and limited. In the fourteenth century Oxford and Cambridge were established, by royal decree, as national institutions—which gave them, in effect, a monopoly over higher learning in England. This was the beginning of constant supervision and interference by the king and his counselors in the affairs of the universities, which continued with successive monarchs through many centuries. Similarly in 1446 the Parliament of Paris became the supreme tribunal of the university by order of a royal edict. While the university protested this and further infringements on its rights in the ensuing years, its days of independence were numbered.

> The university remained contentious, however, until the reign of Louis XI, when its attempt to check the monarch's demand to control its rector was utterly defeated and its autonomy was completely broken. The university's final act of self-assertion came in 1499, when it called a cessation to protest against new infringements on its privileges. This protest was hastily withdrawn in response to dire threats from Louis XII, who revoked the right of cessation itself. Such independence as the university continued to have now existed only on the sufferance of the kings.[26]

There is a tendency, not entirely resisted in the foregoing discussion, to emphasize the positive aspects of the medieval universities, which is to ignore the fact that all masters were not great teachers, all students not intelligent and enthusiastic, all meetings of council not placid and statesmanlike, all freedoms not accepted by those within the university, and all battles with external authorities not won. Indeed, we know there were such deviations. We know also that the dominant system of theological and philosophical teaching of the day, scholasticism—in which there was ceaseless dialogue and debate to refine but not contradict the dogma of the church—gradually became less exciting and, indeed, sterile for many. Similarly, as old texts in law and medicine were fully explored, there was little new to take their place. By the end of the fifteenth century the university was firmly established, but it was clearly a less vital and productive organization than in its earlier days.

But in every institution the formative years are of great importance. It is at these times that ideology is conceived, structure developed, and customs formed that soon become institutionalized and difficult to change. This is true of the early universities, so much so that the English sociologist Halsey said:

> Once the European medieval universities were established there could be only two directions of newness in the idea of a university: one with respect to who should enter, the other with respect to what he or she should learn.[27]

It was natural that the early universities should reflect the society in which they were born. The old knowledge suddenly rediscovered, the need for learned men in new professions, and the expansion of wealth and leisure all stimulated the growth in advanced learning—a learning not hitherto provided in any established school or institution. Thus was the mission of the university formed: advanced sophisticated learning, free of external censure, meeting the interests of individual scholars, yet serving the needs of medieval society.

It was inevitable also that the structure and practices of the university would be drawn from the established institutions of the day—the church, the monastery, the guild or commune. From the church was borrowed the idea of the supranational organization, something above and beyond parochial interests; a hierarchy in the form of a chancellor, a rector, a dean; rituals such as convocation; and colorful dress in the form of academic gowns. From the monastery came the idea of separateness—an institution insulated from the practical world, a self-governing community to make its own rules and develop its own way of life. From the guild came the concept of a community of individuals bound together by an oath of mutual support and common obedience to elected officials and with authority to select its own members.

Other practices emerged perhaps spontaneously as a variety of problems were met and resolved: the lecture method (in the absence of books the master was required to read from or talk about the only existing text); the formation of faculties; a set curriculum; examinations as a means of certifying the qualified; and the awarding of degrees (bachelor, master, and doctor). These became accepted practice in all universities.

The merging of these ideas gave the university its distinctive character and structure: a self-governing community with an elected hierarchy, separated from the world of commerce, involved in a mission to learn and to teach at an advanced level, using mysterious rituals and dress to dramatize its uniqueness, and requiring from its members deep loyalty to and enduring support for each other and the university. This conception of what a university is, or should be, is deeply rooted in academic ideology and has been stoutly defended by scholars in the centuries that have followed.

What is important to recognize is that this ideology and these practices, however often they were ignored, distorted, or abused in medieval times or in the centuries that followed, constituted a model of what a university should be. Like the "American Dream" or any statement of faith, it motivated men to work toward the ideal; it disturbed their conscience when it was not achieved; and it became part of the university mythology, sacred in the lives of traditional scholars.

Universities from 1500-1850

The three and a half centuries identified here constitute a period which many observers consider one of somnolence, even of stagnation and retreat, for the universities in England and North America.[28]

Why this should be so is an immensely interesting question, for while the pace of development in these centuries may have been considerably slower than that to which we are accustomed today, it was, taken overall, one of steady exploration and expansion in terms of physical geography, science, and intellectual outlook. The early medieval universities were the leaders in investigation of ideas in their time; the universities which followed had little, if any, part in opening up the new world either physically or intellectually. This constriction of purpose and form in the university is both significant and puzzling.

That society was alive and vital at this time there can be no doubt. The Renaissance was at its peak in 1500, and the Reformation and the period of the French Enlightenment quickly followed. The effect was to loosen the authority of religious thought, to encourage new fields of investigation, and to nourish fresh scientific speculation. Among intellectuals the cry was to carry on the mission the medieval university had conceived for itself. Men should "take the risk of discovery, exercise the right of unfettered criticism, accept the loneliness of autonomy." [29]

The number of famous names in the arts and sciences during this period is legion: William Shakespeare (d. 1616), Johannes Kepler (d. 1630), Galileo Galilei (d. 1642), René Descartes (d. 1650), William Harvey (d. 1657), Molière (d. 1673), John Milton (d. 1674), Baruch Spinoza (d. 1677), Thomas Hobbes (d. 1679), John Locke (d. 1704), Christopher Wren (d. 1723), Isaac Newton (d. 1727), Johann Sebastian Bach (d. 1750), David Hume (d. 1776), Jean Jacques Rousseau (d. 1778), Voltaire (d. 1778), Samuel Johnson (d. 1784), Benjamin Franklin (d. 1790), Adam Smith (d. 1790), Wolfgang Amadeus Mozart (d. 1791), Edward Gibbon (d. 1794), Robert Burns (d. 1796), Immanuel Kant (d. 1804), James Watt (d. 1819), Thomas Jefferson (d. 1826), and Georg Wilhelm Hegel (d. 1831).

Speculation, investigation, study of many facts of the intellectual world proceeded: philosophy, astronomy, mathematics, metaphysics, medicine, law, architecture, literature, and music were all lively enterprises. New inventions, particularly the printing press (ca. 1440), the telescope (ca. 1608), the microscope (ca. 1590), the pendulum clock (ca. 1656), the thermometer (ca. 1654), and the barometer (ca. 1643) all gave impetus to and widened the field of investigation.[30] These centuries were not dull intellectually or culturally for those sensitive to see and to hear. The universities did not seem to be among the sensitive.

If the universities had been responsive to the social and intellectual movements of the day, they would have been centers of great vitality with imaginative teachers working on the frontiers of knowledge. Instead they were encapsulated by narrow religious dogma and antiquated methods of teaching. They were not for the intellectually brave and adventuresome.

A comment by Sir Sydney Caine on the British universities is equally applicable to universities in Canada and the United States:

> In the area of original ideas it is fair to say that in the seventeenth and eighteenth centuries the universities as institutions contributed little, if anything. Most of those whose names spring to mind were university men, i.e., had attended a university and some held university appointments at one

time or another; but such connections were more in the nature of coincidences than contributory causes to their thinking.[31]

The fact was that most of the creative work in these centuries was carried on outside academic walls—indeed much of it was subject to ridicule and scorn by those in the universities. It would be no exaggeration to say that most of the greatest works in literature, philosophy, science, medicine, law, and music during the period 1500–1850 were produced outside the university,[32] although as suggested by Caine earlier, some of the creators of these works were university graduates and perhaps received early stimulation or inspiration there.

Before we consider the reasons for the partial retreat of the university from the intellectual world, let us look briefly at developments in England, Canada, and the United States up to the middle of the nineteenth century.

England: From the Middle Ages until well into the nineteenth century, Oxford and Cambridge were the only universities in England. The University of London was opened in 1828 and Durham University in 1837, but neither had much influence or status before 1850. It is fair to say, therefore, that Oxford and Cambridge represented formal higher education in England in the three and a half centuries under discussion.

The main function of these two universities, it was generally agreed, was the production of parsons.[33] The universities did, of course, provide a home for many young aristocrats who wished to have a year or two of leisure and diversion, but few of these took their studies seriously and none interfered with the main function of the university,[34] which was to produce a clergy fluent in Latin, knowledgeable in the classics, and devoted to the perpetuation of the church and the monarchy. Oxford and Cambridge were clearly what we would today call "establishment institutions."

There was much criticism of these universities. Not only the narrow functions to which the universities limited themselves was criticized but also the quality of education provided within these limits. Bishop Burnet, an early financial supporter of Oxford, despaired of the young clergy trained at that university:

> In the Universities they for the most part lost the learning they brought with them from schools, and learned so very little in them that too commonly they came from these knowing less than when they went to them.[35]

But it was the narrow perspective and curriculum that disturbed knowledgeable people most. Except for brief flourishes which were not sustained, emphasis was on Greek and Latin. The large evolving fields of natural philosophy, science, social science, medicine, and law were almost completely neglected.

> The ancient and catholic conception of their functions as great schools of all the sciences and of all learning, had narrowed to one whereby they came to be regarded as little more than seminaries for the education of the clergy of the Established Church.[36]

The "low level of thought and life" that seemed characteristic of both Oxford and Cambridge is often said to have been caused by the control and interference of King and Parliament.[37] There was indeed considerable such interference. For example, in 1536 an act of Parliament required that:

> . . . every person proceeding to any degree in any university of the realm to make oath before the commissary of such university, that he from henceforth shall utterly renounce, refuse, relinquish, or forsake the Bishop of Rome and his auctorite, power, and jurisdiction.[38]

This was one of the early, but not by any means the only, act passed or advice given that sought to have the established church dominate the life at both universities in England. Until 1850 the universities and colleges were still ruled by most of the same statutes as in the reign of King Charles I. Up to that time, to matriculate and to obtain a degree a student had to sign a subscription to the Thirty-nine Articles of the established church,[39] and this was still the case in 1840.[40] The effect of constant and close supervision and control was the stifling of any sign of intellectual initiative or unorthodox thinking and the making of the university, in effect, into a servant of the status quo.

Dissatisfaction with Oxford and Cambridge led to two interesting developments. The first was the organization of nonconformist or dissenting academies which received support both from those who refused to sign the Thirty-nine Articles and from those who wished to seek a broader field of investigation and teaching than that provided in the universities. Although prohibited from granting a degree, these academies flourished in the late seventeenth century and for most of the eighteenth, some surviving into the early nineteenth century. One of these was opened in London in 1675 by Charles Morton, who thought his academy "might stir up . . . a greater Diligence and Industry in the Universities," and offered a five-year program of advanced education which gave considerable emphasis to new developments in science.[41] The success of the academies was resented by the established universities, which never ceased to press for action that would terminate their existence. This hostility, a lack of sympathy at court, and inadequate finances gradually succeeded in bringing about the academy's demise.[42]

The second and more permanent development was the organization of the Royal Society in 1662. It brought together men from many walks of life with intellectual interests in a broad range of subjects. Many of its members had been to university but wished now to pursue further studies which the universities could not satisfy. The society became in effect an institute of advanced studies, with its own meeting house, lectures, and publications. It kept alive broad scientific and intellectual interests, a function which had in medieval days been centered in the universities.

Notwithstanding the narrowed vision of the established universities during these centuries in England, they did contribute to the evolution of a concept of undergraduate education that has been a model for, if not a reality in, other universities ever since. This concept had three aspects: (1) the small college and shared domestic life of student and teacher, (2) the tutorial—the regular face-to-face meeting of student and tutor to explore and discuss the lessons or topics of the day, and (3) the idea of *in loco parentis* by which the university assumed responsibility for the care, discipline, and full development of each student. These methods of dealing with undergraduates were early recognized as having great potential for influencing the lives of students and were warmly embraced as the means by which the character of future leaders could be molded.[43]

Another innovation that emerged at Oxford and Cambridge which had considerable influence on the future of universities, particularly in late-nineteenth-century North America, was the solicitation of finances from private donors. Oxford and Cambridge had unusual success in securing very large gifts by which colleges and scholarships were endowed and by which the university as a whole was made secure financially. The idea of appealing for very large sums of money and of creating an endowment fund developed during these years and allowed Oxford and Cambridge to establish a financial base which permitted them to provide facilities and later to secure a degree of freedom that was the envy of universities throughout the world.

While it is not our intention here to deal with British universities other than those in England, it should be noted in passing that four universities were started in the very early years of this period in Scotland[44] and that they contributed to the emerging character of the university in a significant way. Before these Scottish institutions were established, universities had been initiated by scholars, teachers, and students. The new Scottish universities, although started by ecclesiastical authorities, soon provided for a share in governance by laymen. Edinburgh, particularly, developed with a close association of Calvinist ministers and the local town council. This gradually gave the university a new form of governing structure, to which we will refer later, but it provided also, in spite of strong religious influences, a broader and more pragmatic curriculum and outlook than in England.[45]

Canada: While achievements in higher education were not notable in Canada before 1850, there were some threads of interest and importance in the growth pattern.

Before 1850 Canada was made up of a series of sparsely populated British colonies and was in many respects an undeveloped frontier country. That there were universities at all is perhaps surprising. But by 1850 there were ten universities in the British North American colonies representing a variety of interests that gave these institutions somewhat varied forms.[46]

There are some writers who suggest that Canada had one of the first institutions of higher education in North America. A small French school at which Latin was taught was opened in Quebec in 1636, and its curriculum broadened over the years to the extent that it became the first *collège classique* in North America. In 1663, the Bishop of Quebec established the (Grand) Seminaire de Quebec:

> . . . there can be no doubt that higher education of a professional character was offered—and it is legitimate to state that Canada entered the field [of higher education] by 1663.[47]

There are few in Canada, however, who see this as comparable to the emergence of the early English or American universities. Its importance is simply that even in these early days, there was an interest in Canada in formal education.

The major development in Quebec in these early years was a series of seven *collèges classiques* in which the classics were taught, the French language used, and the Roman Catholic faith promulgated. They were colleges in the tradition of the University of Paris after 1500. The colleges:

> . . . were quite independent of each other, but they developed academically and administratively on essentially similar lines; this was to be expected since the classical course had long been clearly defined, the faculty were all clerics, and the great majority of the faculty either had been trained or were in the process of being trained at the Seminaire de Quebec.[48]

Just as the influence of Paris was present in Roman Catholic colleges, English and Scottish influences were present in the protestant colleges. The early King's colleges (in Windsor, Fredericton, and Toronto) were organized by the efforts of the Church of England, which aspired to have these colleges develop on the Oxford-Cambridge model. Others (such as Dalhousie, Queen's, and McGill) were influenced by the Scottish universities. Most of the colleges were aware of the growth of American colleges, particularly those in New England, and it can be said that there was present a United States influence as well. All of this would seem to make for a varied, multipatterned university picture in Canada, but while there were some differences in organization and curriculum, the dominant picture was of a small, rigid, poorly equipped, religion-controlled college whose teachers were clergymen and whose curriculum was based on a study of Latin and the classics.[49]

The major difference was in the manner of control; two of the colleges (Dalhousie and McGill) were nondenominational colleges operated independent of any religious group and open to students of varied faiths. This did not, as suggested earlier, make for marked difference in orientation, but it did provide a basis for competition, flexibility, and expansion that would probably not have prevailed if all colleges had been exclusively religious.[50]

Some evidence that Canadian universities might depart from the bland model of England and relate to the frontier society of which they were a part is seen in a report of a commission on universities (in 1854) in New Brunswick. Two of the members of this commission were J. S. Dawson, who would shortly thereafter be appointed principal of McGill University, and Egerton Ryerson, superintendent of education of Upper Canada. The report said in part:

> In considering the system of Collegiate Education in New Brunswick, we were unanimously of the opinion that it ought to be at once comprehensive, special, and practical; that it ought to embrace those Branches of Learning usually taught in Great Britain and the United States—and special courses of Instruction adapted to the Agricultural, Mechanical, Manufacturing, and Commercial pursuits and interests of New Brunswick; and that the subjects and modes of Instruction in

the Sciences and Modern Languages (including English, French, and German) should have a practical reference to those pursuits and interests.[51]

While this report was not adopted or fully implemented, it suggests a more realistic attitude toward the higher learning necessary for a pioneering country such as Canada than that considered in the prevailing rigid classical education.

United States: Before the Revolutionary War there were nine colleges in the colonies that became the United States.[52] Harvard College was the first, founded by Puritans in 1636, and was followed gradually by denominational groups which established small colleges for youths of their own faith primarily "to train a class of learned men for the Christian ministry, although some aimed also at training a body of men in culture and knowledge for service to the state."[53] The College and Academy of Philadelphia was an exception, because it was originally secular and because, reflecting the interests of Benjamin Franklin, who gave impetus to its founding, it presented a broad plan of education which included mathematics, science, government, law, and in 1765 the first medical department in North America.[54]

After the American Revolution the number of colleges and universities multiplied rapidly. By the time of the Civil War there were approximately eight hundred colleges in the United States, and although only 180 of these survived into the twentieth century,[55] the latter number still represented considerable vitality and a profound belief in the need for the education of youth. Most of the early American colleges were started by religious groups, and while in the latter part of the eighteenth century and first half of the nineteenth seven state universities were organized,[56] these were also much under the influence of religious groups and from the very beginning had Bible classes, daily prayers, compulsory chapel, and revival meetings.[57]

One might expect, nonetheless, with the variety of scholarship both public and private, the influence of men like Franklin on Pennsylvania and Jefferson on Virginia, and the energy and enthusiasm of a new country, that a rich and diversified pattern of higher education would emerge. To the contrary, there was an astonishing sameness of American colleges not only in the curriculum but in all aspects of college life. Among scholars of university evolution most would agree with Jencks and Riesman that:

> During the seventeenth, eighteenth, and early nineteenth centuries, American colleges were conceived and operated as pillars of the locally established church, political order, and social conventions. These local arrangements were relatively stable, widely accepted as legitimate, and comparatively well integrated with one another. Yet while the pre-Jacksonian college was almost always a pillar of the establishment, it was by no means a very important pillar. An American "college" was in some respects more like today's secondary schools than today's universities. It did not employ a faculty of scholars. Indeed, only one or two pre-Jacksonian college teachers exercised any significant influence on the intellectual currents of their time. An always upright and usually erudite clergyman served as president. He then hired a few other men (usually young bachelors and often themselves aspiring clergymen) to assist in the teaching. There were only a few professorships in specialized subjects. In most cases everyone taught almost everything, usually at a fairly elementary level.[58]

The curriculum was heavily, if not exclusively, weighted in favor of the English classical tradition with required Greek and Latin readings. Classes tended to be "recitations" at which the teacher listened to, and corrected, students as they read and translated Adam's *Roman Antiquitus,* Cicero's *De Oratore,* or Griesback's *Greek Testament.*[59] There was little scholarship beyond these efforts. Reflecting the spirit prevailing before 1850, Charles W. Eliot, president of Harvard, as late as 1869 said that his university did not possess "with the exception of the endowment of the Observatory . . . a single fund primarily intended to secure to men of learning the leisure and means to prosecute original researches"[60] and that "the prime business of American professors in this generation must be regular and assiduous class teaching."[61]

The impression is of a campus environment that would stifle intellectual vitality, and it is not unexpected that creative scholars found the colleges and universities unattractive. There was the basis for change and development in the ideas of Franklin and Jefferson, both of whom conceived of a wider range of studies, including professional schools of medicine and law, but the unimaginative, stereotyped college prevailed under the jurisdiction of church and state. It was necessary to break this pattern, and in an important speech in the early nineteenth century, President Quincy of Harvard established the essential conditions for future development:

> The duty of considering science and learning as an independent interest of the community, begins to be very generally felt and acknowledged. Both in Europe and in America attempts are making [sic] to rescue the general mind from the vassalage in which it has been held by sects in the church, and by parties in the state; giving to that interest, as far as possible, a vitality of its own, having no precarious dependence for existence on subserviency to particular views in politics or religion; and, for this purpose, to place it like a fountain opened in religions far above those in which the passions of the day struggle for ascendency. . . .[62]

This was the argument, philosophy, and foundation that formed the basis for the future growth of universities in the United States.

Emergence of distinctions: The limited definition of the function of the university from 1500 to 1850 related to its exclusive identification with the prevailing religious forces of the day. The first medieval universities had responded to a number of pressing social needs. Oxford and Cambridge, which had participated in this early development, soon retreated almost entirely into narrow theological institutions designed to maintain order and tradition. They had little interest in or sensitivity to the needs of a society involved in the opening of new trade routes, with an emerging middle class, or with new ways of studying man and nature. They remained insulated from the major developments of the time, content to support and sustain the social structure of the day.

The pattern of higher learning thus established had great influence on the early universities in North America, where the practical professional schools of Italy were unknown or ignored and the limited classical curriculum of England copied and admired. That this curriculum was hardly relevant to the North American environment made little difference. Oxford and Cambridge represented for the colonies what a university was supposed to be, and this model was supported as a symbol of status. Thus unrelated to the world around them, it was perhaps not unexpected that the universities in the new world would languish and that many in North America would disappear.

Another reason for the lethargy is undoubtedly the method of scholasticism which gripped the universities in the late medieval period. This is a philosophy that nourishes not the expansion of knowledge but rather the containment of knowledge within a rather rigid mold. One does not expect scholars of this school to be adventuresome in the field of ideas or to engage in the exploration of entirely new fields. Thus confined, the tendency is to rely on the known, on the repetition and the justification of old truths. It is a system of closed doors that actively prevents the entrance of new ideas. Thus the universities which adhered to this philosophy were in effect static. The development of fresh vistas and methods inevitably fell into the hands of laymen—amateur scientists and philosophers—who kept thought and learning alive.

Such limitation of ideas may also explain in part the lack of internal vitality in these colleges and universities. Many masters in the early medieval universities were intellectually adventuresome, convinced that the university should explore all topics "unfettered." They actively opposed inertia and the suppression of ideas by either internal or external forces. The teachers in the universities in the later period and before 1850, in comparison, appeared docile and submissive, fearful of their jobs, and at best like "a genial Mr. Chips," anxious to be both firm and kind to their boys. They seemed not to understand or appreciate the ideology of the early universities; they retreated to a conception of a "school" where discipline and character-building were of greater importance than intellectual development.

It needs hardly be said that the colleges and universities up to 1850 were male-dominated, restricted largely to upper-class families. They reflected the dominant culture of the day in terms of social class, race, and religious outlook.

The major legacy of this period is a conception of undergraduate education which is still much revered, if not followed. The university should "know its students one by one," as Cardinal Newman suggested; it should stimulate and nurture the intellectual, moral, and spiritual growth of each; and its curriculum should encourage discipline and strengthen the moral fiber of all. What was fundamental was the development of the student—the study of Latin and Greek was required as much to create good habits of work as it was to expand the mind. Given this objective, what was important was good teaching of that which was already known.

While the colleges and universities in England, Canada, and the United States were very much alike, a very important distinction in the role and purpose of education in these three societies was becoming apparent. It can be seen most clearly in the number of colleges and universities in each. In 1850 England had four universities, Canada ten, and the United States close to eight hundred. The English conceived of the university as a center for training an elite leadership—primarily for the church. The universities in Canada and the United States may well have drawn their students primarily from the upper classes, but they were obviously for a much wider group and for a much broader purpose than in England. In North America the aim was to provide what was considered to be "intellectual and moral training"; education was to be valued for itself, and it was widely supported as a means of developing sound character—in short, to instill the virtues that would make the nations strong. This prevalent belief, nourished by provinces and states determined to build a civilization equal, if not superior, to the older European culture, led to a determined and successful effort to expand educational opportunities far beyond those existing in England.

The German Universities

While English and North American universities languished, major developments in higher learning were taking place in Germany. These were of the greatest import, particularly to the United States, where after the Civil War there was a new outlook which encouraged change in education.

The early exploratory mood of the medieval universities seemed to flow to Germany and to be nourished by various national states, in each of which a university was considered an institution to be respected and supported. In the early nineteenth century the German universities flourished and gave impetus to a new conception of what higher education could do for society.[63]

There were, briefly, four ideas of great importance that evolved in the German universities in the first decades of the nineteenth century: (1) the focus of the university on research and scholarship in all fields (the purpose was the "ardent, methodical, independent search after truth in any and all its forms, but wholly irrespective of utilitarian applications"[64]), (2) the advancement of research in "institutes" in which all senior professors worked with their students, (3) the concept of *Lernfreiheit,* by which was meant the freedom of the student to choose his own program of study, live independent of the university, and move from one university to another, and (4) the concept of *Lehrfreiheit,* by which was meant the freedom of the professor to investigate and teach the results of his researches without government interference.[65]

This was a different university: with four faculties (theology, law, medicine, and philosophy) in which there was eagerness to pursue new subjects such as social science; with research institutes stimulating investigation in many fields; with professors free of inhibiting external pressures; and with students following their own inclinations and way of life, required only to pass a major final examination. The

German university was a model of great attraction to many academics who traveled there to study in the nineteenth century, and it was to have a profound effect on the development of universities in England, Canada, and the United States.

NOTES

1. Rubinoff, 1971, p. 13.

2. Shils, 1972*b*, p. 127.

3. Ashby, 1961, p. 3.

4. McNeill, 1971, pp. 256–265.

5. Mallet, 1924, vol. 1, pp. 2–3.

6. Mullinger, 1884, vol. 1, pp. 333–334; see also Lyte, 1886, p. 1.

7. Ulich comments as follows on the origin of universities: "It is impossible to give the exact dates of the origin of all medieval universities, because many of them arose from more or less informal congregations of scholars. At Salerno famous physicians were already teaching during the ninth century, before the university became internationally famous as a medical center in the eleventh century. At the same time systematic legal studies were being pursued at Bologna, which became the leading school of law. During the twelfth century the University of Paris developed from schools connected with the cathedral on the Ile de la Cité. Oxford and Cambridge can also be traced back to the twelfth century. In the thirteenth and fourteenth centuries there developed in Spain the universities of Valladolid, Seville, and Salamanca. Prague was officially chartered in 1347, Cracow in 1364, Heidelberg in 1385, Cologne in 1388, Erfurt in 1379, Leipzig, a secession from Prague, in 1409, Louvain in 1426, and Budapest in 1475" (Ulich, 1965, p. 46).

8. Halsey and Trow, 1971, p. 34.

9. Rashdall, 1936, vol. 3, p. 456.

10. Hyde, 1972, p. 26.

11. Armytage, 1955, p. 39.

12. Rashdall, 1936, vol. 3., p. 246.

13. Lyte, 1886, p. 68.

14. Armytage, 1955, p. 41.

15. Ibid., p. 41; see also Mallet, 1924, vol. 1, p. 115.

16. Lyte, 1886, p. 25; see also Mallet, 1924, vol. 1, p. 138.

17. Mallet, 1924, vol. 1, p. 25.

18. Nisbet, 1971*a*, p. 34.

19. Mallet, 1924, vol. 1, p. 25.

20. Hofstadter and Metzger, 1955, p. 8.

21. Hyde, 1972, pp. 44–45.

22. Hofstadter and Metzger, 1955, p. 24.

23. McNeill, 1971, p. 262.

24. Haskins, 1957, pp. 360–361.

25. Verger, 1972, p. 62.

26. Hofstadter and Metzger, 1955, p. 42.

27. Halsey, 1974, p. 5.

28. V. H. H. Green in *The Universities* (1969) suggests that the period 1500–1650 was one of transition and 1650–1800 one of decline.

29. Gay, 1967, p. 3.

30. McNeill, 1971, pp. 317–318.

31. Caine, 1969, p. 55.

32. Nisbet, 1971*a,* p. 19. There were a few exceptions, of course. Isaac Newton, for example, produced some of his outstanding work in the years 1661–1701 while he was associated with Cambridge University (Smyth, 1972), but his inspiration seemed to come more from his colleagues in the Royal Society than from those at Cambridge.

33. Hill, 1972, p. 108.

34. Ibid., p. 131.

35. Armytage, 1955, p. 133.

36. Mullinger, 1884, vol. 2, p. 250.

37. Trevelyan, 1923, pp. 26–28.

38. Mullinger, 1884, vol. 2, p. 35.

39. Bill, 1973, p. 39.

40. Halsey and Trow, 1971, p. 42; see also Sparrow, 1967, pp. 82–83.

41. Armytage, 1955, p. 129.

42. Ibid., p. 132.

43. ". . . . As the tutor stood not merely *in loco parentis* in relation to his pupil, but was also his instructor, and to a great extent his companion, the influence he could thus exercise was almost incalculable, and when exerted for good was productive of results that could not be mistaken and were widely felt and recognised. At no period do we find this influence, as exerted by men possessing not merely high culture and intellectual endowments, but also the requisite moral qualities and sympathetic faculty, forming so prominent a feature in our academic history as in the seventeenth century" (Mullinger, 1884, vol. 2, p. 398).

44. St. Andrews, 1411; Glasgow, 1451; Aberdeen, 1494; Edinburgh, 1583.

45. See Beloff, 1968, p. 15; Harris, 1973, chap. 3, pp. 15–16; Smyth, 1972, pp. 70–72. These developments may well be considered the roots from which evolved the role of laymen on courts, councils, and boards of universities, and perhaps even the origin of a curriculum in which the student had a choice of subjects.

46. It is difficult to be precise about dates of founding, since charters were sometimes given to colleges which did not open for several years or even decades thereafter. Following are probably the first Canadian universities and the date each began teaching: King's College, Windsor, N.S. (1805); King's College, Frederiction, N.B. (1828); McGill College, Montreal, P.Q. (1829); Dalhousie University, Halifax, N.S. (1838); Acadia College, Wolfville, N.S. (1841); St. Mary's College, Halifax, N.S. (1841); Queen's College, Kingston, Ont. (1841); Victoria College, Cobourg, Ont. (1841); Bishop's College, Lennoxville, P.Q. (1843); King's College, Toronto, Ont. (1847).

47. Harris, 1973, chap. 2, p. 2.

48. Ibid., chap. 2, p. 10.

49. Harris reports "few college libraries had as many as 5,000 volumes. The largest was Laval's—in 1863, 28,000 volumes. . . . Other figures include McGill 8,000, Bishop's 4,000, Grand Seminaire de Montreal 2,500, Toronto, 15,000, Knox 4,000, Trinity 3,500, Queen's 3,000, Ottawa 2,000, St. Michael's 1,500, Victoria 1,000 . . ." (Harris, 1973, chap. 6, pp. 4–5).

50. *Encyclopaedia Britannica*, 1967, vol. 22, p. 872.

51. Harris, 1973, chap. 3, p. 13.

52. Harvard College, 1636; College of William and Mary, 1693; Yale College, 1701; College of New Jersey (later Princeton), 1746; King's College (later Columbia), 1754; College and Academy of Philadelphia (later University of Pennsylvania), 1755; Rhode Island College (later Brown University), 1764; Queen's College (later Rutgers University), 1766; and Dartmouth College, 1770.

53. *Encyclopaedia Britannica*, 1967, vol. 22, p. 874.

54. Ibid.; see also Armytage, 1955, p. 161.

55. Jencks and Riesman, 1968, p. 3.

56. North Carolina, 1795; Georgia, 1801; Virginia, 1825; Michigan, 1837; Iowa, 1847; Wisconsin, 1848; see also *Encyclopaedia Britannica*, 1967, vol. 22, p. 875; Harris, 1973, chap. 7, p. 31.

57. Hofstadter and Metzger, 1955, p. 297.

58. Jencks and Riesman, 1968, p. 1.

59. Hofstadter and Metzger, 1955, pp. 186–197.

60. Morison, 1965, p. 330.

61. Hofstadter and Metzger, 1955, p. 299.

62. Morison, 1965, p. 256.

63. Ben-David and Zloczower, 1962, pp. 50–65.

64. Hart, 1874, p. 264.

65. Veysey, 1965, p. 384; see also Hofstadter and Metzger, 1955, pp. 386–387.

chapter two

THE EVOLUTION

Wars and Peace (1850-1950)

The hundred years which followed 1850 were among the most momentous in history. Never had there been as many changes which affected the whole of society and the attitudes and behavior of man. What distinguished those years was the accelerating pace of change and the enlarging scope and range of that change. The technical innovations in the mid-nineteenth century were revolutionary in their effect but were few in number when compared to developments a century later. And while the earlier changes seemed confined to only a small proportion of the population, it soon became apparent that no person, no belief, no idea would be unaffected by the results of the new interaction of fertile minds, technical inventions, and scientific discoveries.

The industrial revolution began this process of fundamental change by creating new industries, new cities, and new wealth. Perhaps most important, it created new social classes—a vast new middle class of workers and a new elite of scientists and managers—that profoundly affected social structure and social attitudes. The rapid advance of science and technology was only to accentuate this movement.

Many social scientists believe that the most profound effect of these changes was to move people from the farm to the city. Until the twentieth century the vast majority of men in the Western world lived in rural areas, their lives regulated by the age-old rhythms of the seasons. They lived close to nature and to God, largely unaffected by doubts about their way of life or conflicts in ideology. Urbanization and

secularization called for new attitudes and behavior patterns.
Thus:

> It seems likely that the change in ordinary everyday human
> experience and habit implied by man's wholesale flight from
> the fields will alter society as fundamentally as it was altered
> when men ceased to be simple predators and began to pro-
> duce their food. If so, it is difficult to overemphasize the his-
> torical importance of the industrial revolution and impossible
> to believe that the social organization and styles of life that
> will eventually prove to be best attuned to industrialized
> economies have yet clearly emerged.[1]

With the rise of cities, new work habits, and new patterns
of living, there was the continued growth and spread of secularization. Acceptance of the common explanations of unusual phenomena in religious terms diminished as men
sought secular, rational, and scientific reasons for all events.
The change did not come quickly, but as alert minds grasped
enthusiastically for new secular insights, the authority of religion and of the church was gradually eroded. A new attitude—called the "rational-empirical" outlook—prevailed.
This was ". . . the outlook of independent curiosity, openness to experience, disciplined inquiry and analysis, rea-
soned judgment, and the appreciation of originality." [2] This
approach became the basis of scholarship inside and outside
the university, and while there were many struggles with religious bodies over its legitimacy, it was to become the dominant force in society and in the university.

Ideas that were to alter human thinking began early in the
period between 1850 and 1950. Darwin published his *Origin
of Species* in 1859, Marx his *Das Capital* in 1889, and Freud
and Einstein their major work in the early part of the twentieth century. New conceptions of man and matter were now
at hand. While much of the creative work of these individuals was done outside the university, it was quickly assimilated in the academic communities of the Western world.
There were the expected quarrels with Darwin, the expected
fear of Marx, the expected shock from Freud as old ideas of
religion and the nature of man persisted. But as the new concepts were grasped, assimilated, embraced, an entirely new

34

intellectual climate resulted. Simplistic explanations of complex phenomena were not acceptable; knowledge, observation, study, analysis, and insight were the tools required.

All these developments provided a congenial environment for a reawakening of the university. It could hardly be otherwise. The university not only rose to the challenge but contributed mightily to the shaping of the new society.

The Universities Adjust

England: Perhaps the most remarkable feature of the English universities during the one hundred years after 1850 was the resilience of their idea of what a university should be.[3] The belief persisted that education existed to produce the cultivated, well-rounded member of the elite and that universities should be organized precisely to do just that.

The continuing dominance of Oxford and Cambridge was, of course, responsible for this idea and practice. These universities had been the subject of studies by royal commissions in 1850, 1872, and 1919 and were under strong pressure to offer programs in "many new and distinct branches of knowledge," to offer scholarships to a wider range of students, to develop a more democratic form of government, and to provide more authority and responsibility to the university vis-à-vis the colleges.[4] The result was a breaking away from the Greek and Latin curriculum, the introduction of science and other modern subjects, the admission of more students from state schools, and the recruitment of outstanding scholars for the academic staff. But more remarkable was the persistence of what these universities conceived to be their principal mission, namely, undergraduate education, and of their ability to provide the conditions—small colleges, tutorial teaching, domestic living—that made this possible. There were many who criticized this orientation, but few could deny its quality. And this attitude persisted. Even such a crusty observer as Flexner said in 1930:

> Whatever their defects—and they are neither few nor slight—the concentration at these two seats of learning [Oxford and

Cambridge] of able students, accomplished scholars, and brilliant scientists furnishes England, and indeed the Empire, with . . . two real centres, sufficiently large, varied, strong, and independent to set up and to maintain intellectual standards.[5]

But it was obvious that England could not ignore other pressing needs—for graduate education, for professional education, and for a much larger student population—which Oxford and Cambridge chose largely to ignore. As early as 1868 Matthew Arnold had said:

We must plant faculties in the eight or ten principal seats of population and let the students follow lectures there from their own homes with whatever arrangements for their living they and their parents choose.[6]

New universities were required and were begun. But not without resistance. This latter was related to a deep-rooted belief that there were a very small number of able students and to admit more would merely lower the standard of education. "Narrow the gates of entry," [7] Charles Grant-Robertson wrote in 1930, confirming the view of Herklots, who in an important book a few years earlier had said, "One cannot but deprecate the attempts that are being made to found universities up and down the country." [8]

New universities were, nonetheless, founded.[9] They were spread through the provinces with a good deal of local lay participation in financing and governing. These universities tended to be more practical and vocational than Oxford and Cambridge,[10] offering, besides undergraduate and graduate courses in arts and science subjects, a wide variety of courses in such areas as commerce, household science, public administration, engineering, and applied science.[11]

The civic—"Redbrick"—universities flourished. They served a new constituency, with new curricula, and with many first-class teachers and researchers. In some fields they excelled. "In scholarship and science they take second place to none in the world," said Edward Shils of these universities in 1955. Compared to Oxford and Cambridge, the Redbrick universities were more responsive to the technological and manpower needs of society, more aware of the progress of research in the German universities, and more sensitive to the pragmatic approach of some universities in North America. They incorporated these needs and ideas in their programs to create, for Britain, a distinctive pattern of higher education.

The result was that:

> . . . two university traditions emerged: Oxford and Cambridge were national universities connected with the national elites of politics, administration, business and the liberal professions, offering a general education designed to mould character and prepare their students for a gentlemanly style of life; the rest were provincial, all of them, including London, addressed to the needs of the professional and industrial middle classes, taking most of their students from their own region and offering them a more utilitarian training for middle-class careers in undergraduate courses typically concentrated on a single subject.[12]

If two traditions existed, only one had status. For many years after 1900, even after the Redbrick universities had proven themselves, the dominance of Oxbridge continued. This was in part because of the quality of the life experience provided at Oxford and Cambridge; in part because of what is sometimes called the "Oxford-Cambridge-London axis" [13] (to underline the inner circle of prestigious relationships between the older universities and those persons—mostly Oxford-Cambridge graduates—who held positions of power in London); and in part because of the deep conviction in England that real learning is a one-to-one or small-group experience—a process of osmosis—which is impossible in any large enterprise.[14]

The clear distinction—in wealth, ideology, and social class—between the students of the two different types of schools[15] was disturbing to some. Bruce Truscot in 1943 wrote a widely read book urging greater equality among the universities. It caught the wartime egalitarian spirit and gave impetus to the funding of the Redbrick universities. There should no longer be:

. . . two large residential universities for those who are either well-to-do or brilliant, and nine smaller universities, mainly non-residential, for those who are neither. Let there be eleven, of approximately equal size, all in the main residential and each having certain Schools in which it excels the rest. Let the standards of admission at all universities, as well as the minimum standard for graduation, be raised, as nearly as possible, to the same level. . . . Let every boy or girl entering a university go where his or her particular subject is best taught. And finally, let a levelling of standards pave the way for the interchange of pupils where this is in the interests of the pupils themselves.[16]

This was not to be in Truscot's day. The brilliant record of Oxford and Cambridge in scholarship, in undergraduate education, and in many fields of research was not to be challenged, not to be eroded by expansion, and not to be "watered down" by being merged into a unitary system with other lesser institutions. The superiority of means, of tutors, of status remained. It was not until after World War II that the momentous decision was made by the University Grants Committee to provide capital grants to all universities and thereby begin a new era of development for the newer institutions.[17]

Canada: When Canada became a nation in 1867, she had the ambition to become a great nation. But her ambitions at the time exceeded her immediate resources. True, Canada was a vast country, like the United States, stretching from sea to sea, with substantial but as yet unexplored natural resources. But relative to the United States her population was small and spread thinly throughout the country, and there was little capital to stimulate economic development. The first coast-to-coast railway was not completed until 1885, and then only after a long series of political and financial crises.[18]

Thus it is not unexpected to find Harris, summing up university developments in Canada in 1870, stating that except for the rebirth of Dalhousie University, "the picture is grey—survival and modest consolidation." [19] Canada did not have the resources—potential university students, well-trained faculty members or finances—to support a dozen or more universities. While some successfully struggled to overcome these difficulties, others continued only by offering considerably less than an adequate university program.

An indication of the continuing difficulties of the multiplicity of small colleges in a sparsely populated country is given in a 1921 report prepared for the Carnegie Foundation by Kenneth Sills, president of Bowdoin College in Maine, and by William Learned of the Carnegie Foundation for the Advancement of Teaching. The study, which Harris reports on, was of the educational institutions in the Maritime Provinces.

> . . . . They noted that so far as the degree-granting institutions were concerned government support was limited to the annual grant made by the Province of Nova Scotia to the Nova Scotia Technical College ($50,000) and by the Province of New Brunswick to the University of New Brunswick ($25,000). This meant that all the other universities were entirely dependent upon student fees and endowment. But the combined endowment of Acadia, Dalhousie, King's, Mount Allison and St. Francis Xavier, which together enrolled about 1,000 students, was substantially less than that of any *one* of the three New England colleges, Amherst, Bowdoin and Williams, none of which enrolled more than 500 students.[20]

The reality of the situation was that only those universities that had government grants or substantial private gifts could survive. After 1867, education was made a provincial responsibility, and since most provinces were averse to providing funds for denominational colleges or universities, these were left almost entirely dependent on private donors. It was inevitable that only a few strong universities would emerge and that many would close and some would survive without distinction. Thus it was. In the first part of the century McGill and Toronto were the leaders; others in the east were respectable but not outstanding, and the western provincial universities—Manitoba (1877), Saskatchewan (1890), Alberta (1882), and British Columbia (1890)[21]—grew slowly and developed rapidly only after World War II.

Most of the leading universities were provincial institutions; of the others, Queen's and Western did receive some public funds after 1920. A royal commission on university finance in Ontario in 1920

> . . . recognized that the government's first responsibility was to support the University of Toronto . . . but also since Queen's [now an undenominational university] and University of Western Ontario were providing a special service for the eastern and southwestern districts of Ontario they also should receive regular and substantial assistance.[22]

McGill and Dalhousie are the only two examples of Canadian universities that achieved status primarily with the support of private gifts. Dalhousie had raised some $2,600,000 between 1890 and 1920 from foundations and private benefactors, and while this did not allow it to provide a quality of work comparable to its neighbors in the United States, it possessed a degree of affluence beyond that of its competitors in the Maritime Provinces. Perhaps only McGill, before the Depression years, could be ranked with the leading universities of the United States. Located in Montreal, in the early part of the century Canada's largest and wealthiest city, it had the support of the wealthy English-speaking businessmen in a predominantly French-speaking province. Consciously or not, these men may well have seen McGill as the bastion of British ideas and values. In any case it is clear that they supported McGill generously.[23]

> By 1920 it [McGill] was unquestionably Canada's most famous university, the institution from which Sir William Osler had graduated and at which he had done his early teaching, at which Sir Ernest Rutherford had conducted his Nobel prize-winning experiments in radiation physics, and at which Stephen Leacock taught Political Science when he was not writing his humorous books. The fame of McGill also owed something to the enthusiasm of the many Americans who had been attracted to and graduated from its Medical School.[24]

The two French-speaking universities in Quebec (Laval, 1852, and Montreal, 1919) developed slowly, receiving little help from the Quebec government. They were forced to operate on "remarkably small budgets." [25] They had, nonetheless, a profound influence not only in sustaining the French culture but also in adapting that culture to an industrial society. By 1940 these two universities were comparable in size, in organization, and in range of offerings to McGill and Toronto,[26] offering work in arts and science, law, medicine, and dentistry. Their history is one of long struggle with inadequate financial support but of great import, particularly at Laval, where in the late Depression years a brilliant group of young social scientists under the leadership of Reverend Père Georges-Henri Levesque initiated studies on a series of current social and political problems in Quebec.

The Canadian universities in the first half of the twentieth century demonstrated a peculiar blend of educational philosophies.[27] On the one hand, they had the pragmatic outlook of American universities and embraced professional faculties with alacrity, if not always with enthusiasm. In 1921 degrees were being given in various Canadian universities in law, medicine, theology, engineering and applied science, social work, dentistry, pharmacy, nursing, health and physical education, agriculture, architecture, forestry, veterinary science, and household science. Indeed, in 1921 there were 2,854 students in engineering and applied science—more than 10 percent of the total university enrollment.[28] In this respect Canada was clearly in the North American tradition.

Whether because of lack of resources or suspicion of the validity of the German model—or more probably because of the Oxbridge conviction that the undergraduate was of first importance—graduate education was neglected in Canada. In 1928 J. M. Tory, president of the University of Alberta, wrote:

> . . . my judgment is that the weakest part of our whole system . . . is in our graduate work. . . . We allow other countries to take away our choicest men and train them for their own services.[29]

And writing on scholarship in Canada in 1945, J. B. Brebner, a Canadian teaching at Columbia University, wrote:

> Advanced studies in Canada have only 3 or 4 . . . universities which seriously attempt to provide staff and faculties for

conclusive graduate work . . . that is, to the doctoral level and these do so only in some areas.[30]

Clearly Canada was not following Germany or the United States in graduate work. It was not until World War II, during which the paucity of trained manpower became obvious, that a change in this attitude occurred.

In this respect, and certainly in undergraduate education, Canada was firmly in the British tradition. The undergraduate honors program, which had features unique to Canada, nonetheless is clearly a derivative of Oxford and Cambridge. It was given great emphasis in Canada and was until after World War II perhaps the most distinctive feature of higher education in the country. What evolved was a dual bachelor's degree program: one a general or pass B.A. to be completed in three years after senior matriculation, and the second an honors B.A. requiring four years of study after senior matriculation. The pass B.A. generally required exposure to a number of disciplines, some minimum concentration on one subject, and, given these limitations, some choice of subjects to complete the requirements. The four-year honors course provided for some minimal selection of related subjects, but its emphasis was intensive study in the field selected. The four-year honors program had high standards, it attracted the very best students, and it produced some outstanding scholars. The result was that this program was held in high esteem and given priority in budget allocations and teaching assignments.

Many Canadian universities were to divide their undergraduate students in this way, with prestige and status going to the universities with the largest numbers of students in honors courses as compared to the number of students in the general course. There were other attitudes and practices copied from Oxbridge, such as the belief in the influence of education on character formation, the reluctance to introduce many of the new subjects in social science,[31] and the general reticence to think in Freudian terms or to talk about personality problems. The first half of the twentieth century in Canadian universities is the story—if it could be told in detail—of the gradual erosion of the concept of a "good university" in British terms to a gradual acceptance of the advantages of the American university, and a desperate search for something distinctively Canadian.

United States: After the Civil War (1861–1865) the United States began a long, dramatic, and decisive rebuilding program which accelerated rapidly, until at the end of World War II, the country stood as the wealthiest and most powerful nation in the world. The universities were part of that society, reflecting its desires, its values, and its movement. Their growth was a reflection of the dynamic society: from 1870 until the 1950s, enrollment in universities "doubled about every 15 years with a regularity practically unaffected by anything." [32] There was continuous quantitative growth in both the nation and its universities in this period.

In such a society it was unlikely that the small religious college, which sought to shape the student as the model of a pious, righteous, and educated person, would serve the needs or the demands of an increasingly urbanized, secularized, and industrialized country. There was, therefore, after the Civil War a long period of discussion, often of conflict and tension, about the purpose and the form of colleges and universities.[33] The role of the religious-oriented college as a model, maintained for the last half of the nineteenth century, died slowly. There was no doubt that the day of such colleges had passed, but the hold of piety and religiosity in colleges and universities was relaxed only gradually. Cornell abandoned compulsory chapel in 1865, the University of Wisconsin in 1868, Johns Hopkins in 1876,[34] and Harvard in 1886, but at other private Eastern colleges, compulsory chapel remained: at Dartmouth until 1925, at Yale until 1926, and at Princeton until 1932.[35]

Four competitive ideologies sought predominance after 1865.[36] These were (1) the "mental discipline" school, which assumed that enforced contact with Greek and Latin grammar and with mathematics sharpened the mental faculties and was conducive to strength of character and disciplined work habits (this was, of course, a secular adaptation of the religious college); (2) the philosophy of utility, which sought to make education useful, practical, and of public service; (3) the research concept, which came from German universities and emphasized the need for universities to engage continuously in detailed empirical studies; and (4) the cultural school, with its emphasis on the humanities and the need to develop the aesthetically sensitive "all-around" student.

The debates about these purposes of the university were lively and often heated before the turn of the century;[37] thereafter they continued in ritualistic fashion, but by then the questions seemed irrelevant. The issues were never resolved in intellectual terms. Practical and technical developments took command. As Veysey says about the concept of the cultural school, "It was a popular philosophy with articulate advocates, and won many supporters without winning the contest." [38]

No one won the contest. The vastness of the United States, its diversity, its varied subcultures, its multiplicity of developmental needs, and its large number of various-sized colleges and universities made possible the tolerance of most prevailing philosophies and the enthusiastic support of each of these in some form or another. It is true that the classical model largely disappeared before 1900, but like compulsory chapel, its demise was long and laborious and there were still some advocates and "schools" of this kind for many years after the turn of the century.

At first it seemed that the distinctive character of higher education in the United States was to be its diversity.

> By 1900 there were special colleges for Baptists and Catholics, for men and women, for whites and blacks, for rich and not-so-rich, for North and South, for small town and big city, for adolescents and adults, for engineers and teachers.[39]

But a number of major themes that were to shape the dominant character of the American university were in process of development. One of these was pragmatism. It emerged early and grew in importance.

In 1850 a special committee of the Massachusetts Legislature said of Harvard:

The college fails to answer the just expectations of the people of the State. A college should be open to boys who seek specific learning for a specific purpose. *It should give the people the practical instruction they want and not a classical literary course suitable only for aristocracy.* It should help young men to become better farmers, mechanics, and merchants. [Italics added] [40]

This was a theme heard increasingly in the United States. The desire was not, as in Britain, for an aristocracy but for those practical skills that would contribute to the growth of a developing country. The colleges and universities—all struggling for support and survival—could not afford to ignore this demand. When Ezra Cornell began planning a college in Ithaca in the early 1860s, he said, "I would found an institution where any person can find instruction in any study," [41] and while Cornell's first president, Andrew W. White, was less venturesome, Cornell like others at this time began to provide practical courses in agriculture and mechanics.

A decisive blow for utility was the passage of the Morrill Act in 1862, by which the federal government would provide aid to states which would support colleges whose curriculum included agriculture and mechanical instruction.[42] These land-grant colleges might well have become separate trade schools, but indeed they were used as a basis of support for the development of great state universities in which practical subjects and courses were combined with more traditional studies.

Another major influence was the German university. Americans in increasing numbers had been going to these universities for graduate study;[43] most of them were impressed with the devotion to research and the emphasis given to graduate work in Germany. This influence was dramatized by the founding of three new universities before 1900 which were clearly influenced by the German interest in science and research. Johns Hopkins University (1875), Clark University (1889), and the University of Chicago (1892) all gave emphasis, if not exclusive priority, to research and graduate education. Daniel Gilman, the first president of Johns Hopkins, sought to stress the German techniques of laboratory and seminar work and gathered around him men of similar interests.

> In . . . specific terms the Hopkins atmosphere combined two important qualities. . . . On the one hand, the early Hopkins men prided themselves on the absence of form, ritual or ceremony; they boasted of their liberty to pour forth their energies uninterruptedly into the substance of whatever study engrossed them. Yet simultaneously the pressure toward hard work was intense, for it was enforced by a constant, close-range comparison with one's peers. . . . To a certain degree, these qualities have remained present in the leading American graduate schools ever since. . . .[44]

Clark University began as an exclusively graduate school for advanced scholars, and while this idea could not be sustained, it had at the time of its origin considerable impact on higher education.[45] William Rainey Harper at Chicago was more realistic, perhaps because his school was later in opening, and he built a firmer base of undergraduate studies, but his constant effort was to seek out and recruit the finest scholars available so that Chicago might represent the highest standards of scholarship.[46]

The various trends and influences in shaping the new American university were to be combined and given impetus by Harvard University and its president (from 1869 to 1909) Charles Eliot. Harvard had the prestige and Eliot the foresight to initiate changes that were decisive for the future. These were (1) to introduce the elective system in the undergraduate curriculum and thus not only free students to choose the courses they wished to study but to loosen the curriculum, to introduce new subjects, and to engage eager young scholars, many of whom had been trained in Germany, to teach these new subjects;[47] (2) to support professional faculties (hence the introduction of new schools such as business, which opened formally in 1908);[48] and (3) to build up gradually graduate studies in the arts and sciences. By these means new impetus was given to a broadened curriculum in arts and science, to scholarship and graduate work, and to professional "practical" schools. A new model for the university was emerging: it was large, diverse, flexible, and gave support to both practical and theoretical studies at both the undergraduate and graduate levels, to research focused on immediate problems and to research undertaken for its own sake.

There were other factors present that made the American university vital. These were the drive, the organizational capacity, the enterprise, and the competitive spirit of its people; the dynamic mood of the nation; and the wealth that was accumulating in a growing economy. All these impinged on the university and stimulated its growth. The university structure with its lay board of trustees encouraged an entrepreneurial, businesslike enterprise that placed great responsibility on the president for the university's growth. Individuals of great energy and vision appeared to head and build outstanding universities: Eliot at Harvard, White at Cornell, Angell at Michigan, Harper at Chicago, Gilman at Johns Hopkins and California, and Jordan at Stanford. The ambition of society was reflected in these individuals, whose talents, sharpened by competition and the desire to excel, were centered on building great universities. The prestige of these individuals, the centrality of their role in the university, and their driving ambition gave a focus to the enterprise that overshadowed differences in the university about purpose and direction.[49]

All these developments led in the period 1900–1950 to the growth of a unique type of institution: the multiversity. The various concepts for models of higher education were, with appropriate adaptations, merged in the one institution. The trend since the turn of the century clearly has been away from specialized institutions of higher education to universities performing an increasingly greater variety of functions.[50]

Our instinct, time and again, was to turn to higher education whenever there was a new job to be done, and as a consequence both the functions of higher education and the varied activities these functions tended to spawn steadily multiplied, with little thought on anyone's part of the consequences, or of the alternatives.[51]

Thus the dominant feature of higher education in the

United States after World War I was the large institution that combined a liberal arts college, graduate schools in the arts and sciences, and professional schools (usually and preferably at the graduate level). While there developed an ever-increasing number of colleges and universities after 1900, the field of higher education was dominated by a very small proportion of these institutions. Jencks and Riesman calculate that there were only about twenty-two major universities in the United States in the period 1926–1947.[52] The prime objective of many of the small colleges seemed to be to prepare students for graduate work or for professional schools in the larger universities. For this reason the curriculum and standards in these colleges were greatly influenced by the demands of the large universities. And while these few major universities had remarkably large and varied programs, they were very similar to each other; all

> . . . had the same internal rationale as large industrial concerns that combined different kinds and levels of production for the purpose of minimizing their dependence on other firms and on the vagaries of the market. Just as those industrial combinations did, the multiversity arose under the conditions of a relatively competitive market in education, research and professional services.[53]

Some General Observations

The revitalization of the university between 1850 and 1950 was due to a combination of factors: (1) industrialization, the resulting growth of the economy, and the need for technology and trained manpower; (2) the shift from authoritarian to empirical thought, which provided a new method of studying natural and social phenomena and thereby not only provided new knowledge but also a limitless opportunity to expand knowledge; (3) increasing dissatisfaction with the religious-oriented colleges which to many seemed oblivious to the changes taking place around them. The union of these forces in the early part of the nineteenth century, to which the universities responded in varying degrees and at an uneven pace, led to the formation of the modern university with its emphasis on research, expanding enrollments, and public service.

It will be noted that some of the same forces that stimulated the growth of the medieval university were, in more dramatic form, to nourish the rebirth of the university after 1850. The need for "advanced training" beyond anything that could be provided by the cathedral schools, the growth of commerce, and the new knowledge gave impetus to the medieval university. What was significantly different in the university after 1850 was the nature of the "new knowledge." The sources of knowledge for the medieval university soon dried up, and the scholasticism of the day was designed to refine existing, but not to add new, knowledge. It was inevitable that a university so encapsulated would lose its vitality. But the work of the "amateur scientists" and particularly the methods of the German professional scientists were designed to expand consistently the whole field of knowledge. By identifying itself with this method, the university thus embarked after 1850 on a great intellectual exploration, in the course of which there would be only endless vistas. Fresh discoveries provided new opportunities for further revelations.

Apart from this, much of the ideology, a good deal of the structure, and most of the forms and traditions of the first medieval universities continued almost unchanged. The university was for advanced cognitive learning—a more sophisticated and complex learning than was or could be provided in cathedral or secondary schools. Professors were loyal to their colleagues, to their university, to their students, and to learning. Knowledge was divided: there were faculties and departments. There were courses, exams, degrees, and convocation ceremonies. In the midst of expansion, of new ways of thinking and learning, and of a changing social environment, much in the university remained unaltered.

But in a society seized with the inevitability of growth and progress, the new university moved apace. The goals of society and the university appeared consistent and compatible. Each helped the other. The university was seen as an institution of status and prestige essential to the well-being of an advancing society. Its influence and its usefulness were gradually to increase and to move dramatically upward as the result of two world wars.

Something approximating an informal system of higher education began to appear in the early part of the twentieth century. At one end of the spectrum were the early junior community and the technical colleges; further on were the established universities (the Redbrick, the not-quite-developed state universities, and the post-1900 Canadian universities); and at the end of the spectrum were the graduate schools in the prestigious universities. There was the beginning of a plan to accommodate almost every high school graduate with almost any interest. But it was clear that a class system both in respect to people and to universities was emerging. There was a clear class distinction between those who attended junior or technical colleges and those who attended universities such as Oxford or Harvard. The colleges in the lower ranks more frequently drew their students from families of lower-income groups and prepared them for sub-elite positions in the occupational hierarchy, whereas the students in established universities frequently came from professional and upper-class families and graduated into the elite professions.[54]

Similarly, universities tended to be rated on a prestige scale, those with greatest status being Oxford and Cambridge in England, McGill and Toronto in Canada, and those dozen or so graduate schools with the highest reputation in the United States. These universities came to constitute almost a control center for the whole system that has been described. They selected the best students, kept the best of these for themselves, sent others to teach at the best colleges, and sent still others to lesser centers of learning, but in all they sought to teach those who would teach in all parts of the system. These prestigious universities established standards (ideals, myths, and practices) passed on down the line, even into the grade school.[55] One of the reasons for the growing popularity of the university was that many parents saw it as a means of social mobility. As we will see later (Chapter 4), it is clear that the universities of the day were highly class-structured and that a much greater proportion of the children of upper-class people were in universities than children of lower-class families.[56] In the United States it was particularly evident that blacks were discriminated against, not only in terms of numbers enrolled in college but also in terms of the quality of education provided in black colleges.[57]

It can be said in general that the universities in Canada, England, and the United States responded to new opportunities and new resources between 1850 and 1950 and that they enlarged their horizons, their curricula, and their constituency. They became all-powerful in the educational system, exercising almost monopolistic control over that system in each country. Withal they remained conservative, ideologically bound to established goals, class-structured, and peculiarly unprepared to face new demands for reform after World War II.

While the above comments can be made with some justification about the universities in Canada, the United States, and England, there were nonetheless significant differences. Illustrations of these differences may be seen in Tables One, Two, and Three.

The fundamentally different philosophies that dominated the universities of the three countries are seen in these tables. As the data show, the dynamic thrust of higher education in the United States—a tenfold expansion of enrollment between the years 1900 and 1950, the gradually expanding graduate program, the greater acceptance of women students—suggests a more open and democratic system than that in either Canada or Britain. The latter retained its elitist character into the postwar period, reflecting the belief that higher education was for the small group who could be expected to give leadership to the country in the future—and this in British terms was not likely to include many females. In curriculum and general orientation Canada was in the British tradition, but its movement toward the American system is apparent as, in terms of per capita enrollment in both undergraduate and graduate programs, it surpassed Britain and bore comparison with developments in the United States. For a small country, some decades behind Britain and

TABLE ONE

| | 1900 (circa) | | |
	Britain*	Canada†	United States‡
Population	37.0 m	5.3 m	76.1 m
Number of universities	11	20	977
Number of students	14,870	9,700	237,592
Number of women students	n.a.	n.a.	85,338
Number of graduate students	n.a.	n.a.	5,831

TABLE TWO

| | 1920 (circa) | | |
	Britain*	Canada†	United States‡
Population	42.7 m	8.8 m	106.4 m
Number of universities	15	23	1,041
Number of students	36,996	22,292	597,880
Number of women students	10,110	3,824	282,942
Number of graduate students	1,273	423	15,612

TABLE THREE

| | 1950 (circa) | | |
	Britain*	Canada†	United States‡
Population	48.9 m	14.0 m	151.7 m
Number of universities	17	46	1,851
Total enrollment	85,314	63,719	2,639,021
Number of women students	19,483	11,642	805,953
Number of graduate students	11,327	4,559	237,208

* These figures were supplied by the Department of Health and Science, London. It should be noted that the figures are for the years 1901, 1921, and 1951. Figures for 1951 are for full-time students only.

† These figures are provided by Statistics Canada, but it should be noted that the population is for the years 1901, 1921, and 1951. The figure for chartered universities was 80 in 1950. But many of these were colleges merged in larger universities. I think my revised figure (46) gives a more accurate picture of the situation.

‡ These figures were supplied by the Department of Health, Education, and Welfare, Washington, D.C. It should be noted that the figures are for the academic years 1899–1900, 1919–20, and 1949–50.

the United States in economic development, the advances in Canada suggest a strong belief in the importance of higher education and a considerable willingness to make financial sacrifices to support this conviction.

Perhaps the major difference was in the conception of what a university should be. Oxford and Cambridge with superior wealth, special privileges, and leading scholars dominated the English university system.[58] For Oxbridge the university was a place where the best minds—of which there were few—would interact in an intimate domestic setting to produce knowledgeable and cultured leaders of society. To this idea they held with great tenacity throughout the period. The newer universities in both England and Canada were greatly influenced by the elitist conception, and while they responded to other forces by introducing many practical subjects, most of their students were enrolled in undergraduate courses in arts and science or in medicine or engineering.[59]

The universities in the United States were much more responsive to the social needs of the day. There was admiration of and respect for Oxford and Cambridge, especially in the New England colleges, but the system as a whole was more utilitarian, providing a vast array of vocationally oriented courses and relating a portion of its research activity to practical community needs. The university became a multipurpose and multifunctional institution, sharply criticized for its lack of clear parameters,[60] but it developed as a system which in terms of numbers served, productive research, and quality of graduate programs was unequaled in the world. The role of the businessmen on the governing boards and the central role of the entrepreneurial president in the highly competitive academic marketplace in the United States was unquestionably an extremely important factor in this result.[61]

Peace and Revolution (1950–1975)

And what can one say briefly about the university in the turbulent twenty-five-year period between 1950 and 1975? The university had not before been subjected to such great pressure, in a short period, to adapt quickly to a new situation. Since each of the chapters which follow will deal with some aspects of the dramatic developments in the postwar period, we will deal here only summarily with three of the forces operative in this period: enrollment expansion, research development, and the student revolution. The universities in England, Canada, and the United States were all deeply involved and in the same manner with these issues, but their method of coping with them was somewhat different.

The universities in these countries had been growing steadily since the turn of the century (although to some, painfully slowly in Britain), and in all there was a sharp rise in enrollment as veterans swarmed to the campus after World War II. If there was any expectation that this was a temporary bulge in the size of the student body, it was soon dispelled by the obvious change in postwar birthrate and in the social climate which demanded greater and more equal opportunity for youth to secure an education and all it meant: possession of the "high culture," membership in the elite professions, status in the community, opportunity for prestigious jobs.

In all three countries, there were detailed studies of present university and future student enrollment. In all three countries, a sharp rise was predicted, and the assumption of the postwar egalitarian society that a much higher proportion of youth should go to university seemed not to be seriously questioned in Canada and the United States and was only moderately questioned in Britain.

In the United States the president's commission on higher education reported in 1947.[62] It suggested that there should be far more than the 16 percent of the nineteen to twenty-one age group in university [63] and calculated that:

> . . . at least 49 percent of our population has the mental ability to complete 14 years of schooling . . . and at least 32 percent . . . has the mental ability to complete an advanced liberal or specialized professional education.[64]

On the basis of these assumptions, it made some projections:

The Commission believes that in 1960 a minimum of 4,600,000 young people should be enrolled in nonprofit institutions for education beyond the traditional twelfth grade. Of this total number, 2,500,000 should be in the thirteenth and fourteenth grades (junior college level); 1,500,000 in the fifteenth and sixteenth grades (senior college level); and 600,000 in graduate and professional schools beyond the first degree.[65]

The commission took a strong position against what it considered discriminatory practices in the university in respect of the poor, blacks, and women, and it urged realistic admission standards and scholarship aid to remedy this situation. The commission document was a bold stroke for "the democratization of higher education." And the American people were ready for it.

In Britain the royal commission on higher education headed by Lord Robbins took a more cautious line, but one which was nonetheless revolutionary in the community to which he was reporting. His proposal was that the approximately 130,000 student places in 1962 should be increased to 220,000 in 1973 and close to 350,000 by 1982. This in a country in which university enrollment was about 50,000 in 1939!

In Canada each province had its own study of future enrollment, but all were influenced by a study issued by the Education Division of the Bureau of Statistics, which forecast that "a gradual increasing proportion of a rapidly growing youth population" would double university enrollment in ten years.[66] There was general acceptance throughout Canada that this forecast should become reality.

All the projections to 1970 proved to be modest, as Table Four suggests.

In each country there was a doubling of enrollment between 1960 and 1970 in what was undoubtedly the greatest acceleration of enrollment in university history. But the manner in which this expansion was met differed and is significant. In the United States there were relatively few new universities (in the sense of being independent of other colleges and universities) created. The problem was met by modest expansion of many of the prestigious private universities

TABLE FOUR

Year	Britain *	Canada †	United States ‡
	Number of colleges and universities		
1950	17	46	1,851
1960	21	48	2,008
1970	45	67	2,557
	Enrollment in colleges and universities		
1950	85,314	63,719	2,639,021
1960	107,699	116,466	3,215,544
1970	228,131	303,510	7,545,340

* Data supplied by Department of Education and Science, London. It should be noted that figures are for the years 1951, 1961, and 1971 and are for full-time students only.

† Data supplied by Statistics Canada. The figures for chartered universities were 80 in 1950 and 77 in 1960. But many of those were colleges merged in larger universities, such as the University of Toronto. I think my revised figures give a more accurate picture of the situation.

‡ Data supplied by Department of Health, Education, and Welfare, Washington, D.C. Figures are for the academic years 1949–50, 1959–60, and 1970–71.

such as Harvard and Yale; by creating new branches of existing universities such as Illinois's Chicago campus or the Riverside, San Diego, etc., campuses of the University of California; and by substantial increases in enrollments at many universities, particularly the state ones.

The dilemma faced by Britain was considerable. Her tradition was the "small ancient college," and there was no way, it seemed, that this concept could meet the demands of mass education. The compromise was minimal. The problem was met by (1) some increase in the enrollment at the ancient and civic universities, (2) creation of a dozen new universities located in various parts of the country, many of them designed originally to accommodate a maximum of 3,000 students, and (3) the upgrading of many technical colleges into universities and the expansion of their faculties. While such expansion and growth inevitably affected traditional practices (e.g., at least half the Oxford college undergraduates were required to "live out"), still the English were remarkably persistent in protecting and continuing many of their traditional ideas of what a university should be like.

Canada had its own unique solution to surging enrollments. As in the United States, junior or community colleges were started as a way of relieving pressure on the universities and of providing a different type of postsecondary education for many students. Existing universities also expanded, and new universities were started in all provinces except two of the Maritime Provinces. The new universities appeared to be designed in size less by philosophical or educational considerations than by the probable demand for student places in the immediate vicinity. Thus York (in Toronto), Waterloo (in Kitchener-Waterloo), Simon Fraser (in Vancouver), all in centers of large population, grew much more rapidly than Lethbridge (in Alberta), Laurentian (in Sudbury), and Trent (in Peterborough), which were located in relatively small cities.

The size to which universities grew in the three countries is of import. In 1958 there were ten universities in the United States with an enrollment of over 20,000 students; by 1969 that number had grown to sixty-five, of which twenty-six universities had over 30,000 students.[67] Except for the University of London, which was a federated multicampus organization, no university in England in 1960 had as many as 10,000 students, and this was still true in 1970.[68] The Robbins report considered 9,000 to 10,000 an upper limit for student numbers, and this was widely approved in the university and by the public. In 1960 Canada had only ten universities with over 2,000 students, and of these only three had enrollments of 10,000 students. By 1970, twenty-two Canadian universities had over 5,000 students, ten had enrollments of over 10,000, and two were well over the 20,000 student figure.[69]

Arguments about "optimal size" raged on the campus, but there were few studies and no convincing data to prove that "1,000 is too small" or that "40,000 is too large." In the academic community generally there was sympathy with the British position and concern with the loss of intimate contact on the large North American campus. But the pressure at the latter was to give all youth an opportunity and therefore to expand endlessly to meet this need. The British tended to merge this revolutionary new force with traditional practices and were most reluctant to give up any of the latter. The North American university responded much more to the new revolutionary force of egalitarianism and perhaps surrendered more of its tradition, although this tradition was much less coherent and firmly rooted in America than in Britain before World War II.

The second major change in this period related to the high priority given to graduate instruction and to research. The need for new university teachers alone would give impetus to graduate work, but the demands of society, and especially government agencies, for highly trained scientists and social scientists, for expert consultants, and for researchers spurred the growth of graduate work in universities in these three countries. The growth was impressive (see Table Five).

TABLE FIVE

Country	Graduate school enrollment		
	1950	*1960*	*1970*
Great Britain*	11,327	17,836	42,084
Canada†	4,559	9,120	33,172
United States‡	237,208	341,820	900,032

* Data supplied by Department of Education and Science, London. It should be noted that figures are for the years 1951, 1961, 1971.

† Data supplied by Statistics Canada.

‡ Data supplied by Department of Health, Education, and Welfare, Washington, D.C. Figures are for academic years 1949–50, 1959–60, 1970–71.

The dramatic growth of graduate work in Britain raised the question, as it had for American universities earlier, of the balance of priorities between undergraduate and graduate education and, less directly, the balance between teaching and research. Close to 20 percent of students in Britain in 1971 were graduate students, compared with about 14 percent in the United States and 10 percent in Canada. Clearly the British had responded vigorously, if somewhat belatedly, to the requirements of modern society for advanced knowledge and skilled manpower. Whether this would adversely affect the excellence of the undergraduate program was not immediately apparent.

A companion development relevant to this question in the three countries concerned was the remarkable growth of research programs in universities. The World War II demand for scientists, particularly, but also for economists, linguists, anthropologists, experts in communication, and students of leadership and morale, brought the university and its scholars into public view as never before. Much of the knowledge and the manpower required during the war and later in the postindustrial age was centered in the universities, and to these governments and industry turned for help. Money was not a problem; huge grants were made to individuals and to newly organized research institutes in the universities.[70]

The expansion of graduate work and of research activity inevitably affected the orientation of the university. Research and graduate work was "where the action was," and the action was often related much more to the outside world than to the university. For many professors the university was less of an all-absorbing center for their time, their loyalty, and their interests than in previous times.

Inevitably, the structure of the university would be affected. As enrollments, budgets, and research grants increased, existing arrangements for governance and administration were strained. Bureaucracy and regulations, with their accompanying irritations and impersonality, increased. In the early 1960s the university status was very great, but the shift in frontiers, the change in roles, the multiplication of functions, the administrative strains of growth that were becoming evident, all foreshadowed a major threat to stability, if not a complete collapse.

This was the period, also, of the "student revolution." In the academic year 1969–70 in the United States, it is said there were "9,000 protest demonstrations at two-thirds of the American colleges and universities." [71] In Canada in the sixties there had been a $2 million computer fire started by students at Sir George Williams University in Montreal, and almost every university in the nation faced some kind of student demonstration and uprising during the latter part of the decade. The demonstration and sit-in at the London School of Economics was perhaps the most dramatic incident in England, but most universities there also felt the rumble of the revolutionary movement.

We will discuss this movement and the implications for the university in Chapter 5. Here it is enough to say that the student revolution, some aspects of which were supported by faculty members, shook the very foundations of the university. On the surface, by 1970–71 the campus in all countries was relatively quiet, and some reforms had been made in light of student demands, although on the whole these were not significant.[72] On the surface the university looked much as it did in 1960.

If one probed deeper, however, serious crevices in the university fortress became apparent. Part of the thrust of the revolution had been toward what Karl Mannheim called "the democratization of genius," the belief that all are equally equipped to move in and through the university and to reap its highest rewards. This was a direct attack on a fundamental principle of the university, its certifying and accrediting function, its insistence on standards, and its search for excellence. But in these revolutionary days,

> . . . everything is under attack: authority, since no man is better than any other; the past, since learning tells us nothing; discipline and specialization, because they are constricting. What results is a fierce anti-intellectualism, since what counts is feeling and sentiment, not cognition. Education, then, is not the transmission of learning, but a search for "meaningful identity," to be gained by "dialogue," "encounter," and "confrontation." [73]

The result of such a movement was to create confusion, doubt, and uncertainty in the university. It had lived for centuries on the basis of assumptions seldom challenged—and never with the vigor or the success of the current critics. Profound differences of view were evident within the universities. The many specializations, faculties, and functions had divided the university, particularly as it expanded after 1950.

Now it was further divided by differing educational and political philosophies.

The loss of consensus and self-confidence within the university quickly communicated itself to the public. It was at a time (1970–1975) when the rate of increase in enrollments was declining and when the public was concerned about the escalating costs of education in a period of economic recession. The university appeared to be an appropriate whipping boy, and questions about university budgets and autonomy were frequently raised in the press and in elected assemblies. Most of these implied criticism of the university, with the result that by 1975 almost all universities were confronting smaller budgets than they felt essential.[74] There seemed little public sympathy for their financial difficulties.

The inability of the university to reply clearly and vigorously to public criticism reflected the confusion within its own ranks. The differences of view about the role of the university were fundamental and complex. One might well question in 1975 the probability of the university surviving with any of its traditions intact. To paraphrase a question posed by Edward Shils: Can a modern university maintain a stable and orderly structure when its professors, and others who share power with them, have lost their self-confidence and are dominated by a clamorous hostility against the university and those who operate it? [75]

NOTES

1. McNeill, 1971, p. 417.

2. Shils, 1972*b*, p. 71.

3. Halsey, 1962, p. 91.

4. Kneller, 1955, pp. 20–21.

5. Flexner, 1968, p. 264.

6. Arnold, 1868, p. 176; Halsey and Trow, 1971, p. 53.

7. Grant-Robertson, 1930, p. 75.

8. Herklots, 1928, pp. 87–88.

9. Manchester, 1851; Birmingham, 1900; Leeds, 1904; Bristol, 1909; Liverpool, 1903; Sheffield, 1905 (*Encyclopaedia Britannica,* 1967, vol. 22, pp. 871-872); and after the Second World War charters were given to former provincial colleges at Nottingham, Southampton, Hull, Exeter, and Leicester (Halsey and Trow, 1971, p. 58).

10. Ben-David and Zloczower, 1962, p. 67.

11 Armytage, 1955, p. 244.

12. Halsey and Trow, 1971, p. 40.

13. Ibid., p. 214.

14. Shils, 1972*b*, p. 77.

15. The students at Oxbridge were 45 percent from public schools, whereas boys from state schools made up 75 percent of the overall university population in 1960 (Beloff, 1968, p. 16).

16. Truscot, 1943, p. 37.

17. Beloff, 1968, pp. 19-20.

18. Berton, 1971, p. 51.

19. Harris, 1973, chap. 9, p. 1.

20. Ibid., chap. 14, p. 2.

21. Ibid., chap. 9, p. 18.

22. Ibid., chap. 14, p. 27.

23. Harris, 1973, chap. 14.

24. Ibid., chap. 14, p. 14.

25. Ibid., chap. 23, p. 29.

26. Ibid.

27. An interesting comparison of attitudes to education in

Canada and the United States was reported in *Canadian Society;* it suggested that Canadians tend to be more concerned with individual needs and humanistic studies than the Americans to their south (Blishen et al., 1968, p. 214).

28. Harris, 1973, chap. 19.

29. Quoted in ibid., app., n. 18.

30. Ibid.

31. S. D. Clark, 1974, p. 16.

32. Ashby, 1971, p. 4; see also Ben-David, 1972, p. 1.

33. Ben-David, 1972, pp. 50–60.

34. Ibid., p. 55.

35. Hofstadter and Metzger, 1955, p. 361.

36. Veysey, 1965, pp. 21–233.

37. Ben-David, 1972, pp. 50–60.

38. Veysey, 1965, p. 257.

39. Jencks and Riesman, 1968, p. 3.

40. Morison, 1965, p. 287.

41. Veysey, 1965, p. 82.

42. Ibid., p. 15.

43. During the period 1815–1915 it has been estimated that approximately 10,000 students from the United States matriculated in German universities (Smyth, 1972, p. 277).

44. Veysey, 1965, p. 164.

45. Ibid., p. 165.

46. Storr, 1966.

47. See Morison, 1965; Veysey, 1965.

48. Morison, 1965, p. 471.

49. Veysey, 1965, pp. 311–312.

50. Ben-David, 1968–69, p. 27.

51. Pifer, 1971, p. 10.

52. They define a major university as one which turns out more than 1 percent of the nation's Ph.D.'s (Jencks and Riesman, 1968, p. 14).

53. Ben-David, 1972, p. 46.

54. Archer, 1972, pp. 22–23; Touraine, 1974, pp. 104–105.

55. Sexton, 1974, p. 298; Touraine, 1974.

56. Blishen et al., 1968, p. 253.

57. Touraine, 1974, p. 100.

58. Ben-David and Zloczower, 1962, p. 67.

59. Ibid. Harris reports 1960 enrollment in all Canadian universities as follows: forestry—1,686, physical and occupational therapy—476, nursing—1,630, household sciences—1,598, social work—775, music—397, fine and applied art—91 (Harris, 1973, chap. 30, p. 9).

60. Ben-David, 1972.

61. Ibid.

62. *Higher Education for American Democracy,* 1947, vol. 1.

63. Ibid., p. 5.

64. Ibid., p. 41.

65. Ibid., p. 39.

66. Sheffield, 1955.

67. Sutherland, 1973, p. 62.

68. Ibid., p. 62.

69. Harris, 1973, chap. 35, p. 6.

70. Federal expenditures on research in the United States were 1.59 billion in 1945, rose to 4.46 billion in 1956, and to 14.87 billion in 1965 (Ben-David, 1972, p. 106).

71. Schick, 1972, p. 93.

72. D. R. Ladd, 1972, p. 210.

73. Bell, 1971, p. 161.

74. "Let the Professors Work Harder," 1974, p. B4; see also MacArthur, 1974, p. 3.

75. Shils, 1972a, p. 9.

part two

THE PEOPLE

chapter three

●

STUDENTS

While it has always been agreed that one could not have a university without students, there have been quite different opinions—and never more so than in the past two decades—about the role of the student in the university.

Is the student's role similar to that of an *apprentice*—working closely with a master—believing the master, studying the master's ways, and gradually becoming a master? Or is the proper relationship one of a *ward* of the university—placed by one's parents or society in the custody of the university, which is responsible for the student's welfare and moral and intellectual training? Or is the student a *client* of the university—involved in a professional relationship in which the student seeks out professors (as he or she would seek out a physician) to help in areas of interest and need? Or is the relationship one of a *customer,* who, having certain needs locates places where services to meet these needs can be purchased? Or, is the student a *member* of the university and therefore a citizen of that community with rights and obligations like those of other members? Or does the student role include some aspects of all of these?

It cannot be said that these were burning questions in the university until 1960, but they have, by practice, been answered in rather different ways at different times in the gradual evolution of the modern university. It is probably safe to say that in England, Canada, and the United States, until recent years, there has always been a sharp distinction between the role and status of the teacher and the role and status of the student—a simple recognition of the fact that the former by virtue of his knowledge, age, and experience should exercise some domination and direction over the latter. The confrontation of the sixties was in part to challenge the validity of this distinction and to raise consciously and overtly, for perhaps the first time, the question of the role of the student in the university.

Students in the Medieval Universities

There was among the earliest universities a major distinction in respect of the role of the student. In the Italian universities the students, through their student guilds, exercised unique authority. There was never any question of disciplining students; rather it was a matter of discipline for the masters. The university was controlled and operated by students.[1] At Paris it was the guild of masters that exercised control, and most questions of discipline and policy were "settled by the Masters alone." [2] Oxford, greatly influenced by Paris, followed the pattern in which the university was controlled by the masters and students were subject to their direction.

During the student revolt in the 1960s there were many references to the dominant role of students in the medieval universities. This was not generally the case. It was so at Bologna and Salerno, but as we have said, these were primarily professional schools organized by older students who hired masters to help them further their professional life.

> The professor . . . was simply a private-adventure lecturer . . . whom a number of independent gentlemen of all ages between seventeen and forty had hired to instruct them. If many of the students were ecclesiastics, they were most of them already beneficed—many of them archdeacons or dignitaries in cathedral churches; and they owed no ecclesiastical obedience to their teachers.[3]

It is accurate to say that a tradition which placed the student in the center of the life and operation of the university was begun in the earliest Italian universities. But this tradition seems to have been gradually diluted and to have moved to Spain and to Latin America. It was not accepted nor did it have any effective influence in the early universities in Britain, Canada, or the United States. In these the master was the dominant figure.

The most significant development of the day in respect of the life of the student related to some of the special privileges the medieval university achieved for itself. The university was largely an autonomous corporation whose members were free from most, if not all, of the usual civil regulations and laws. The university thus became almost an independent community responsible for disciplining its members for their conduct both inside and outside the institution. There emerged therefore in the minds of civic and academic authorities alike a concept of the university as a separate entity in the larger community, responsible for the conduct and behavior of its own members. As a result, public misconduct of students or masters was not tried in civic courts but was referred to university authorities for consideration and/or discipline. This freedom was clearly and freely abused in the medieval period.

> Another . . . illustration of academical morals in the thirteenth century is the proclamation of the official of Paris in 1269 in which he denounces a class of scholars, or pretended scholars, who "by day and night atrociously wound and slay many, carry off women, ravish virgins, break into houses," and commit "over and over again robberies and many other enormities hateful to God." Such were the kind of crimes in which the clerical tonsure enabled the Parisian scholar to indulge without the smallest fear of the summary execution which would have been the fate of an apprentice or a "sturdy beggar" who essayed such pranks. As a means of preventing such outrages in future the official has nothing more deterrent to hold over the offender's head than the ineffectual threat of excommunication.[4]

This idea—that students were less subject to civil law than nonstudents and responsible only to university authority—which emerged in this time and persisted to a degree until 1960, was decisive in defining the student's role in the university. By accepting the authority of the university (rather than the civic authority), the student accepted a position in which obedience to the university hierarchy was required. It was a position of advantage, for generally discipline in the university was less harsh than in the larger community. But this special status of the student was the cause of frequent "town versus gown" tension and conflict in medieval days and in centuries thereafter.

It established also in the university a specific attitude to students, for whom it was responsible in every respect. For society, students might be seen as "members" of the university, but to the university the student became, in effect, a "ward" of the academic community to be nourished, protected, and disciplined by the parent.

The early records suggest a highly mobile student population. Students were able to move from teacher to teacher, to crowd the lectures of the great masters, and to travel far afield to sample the wares of many universities.[5] But as the university became more established and institutionalized, a more restrictive concept of student life emerged. This was particularly the case as "nations" developed student hostels and, at Oxford and Cambridge, "colleges." The aim of the latter was to provide a complete education *within* the college. It was a movement back to the monastic ideal—even the physical structure of the early colleges suggests a retreat and separation from the outside world.

> The intellectual as well as physical enclosure of Magdalen College contrasted sharply, and not insignificantly, with the early days of unbounded university freedom. With the establishment of Brasenose, 1509, *it was an accepted principle that the student need not go outside his college precincts for an education.*[6] [Italics added]

This movement to encapsulate the student in a single university community took deep root in England and was to become accepted practice in North American universities as well. It was based on the belief in "total immersion," and while it may have had advantages for some, it not only greatly restricted the mobility of the student but made him more dependent on, and more subject to the will of, the authority of the university to which he was bound.

While medieval universities were open to all classes, the

number of students from the less advantaged families was probably quite small. The church and the monastery had always sought out "promising youths" for clerical training, and this probably continued to be the case in the universities. But:

> . . . as we see from the university records, it was only a very small proportion of the students in a university and a still smaller proportion of university graduates, who belonged to the pauper or servitor class. The vast majority of scholars were of a social position intermediate between the highest and very lowest—some of knights and yeomen, merchants, tradesmen or thrifty artisans, nephews of successful ecclesiastics, or promising lads who had attracted the notice of a neighbouring abbot or archdeacon. So habitual was this kind of patronage that a large proportion of university students must have been supported by persons other than their parents, whether related to them or not. The colleges represent simply an extension of this widespread system.[7]

Important if not decisive steps were taken in medieval times to define the university constituency and the student's role. Most students were from the "better classes," given unusual freedom and privileges in the public domain, protected by the university authorities, gradually taken under paternal guidance and encouraged, if not required, to stay "at home"—that is, to stay in one's own university. Undoubtedly indoctrination to a way of life and to one's college was present. There was considerable tolerance of the "sowing of wild oats" and gentle parental guidance. But by 1500 the role of the student was clearly that of a ward of the university family. The student was a member of this family, but there was no question who made the major decisions in the family.

Students in the Period 1500-1850

The role of the student changed but little in these three and a half centuries. Oxford and Cambridge were "cloistered preparatory schools tutoring apprentice clerics." [8] The early American and Canadian colleges were almost all under the patronage of some religious group or, if not, were affected by the religious mood of the day. There was a remarkable sameness in the aims and attitude of the colleges in respect of their students. Classical studies and strict discipline were thought to produce mental and moral power. Rules and regulations were developed to restrict and guide the behavior of the student. The statutes and laws of Harvard College, which had been developing since the school began, had by 1866 some sixteen chapters and 204 articles to control all possible deviations.[9]

Every college had elaborate regulations for its students. The rules were precise. At the University of Georgia the laws stated:

> If any scholar shall be guilty of profaneness, of fighting or quarreling—if he shall break open the door of a fellow student—if he shall go more than two miles from Athens without leave from the President, a Professor, or a Tutor—if he shall play at billiards, cards, or any unlawful game . . . he shall . . . be punished by fine, admonition, or rustication, as the nature and circumstances of the case may require.[10]

The attempt was to mold the student's life to that of a rigid model of a pious, righteous, and educated gentleman. Greek, Latin, and discipline were the means to this end.[11] Penalties of rustication or suspension were always present for students who could not conform.

At Cambridge (England) in the early seventeenth century it was said:

> The ideal undergraduate contemplated by university and college codes, was a decorous, modest, soberly attired youth who made his college his habitual home. Whenever he issued forth beyond its gates, it was only with the express permission of his tutor or the dean. Unless it devolved upon him as a sizar or poor scholar to perform some menial errand for a superior, he was always accompanied by a fellow collegian. He wore his academic gown, reaching to his ankles and, unless a scholar, a round cloth cap. His hair was closely shorn and he eschewed tobacco. He loitered neither in the market-place nor in the streets and shunned alike the lodging-house and the tavern.[12]

This model student was to be nurtured by a carefully developed schedule which allowed little time for high spirits or for mischief. Thus the daily schedule at Harvard in the late seventeenth century:

> Morning bever (breakfast) was preceded by college prayers at five o'clock and followed by a study hour before the eight o'clock lecture. Lectures were generally of the medieval sort: the class tutor read aloud from some prescribed textbook in Latin, and the students took notes, or followed the reading in a text of their own. Dinner came at eleven, or at noon late in the century. . . . Resident fellows and fellow-commoners sat at a head or high table adorned by silver . . . the undergraduates eating from wooden trenchers, drinking beer from pewter "cur-cups," and providing their own knives and spoons. . . .
> After dinner came the recreation hour; then recitations in your tutor's chamber, where you were quizzed on the morning lecture, or disputations in hall for the sophisters, moderated by the President. Around half-past four or five the college bell tolled for "afternoon bever," and the welcome creak of the buttery hatch opening was heard, as the graduate-student butler stood ready to serve out more "sizings" of bread and beer. Evening prayers came at five; then a study hour; and supper at half-past seven. A recreation hour extended after supper until nine; and except in summer it was probably spent around the hall fire, talking and smoking. "Taking tobacco," at first allowed only with parent's permission or doctor's orders, became so general before 1660 that the Steward sold the baneful herb.[13]

The general impression is of an environment dominated by strict paternalistic disciplinarians that bears more relation to a boarding school or to a military college than to a modern university. But this is to overlook the natural inclinations and resourcefulness of college youth and their capacity to find outlets for their energies and desires regardless of rules and regulations. For there is no doubt that the elaborate schedules and rules were disregarded—and consistently—by students everywhere. Where intolerant and inflexible masters and professors prevailed, it appears there was constant tension on the campus; where a more tolerant spirit prevailed, breaches of the rules were either overlooked or punishment was meted out in a compassionate spirit. But it is quite clear that no group of youth could be deprived of some of the excitements that have been of interest to man throughout the ages. Thus "the Faculty records—are full of 'drinking frolicks,' poultry-stealing, profane cursing and swearing, card-playing, live snakes in tutors' chambers, bringing 'Rhum' into college rooms, and 'shamefull and scandalous Routs and Noises for sundry nights in the College Yard.' "[14]

> Until well on in the nineteenth century, college students had no opportunity to visit or dance with young girls, except in vacation. Consequently, true to the medieval tradition, the older and less restrained among them resorted to wenching. There are several complaints in the records of a tavern on the road to Charlestown, just over the present Somerville line, where students made rendezvous with ladies of easy virtue, whom the Charlestown selectmen were requested to warn out of town. And in 1770 "2 women of ill Fame" were discovered to have spent the night in a certain college chamber.[15]

At Oxford and Cambridge there were the same kinds of regulations and a similar recognition that these would be broken on occasion. The effort was to provide "a modest and sensible discipline to the surging liberties of youth."[16] Sir Ernest Barker, who served as one of the university proctors and thereby had the duty and the right to enter any tavern or lodging house and "to capture" students, reports that he made some of his most cherished friendships with undergraduates whom he "caught" on his tours as proctor.[17] And similarly at Harvard:

> The Faculty consistently maintained the Christian principle of forgiving any offense, however grave, if the culprit made a public confession and satisfied them that he repented of his sins. There are several instances of students' being expelled for fornication or other "atrocious" crimes who were readmitted after a year or so, graduated with their class, and became useful and respected citizens, even ministers of the gospel. Tutor Flynt was right; wild colts often did make good horses.[18]

As already implied, the disposition of the student was to

accept and not to challenge overtly the authority of the university: the president, the professor, or the tutor. There are many examples of schoolboyish tricks such as ringing the chapel bell at peculiar hours or leading a cow into chapel. There are also numerous illustrations of rebelliousness—of protests about food or compulsory chapel. But these were designed to irritate the authorities or to have them change their ways. The purpose was never to confront authority directly with a demand that the authority be otherwise located or shared in any way with students.

Perhaps the incident closest to practices common in the 1960s occurred at Harvard in 1834. It is of particular interest because it relates to the relationship established by the medieval universities with civic authorities regarding the disciplining of students. In the 1834 incident, when a student petition was denied, students broke the windows and destroyed the furniture of a tutor who was the focus of their discontent. All the sophomores—the class involved—were dismissed for the year and ordered to leave town at once. This severe penalty would probably have been accepted without protest, but President Quincy decided that civic authorities should root out and further punish the offenders.

Then, hell broke loose! *Quincy had violated one of the oldest academic traditions: that the public authorities have no concern with what goes on inside a university, so long as the rights of outsiders are not infringed.* The "black flag of rebellion" was hung from the roof of Holworthy. Furniture and glass in the recitation rooms of University were smashed, and the fragments hurled out of the windows. . . . A terrific explosion took place in chapel; and when the smoke had cleared, "A Bone for Old Quin to Pick" was seen written on the walls. A printed seniors' "Circular," signed by a committee who were promptly deprived of their degrees, gave their version of the Rebellion in language so cogent that the Overseers issued a forty-seven page pamphlet by Quincy to counteract it. . . . Quincy never recovered his popularity.[19] [Italics added]

Such protests were infrequent, and even this one fizzled out, for no one seriously doubted the right of the authorities to decide what should be done.

The attitude and practice that emerged from the clergy-dominated colleges of this time was paternalistic in the extreme. It accepted responsibility for shaping the character of its students and this by the most detailed regulations. Perhaps fortunately for these colleges, they were able to overlook or ignore many deviations from established norms and gradually to liberalize their concept of "proper behavior." But there emerged a double standard: what the student was required to do; and what the student actually did. This was to divide the student and the master and to overlay their relationship with a degree of hypocrisy. There was some unarticulated understanding of each other's world, but seldom was there intimate sharing of these worlds. But the role of students as wards of the university was further nourished in this period. They had, in effect, no rights not bestowed upon them by their masters.

The idea of the separation of the university and the city authority was sustained during these years. In the latter, difficulties with students were usually referred to the university rather than civil officials, and the university was self-contained as far as disciplining problems on campus were concerned. As the Harvard incident indicates, outside interference was not to be tolerated.

Students in the Period 1850–1950

The hundred years after 1850 was a period of great change in the status of the students at the university. In Britain, Canada, and the United States they were to have increasing freedom from strict rules and regulations, but in none of these countries would they have the freedom of the German students to choose their courses, to move from university to university as they wished, and to regulate their own lives as they pleased. The universities in Britain, Canada, and the United States gave or were forced to give by changing circumstances much more freedom to the student, but they never abandoned their paternalistic authoritarian stance.

But while student life was much alike in the three countries prior to 1850, when all were mired in religiosity, there began to be marked differences after that year—differences that were to be accentuated during the century that followed.

England: The college concept at Oxford and Cambridge emphasized a close relation between student and teacher. In the intimate atmosphere of the college family, there was constant interaction and a considerable degree of knowledge about, and understanding of, each other. There were, of course, college regulations, but once the universities were freed from strict church control there seems to have developed a high degree of tolerance of eccentric behavior, little disposition to destroy lively spirits, and a very considerable degree of freedom for the individual student. There was never any question of where authority resided: final decisions on academic and all other aspects of college life were made by the college fellows.[20] But the liberal attitude of the fellows and their close relation with students made for an unique environment in which resentment of authority or lack of mutual understanding was kept to a minimum.

As already intimated, the Oxbridge model had considerable influence on the Redbrick universities. While the latter could not duplicate the tutorial arrangements or superb facilities of the former, nonetheless the importance of an intimate undergraduate experience (the osmosis process assumed to take place in a tutorial) was firmly implanted in these newer universities, in all of which close student-faculty contact was encouraged.[21] The English professors took their *in loco parentis* responsibilities seriously, and there was not up to 1950 the distinct student and faculty cultures that developed in universities in some other countries.

Two features of the British universities that emerged during this century need to be noted. One was the absence of the fierce athletic rivalries which began in the United States. There were games and contests—indeed some of these such as the annual Oxford-Cambridge boat race created great public interest, and winners of the "double-blue" were popular and important figures—but on the whole these games and contests were low-key events, amateur in spirit and, in fact, arranged and conducted largely by students themselves. The universities, the professors, the tutors, however great their interest, never financed or formally sponsored the athletic programs. This was a student prerogative and responsibility.

A second element of importance was the beginning of student unions—the organization of students into representative bodies to guard students' welfare and rights. The first such group was organized at the University of Edinburgh in 1884 by a student (Fitzroy Bell) who had studied in Germany.[22] Bell was able to organize a student representative council on which sat elected representatives of all faculties to bring "firm but friendly pressure on university authorities." Specifically the council:

> . . . secured improvements in the library; it organized a staff-student consultative committee to reform the clinical instruction in the faculty of medicine; it criticized the high failure rate for the M.A. degrees; . . .[23]

Similar councils or unions were started at English universities and in time became influential and to some extent powerful. Between the two world wars they instituted inquiries into teaching methods and curricula at Manchester, Birmingham, Nottingham, and Bedford colleges. A national union of students was begun. It organized annual conferences and at one of these (in 1938) issued *A Challenge to the University: A Report on University Life and Teaching in Relation to the Needs of Modern Society,* in which a wide range of modest curriculum reforms were proposed.[24]

By 1940, a more militant attitude was evident. The first "Charter of Student Rights and Responsibilities" was published. It warned of "recent encroachments on student liberties" and called for the establishment in the university of certain rights such as "the right to share in the government and administration of the university" and "the right to belong to any organization whether cultural, political, or religious." [25] World War II interrupted the further growth of student organizations, but the groundwork was being laid to alter the traditional role of the student to one in which he had status and rights, including the right to participate in university government, not heretofore considered reasonable in the English context.

Opinion regarding the effectiveness of the councils, the union, and congress differs. Ashby thinks the early councils had "an indubitable influence on higher education in Scotland" and that on the whole the councils "acquired for the student movement . . . valuable and lasting rights." [26] There can be little question that the constant pressure of students had some effect, but in respect of the crucial sharing in the government of the university it made little progress:

> Student participation in university government has been negligible for a long time in English universities and little more than a vestigial formality in Scotland.[27]

The English attitude was to encourage student initiative and expression but to draw a sharp line between student extracurricular activities and the authority and operation of the university. Even Ashby, who spoke with favor of the 1940 student's charter, drew this distinction:

> . . . participation must rest on one axiom of consent, which is that the university exists so that those who know more can transmit knowledge and the techniques of scholarship to those who know less; therefore the Scholars come to learn and the Masters are there to teach. Any pattern of participation which weakens this authority of the university must be resisted.[28]

Canada: That which most influenced student life in Canada was a duality which emerged as the most distinctive feature of higher education in that country:[29] the "pass" and "honor" course programs. The relevance of this system is that it separated the serious student into an intense, demanding, and highly specialized program of study. Honor students may have had some time for social and athletic activities if they chose, but there was little question about the reason they were in university. Speaking about a time just at the end of the hundred years being considered here and after a long discussion of extracurricular activities, one student said:

All these preoccupations belonged to the realm of what the academic staff amusedly called "the college's ancillary social life," and serious students were supposed to regard them as unimportant. What was important was "the course." The subject we were studying. English literature. Undergraduates in other disciplines were conscientious, even engrossed. But we were obsessive; everything else we studied—philosophy, French literature, history—was regarded in terms of whatever bearing it had on the English literature of its period.[30]

One can overemphasize the influence of the honors course, but there are many to testify to its compelling and all-absorbing attraction. It gave Canada a layer of serious students, which affected the ethos of the university; it made study and scholarship respectable and even exciting.

The major focus of interest of the honor student in the university was his "subject," an interest which he shared with other students and professors in the same specialized field. The result was something approximating the intimate environment of the English universities. Honor students and their professors were united in pursuit of a common interest.

There were, of course, the usual student activities: clubs, athletics (the University of Toronto Athletic Association was organized in 1893),[31] and student publications. But Canada seemed more firmly in the British pattern than that of the United States until the latter part of this hundred years. Great football rallies and fraternity and sorority life, while present, never gained the same prominence as they did on the American campus.

There were, in Canada, many student clubs with intellectual interests: Dr. Daniel Wilson organized the University Literary and Scientific Society in 1854,[32] and this practice of professors taking the initiative in organizing such clubs seems to have been prevalent on early Canadian campuses. In any case, there emerged many such clubs (the literary society, the history club, the French club, etc.), which gave impetus to the intellectual life of the university. In respect of athletics, it became the practice to have these supervised by a committee or board which had on it representatives from the student body, the faculty, and in some cases the alumni. While these committees went a good deal further than the British in providing for coaches, trainers, and facilities, "big-time athletics" was not a major force on the Canadian campus.

Students followed the British practice of organizing student councils; these gradually came to assume responsibility for the principal student activities on campus. The first student council was organized at the University of Toronto in 1905.[33] As far as is known, no student council in these early days seriously sought to participate in the government of the university, and, on the whole, councils were quiet, inoffensive bodies that looked after student affairs without ever directly confronting the authority of the university. The National Federation of Canadian University Students was organized in 1927, lay dormant during the war, and was revived in the early postwar years.[34] Until the 1960s it was a relatively moderate organization concerned more with cooperation and coordination than with student rights or social issues. The radicals on the campus—many of them in the late 1920s and 1930s in the Student Christian Movement—were concerned with social injustice, and their very considerable abilities and aggressiveness made an impact both on the university and on the country. But few of them thought, as their successors in the sixties did, that the university, like the government or the industrial corporation, was a proper object of attack.

While separate student programs were developed on the Canadian campus, these were seldom divorced from faculty and administration interests. The leadership of many clubs and athletic programs was shared by student and faculty. The practice was for even relatively independent student activities, such as the student council or newspaper, to have faculty advisers. And the university retained ultimate authority over all student clubs and activities. There seemed to be little resentment by students of the role defined for them by university authorities.

United States: When Dean Andrew West of Princeton wrote an article in 1885 asking "What Is Academic Freedom?" he answered: the elective system, scientific courses, voluntary chapel attendance.[35] This is far from that freedom provided by the concept *Lernfreiheit* for the student in Germany. Nonetheless the elective system in which the student had the opportunity to choose some of his courses; the introduction of science courses, which broke the tradition of the rigid classical program; and voluntary chapel, which symbolized new freedom for the student, were all significant steps in liberating the student in the United States.[36]

But the result, to judge by many accounts,[37] was not to bring intellectual zest and maturity to the American campus. Veysey, in his excellent and detailed book *The Emergence of the American University,* describes students in the early twentieth century as mainly childish, frivolous, romantic, and in many cases anti-intellectual.[38] "To most American undergraduates at the end of the nineteenth century, colleges meant good times, pleasant friendships, and, underneath it all, the expectation of life-long prestige resulting from the degree." [39]

Between professors and students a division of interests was to be seen: the former, more scholarly than in the days of the religious college, more interested in serious study, moved psychologically and spiritually away from fun-loving undergraduates with little interest in academic work. An "awful chasm" [40] developed between students and faculty. Of this situation Woodrow Wilson wrote:

> The work of the college, the work of its classrooms and laboratories, has become the merely formal and compulsory side of its life, and . . . a score of other things, lumped under the term "undergraduate activities," have become the vital, spontaneous, absorbing realities for nine out of every ten men who go to college.[41]

What emerged on the American campus in the first few decades of the twentieth century was a distinctive student culture which existed apart from what many considered the main function of the university, academic study. Students were involved in a world created and controlled by students. It was a world of sports, debates, theater, clubs, fraternities and sororities, dances, and activities unrelated to scholarly pursuits. And yet this vast activity-oriented student culture was not without value, for it provided students with a period of isolation from home and from adults in which it was possible for them to make new friends, to find new experiences, and to try different identities in order to decide what kind of persons they wished to be.[42] Often it was said that it was on a team or in a club that a student "found himself." Ben-David expands this idea:

> Membership in these groups often evoked great loyalty and warm feelings of friendship and brotherhood towards the group and fellow members, great devotion to the purposes of the groups, and intense competitiveness toward other groups. Achievement in these various group activities and in pursuit of the universal interests of youth, such as sports, sex, and love, counted in this culture more than scholarship. This culture was not created by educators and did not serve any specific purpose of study or training. Yet, as has been pointed out by Talcott Parsons, the values implicit in this culture were consistent with the beliefs and purposes of American society. Participation in these group activities was a good preparation for the combination of ruthless competitiveness and personal loyalty to one's team of co-workers, which were so important in business. . . . In this sheltered freedom of collegiate culture, the young man could find, or rather, learn to know, himself. The activities in which he engaged were interesting and challenging enough to get him involved. At the same time, however, the activities took place in a controlled environment and were regarded as play, so that one could go far out in experimenting with oneself without running the risk of incurring lifelong liabilities.[43]

All of this represents perhaps the dominant theme in undergraduate student life in American higher education in the 1850–1950 period. The typical male student was fun-loving, prankish, sports- and club-minded, and, as far as studies were concerned, wanted only to get his "gentleman's C" and his degree, which held promise of improved class status and prestigious job potential. But this interpretation—generally accepted as the norm for American student life in this period—is to miss two themes of growing influence and importance.

The first is that there was always a group of students, both graduate and undergraduate, with serious intellectual interests. There were always good students—potential scholars—who gave the classroom and the campus intellectual vitality. In many colleges and universities they may have been a small and even unpopular minority, but at the prestigious universities they were by no means isolated and perhaps not a minority. It is useful to emphasize this point. There were subcultures in the student world, some of which were anathema to the dominant culture described above.[44] For example, here is a report of a student at Harvard in 1910, as quoted by Morison:

> All sorts of strange characters, of every race and mind, poets, philosophers, cranks of every twist, were in our Class. . . . What is known as "college spirit" was not very powerful; no odium attached to those who didn't go to football games and cheer. There was talk of the world, and daring thought, and intellectual insurgency; . . . Students themselves criticized the faculty for not educating them, attacked the sacred institution of intercollegiate athletics, sneered at undergraduate clubs so holy that no one dared mention their names. . . . Of course all this made no ostensible difference in the look of Harvard society, and probably the clubmen and the athletes, who represented us to the world, never even heard of it. But it made me, and many others, realize that there was something going on in the dull outside world more thrilling than college activities, and turned our attention to the writings of men like H. G. Wells and Graham Wallas, wrenching us away from the Oscar Wildean dilettantism that had possessed undergraduate litterateurs for generations.[45]

The second important theme is that as enrollments grew, as graduate and professional education became more prestigious, and as universities became more selective, competition for places in the university, for maintenance of one's standing in the university, and for entry to graduate or professional school grew markedly. The old "gentleman's C" was made difficult to attain, and even it, while it might allow one to graduate, was not adequate for entry to the best professional and graduate schools. Thus, pressure of numbers and the competition among these numbers began to change the character of the American campus. The best professional and graduate schools recruited serious and intellectually able students and provided an atmosphere and environment inconsistent with the older student culture. The most prestigious universities became much more selective in their admission policies, and only students with very good academic records were admitted. Perhaps for this very reason these universities became even more respected and admired. Other universities tried to follow their practices that they too might become prestigious. In any case, it seems clear that academic standards were gradually being raised, and while the dominant student culture persisted throughout this period, it was obviously of somewhat lesser import and it found a less congenial home in those universities in which academic concerns—particularly graduate study and research—were becoming increasingly important.[46]

The first sign of student government in the United States was at Amherst College in 1877, when President Seelye gave the undergraduate body considerable responsibility for the conduct of student affairs but with the proviso of a presidential veto.[47] This practice of student organization was to spread to almost all colleges and universities, always with the provision that student decisions—even in extracurricular matters—could be overruled by the president or the faculty. And there was never serious question of students having a say in academic affairs:

> "Student government," as it developed almost universally on campuses across the nation, remained entirely extracurricular. The officers of student organizations enjoyed neither the right to nor the responsibility for collaborations with the faculty in determining academic purposes, policies, or practices.[48]

Indeed, one can say of the whole 1850–1950 period that from the point of view of the student, "the academic community can only be described as authoritarian and utterly paternalistic."[49]

As already intimated, the American campus became deeply involved in athletics. At first (before 1900) athletic contests were friendly games and stemmed from the idea of developing the whole individual. But the American passion for competition took command of the athletic program, made it in effect "big business," and pushed it more closely to the professional than to the amateur spirit. Highly paid coaches, immense stadiums, and elaborate rituals were part of the athletic program in all major universities before World War II. While students were the participants in, and the supporters of, these programs, they had little if any voice in, or control over, the operation of the athletic program.[50]

Summary and Conclusion

A person's role in any given situation is defined not only by the individual but by other people and institutions in the environment. Up to 1950 there seemed few differences in the views of students, professors, or the university in respect of the student's role in the university.

Quite clearly the student was not a member of the university if membership is defined as having a shared responsibility for the program, regulations, and welfare of the institution. In these respects the student was without status or recognition. Students' views may have been taken into account by authorities, but there is little evidence to suggest this was generally the case. Not until the latter part of this period was the possibility of sharing in the governance of the university even raised by students. Except in a few experimental colleges in the United States, this idea was not taken seriously by university leaders.

The attitude of the university was paternalistic and authoritarian; this was accepted by all concerned. Student protest was over minor regulations or irritants; it never directly confronted the legitimacy of the university's authority. This attitude was sustained, in part, by the university's generally liberal attitude, which gave the student increasing freedom and special protection from all but the most grievous of crimes in the community. Students had special status and privileges; their deviant behavior was tolerated to a degree that was not possible in other organizations, such as business or government. Perhaps for this reason, students accepted their position in the university without serious protest.

The emerging concept of the university's relation to the student was *in loco parentis,* which meant that the student was in effect a ward of the university, which was responsible for guiding and nurturing his or her development. Undoubtedly other roles emerged: the brightest students in both undergraduate and graduate schools often became "apprentices" in the full meaning of that term; others were simply customers shopping for the easiest courses by which to earn a degree; others were bohemians or separatists who lived on campus but divorced themselves from the academic life of the university. But for all of these the idea of *in loco parentis* prevailed, and before 1950 there were few to dispute the implications of this philosophy.

There were, however, significant differences between Canada, England, and the United States. In the latter, perhaps because of more rapid growth, the more liberal curriculum and program of options, and the reliance on the lecture method, student-faculty relations were generally less intimate than in either Canada or England. The "awful chasm" used to describe the separation of professor and student in the United States facilitated the growth of a separate student culture hostile to the aspirations of many of the best professors, who, as frequently as possible, took refuge in graduate schools and sought to confine their teaching to that level. Only gradually was the dominance of this culture eroded as academic competition intensified and scholarship given greater status.

In 1950 it was generally assumed in all universities that there should be a close paternal relationship between professor and student. But larger classes and increasing professional responsibilities made this relationship difficult except at the wealthiest universities that could afford to retain a semblance of the tutorial system. *In loco parentis* was becoming an unrealistic and unattainable objective. Its demise will be described in Chapter 5.

NOTES

1. Rashdall, 1936, vol. 1, pp. 148-150; see also Mallet, 1924, vol. 1, p. 25.

2. Rashdall, 1936, vol. 1, p. 148.

3. Ibid., vol. 1, p. 150. "Writing soon after 1200, Boncompagno relates how the young Bolognese teacher Ugolino Gosia was invited to become *podesta* of Ancona. 'If the governorship of this city is given to me at this time,' Boncompagno has Ugolino say, 'I would not dare to accept it without the permission of my students (*socii*), to whom I teach the laws and to whom I am held, and am both in authority and subservience" (Hyde, 1972, pp. 41–42).

4. Rashdall, 1966, pp. 279-280. Armytage reports: "The northern scholars at Oxford, unofficially organised as a 'nation,' were in continual conflict with those of the south—also a 'nation.' One of their great fights in 1274 led to 50 persons being accused of homicide and sent up to London for trial. As a result of this, the chancellor of the university was invested with a control over scholars, whose halls and hostels were freed from civic and fiscal liabilities and placed under his rule. This right, taken in 1275, was a prelude to many others which elevated the university above the normal jurisdiction of the Oxford civic courts and gave it a set of rules and a jurisdiction of its own" (Armytage, 1955, p. 43).

5. Mallet, 1924, vol. 1, p. 14. "The tireless scholars of the Middle Ages were not content to study at a single university, they travelled far afield in search of teachers—'wont to roam around the world—till much learning made them mode' " (vol. 1, p. 138).

6. Kneller, 1955, p. 9.

7. Rashdall, 1936, vol. 3, p. 444.

8. McGrath, 1970, p. 15.

9. Morison, 1965, p. 357.

10. Hofstadter and Metzger, 1955, p. 306.

11. Ben-David, 1972, p. 52.

12. Mullinger, 1884, vol. 2, pp. 391-393.

13. Morison, 1965, pp. 27-28.

14. Ibid., p. 78.

15. Ibid., p. 116.

16. Kneller, 1955, p. 36.

17. Ibid.

18. Morison, 1965, pp. 112-113.

19. Ibid., pp. 252–253.

20. Robbins, 1971. See also Caine, 1969; Halsey and Trow, 1971; and Kneller, 1955.

21. Armytage, 1955.

22. Ashby, 1970, pp. 27–28.

23. Ibid., pp. 28–29.

24. Armytage, 1955, pp. 275–276.

25. Ashby, 1970, pp. 53–54.

26. Ibid., p. 32.

27. Caine, 1969, p. 157.

28. Ashby, 1970, p. 63.

29. Harris, 1973, chap. 10.

30. C. Newman, 1972, p. 58.

31. Reed, 1944, p. xi.

32. Ibid.

33. First called the Student Parliament, the name was changed in 1906 to the Undergraduate Parliament, and in 1913 to the Student Administrative Council (*U of T Monthly*, Archives).

34. Harris, 1973, chap. 30, p. 3.

35. Hofstadter and Metzger, 1955, p. 397.

36. In 1886 the 204 articles guiding student behavior were replaced by a new code which occupied fewer than five pages (Morison, 1965, p. 357).

37. See Veysey, 1965; Ben-David, 1972; Jencks and Riesman, 1968.

38. Veysey, 1965, pp. 334–337.

39. Ibid., pp. 269–270.

40. Ibid., p. 294.

41. Wilson, 1909, p. 574. Also quoted in Veysey, 1965, pp. 294–295.

42. Gusfield, 1970, p. 24.

43. Ben-David, 1972, pp. 78–79.

44. Burton Clark and Martin Trow (1966, pp. 20–23) have distinguished four types of student subcultures; the collegiate (the pleasure-seeking group); the academic (the serious students); the consumer-vocational (the time-servers seeking a good job); and the nonconformist (a group placing high value on ideas but having low regard for the university).

45. Morison, 1965, pp. 434–435.

46. Jencks and Riesman, 1968, pp. 10–40; see also Veysey, 1965, p. 272.

47. McGrath, 1970, p. 19.

48. Ibid.

49. Nisbet, 1971*a*, p. 58.

50. Ulam, 1972, p. 54.

chapter four

●

PROFESSORS

here are many expectations of the role or roles the professor must play in the university. Students expect the professor to be a good teacher—knowledgeable, well-prepared, and articulate. Some parents expect the professor to serve as a guide and counselor—a parent substitute. Colleagues expect the professor to be a "productive scholar" engaged in research of some significance. The administration of the university requires that the professor take part in the committee work of his or her department and carry his or her share of administrative work. The professor's professional associations expect his or her interest, participation, and adherence to their standards. The community and society expect the professor to make his or her expertise available when it is required. These multiple expectations place a very considerable burden of work on all academics in the university. How do they manage?

In general there are two ways in which work may be organized. One is by dividing the task or tasks into separate units and training each worker to carry responsibility for a particular unit of activity. This is essentially the bureaucratic organizational model, in which there is a specialized worker for each specialized task. The second method is one in which each worker performs *all* the tasks involved; while he or she may have assistance, it is the worker's norms and standards that control the whole operation. This is essentially the professional organization model.[1]

The university has traditionally organized its academic program on the professional model; that is, the academic staff has assumed responsibility for all aspects of the university's academic program. This practice is deeply embedded in British universities but is present in Canada and the United States as well:

> . . . Although there are some notable exceptions, most professors on tenure in the faculties of arts and sciences are expected to teach graduate and undergraduate courses, carry out research or scholarly inquiries and write them up for publication, provide consultant, advisory or other service functions related to their specialties, as well as advise undergraduate and graduate students, supervise doctoral theses, and serve on departmental, graduate faculty, and university committees. And the same conditions largely appear to exist in the professional schools at the universities.[2]

The responsibilities of the professor are thus very diverse. Whereas other organizations have frequently met the problem of expanding responsibilities by a further division of labor, the university in its academic program has not deviated from the path on which the professor is responsible for the whole. Only in the postwar period has there been the beginning of bureaucracy in academic affairs: the teaching assistant, the research assistant, the executive assistant, and the well-organized secretary. But this intrusion on the traditional pattern is still far from dominant. The vast majority of professors carry multiple responsibilities in the operation of the academic program as a whole.

In this chapter the development of the role of the professor is briefly reviewed up to 1950, the professor's professional associations are examined, traditional definitions of the obligations of the professor are reviewed, and in conclusion, an account is given of changing concepts and practices since 1950.

The Role of the Professor to 1950

It is quite clear that the medieval universities sought "learned teachers." The two words were intimately associated; one would not think of a teacher who was not "learned," nor of a scholar who was not a teacher.[3] Students throughout Europe sought out men with such talent: knowledgeable and articulate teachers. The model master was both a scholar—a man of great learning in his field—and a teacher able to interest and communicate with many different kinds of students. What must be emphasized is the inevitable linking of "learning" and "teaching." "To style a man Master, who had not actually been a teacher, would have seemed a gross anomaly to the scholars of the twelfth and thirteenth centuries." [4] And concerning teaching, it:

> . . . demands that the instructor learn clarity and brevity, that he know how to arouse the learner's interest through right motivation, that he have a sense of moderation and humility, and that he learn to distinguish between that which is significant and that which supports the vanity of erudition.[5]

As we have seen, this concept of master or professor in the university declined in the centuries between 1500 and 1850, when colleges and universities tended to be dominated by religious groups and religious teaching, when most teachers were clergymen, and when most teaching tended to be arid recitations of text material. Their responsibilities tended to be defined as follows:

> . . . to keep recalcitrant and benighted undergraduates in line, exacting a certain amount of work and imposing a measure of discipline. These men were more often trained as clergymen than scholars, though some saw themselves as both. They found it natural to justify their work more in terms of improving the social and moral character of the young than of their intellectual attainment.[6]

In Canada and England, as well, the teacher or tutor in this period was concerned with the welfare of the whole student. There emerged therefore that strand in the matrix of the professor's responsibilities which required him to give attention to the students' need for guidance and supervision in many matters other than intellectual. The concept of *in loco parentis* took deep root in the life of the university prior to 1850, and the Mr. Chips model of the teacher's task became part of the mythology surrounding the professor's role. This myth, never appropriate or realistic in the modern university, persisted nonetheless up until World War II; indeed, numerous student radicals in the 1960s seemed to be suggesting this was the kind of person a professor should be. In any case the kindly but firm schoolmaster concept emerged in the period 1500–1850 and was merged with the medieval teacher-scholar idea to make a confusing, if not conflicting, series of roles for the professor.

After 1850 priorities among the responsibilities of the professor began to emerge. The best universities began to search out and to recruit the finest scholars available. The common criteria for selection were eminence in a specialized field, ability to pursue independent research, and ability to inspire students with enthusiasm for study.[7] This was true at both Oxford and Cambridge (as at Harvard or McGill), where in spite of informality and unorthodoxy in organization, brilliant research was carried on to the amazement of German scientists accustomed to more orderly ways.[8] From this point forward scholarship and research competence came increasingly to be the first criterion of most universities in hiring or promoting a professor. It was inevitable therefore that professors would themselves gradually give scholarship and research priority in ordering and organizing their own responsibilities.

But at the turn of the twentieth century important differences were beginning to appear in the English and American universities. In England the emphasis was clearly on undergraduate teaching and the development of the whole man. Honors programs were given full reign, and a "first" in one of these programs was considered a sufficient start on an academic career. The most influential, if not the clear majority, of university professors were trained at Oxford and Cambridge. They had the experience of sustained, intimate work with individual teachers, and those students with ability were encouraged to strike out on their own. There was little enthusiasm for graduate instruction or courses. The English professor who emerged was likely to be, therefore, a scholar of more than average talent with a capacity to work independently. But he had been nurtured in the environment of the college, the "community of scholars," and the tutorial. He was likely to conceive of his job as continuing those traditions in which emphasis was given to the student, character, and culture. Indeed, the lack of any substantial graduate program in England before World War II is perhaps indicative of the professors' priorities in English universities.

In the United States a rather different trend began to appear. Serious scholarship and research came to be focused in the graduate school; the undergraduate fun-culture was a thing apart and of little interest to scholars who found more inspiration and opportunity working with alert graduate students. The Ph.D. became a prestigious degree in the United States and a prerequisite for a teaching appointment in the university. But the Ph.D. was fundamentally a research degree, and those who attained it were often more interested, and certainly better trained, in research design and process than in teaching.[9] The emphasis in this program seemed to some to move the graduate student away from the life of the university as a whole to work with a small group of colleagues and peers in highly specialized fields. What came to be important was the subject, the project, and the research process.

It would be an exaggeration to say that the English professor stood for the student, the college, and the tutorial while the American professor was attracted to the graduate student and to the advancement of knowledge. Nonetheless, a difference in emphasis did exist, and each country trained its future staff with somewhat different priorities and conceptions of the professor's role.

Canada was to move toward the American pattern. In the early years of the century those students who did proceed to further study tended to do another two or three years' study at Oxford or Cambridge, but gradually the great universities in the United States became the focus of interest and attraction. Just when the balance shifted to the United States is not known, but after World War II there was no question that many more Canadians took advanced degrees in the United States than did graduate work in Britain.[10] By 1950 the Ph.D. was firmly established as a requirement for a teaching position in the prestigious Canadian universities.

The manner in which people are "socialized," that is, inducted into the intricacies, traditions, and purposes of their work or profession, is a determining factor in the way they function "on the job." From the turn of the twentieth century to World War II it was apparent that English and American professors were undergoing rather different kinds of preparation for a career in the university.

The inevitable result was some difference in role conception. The distinction was in emphasis and not in absolute terms. It was nonetheless real, and it kept the professor in England in much closer contact with undergraduates than his counterpart in all but a few universities in the United States.

But in the rhetoric of the day, there was little to suggest any disagreement about the role of the professor. He was a professional, and his work was organized on the professional model. While there would be different emphases by different individuals, universities, or countries, there was agreement on the need for professors to teach, to do research, to be interested in and concerned about the welfare of their students, and to share in the committee and administrative work of the university. Almost all university professors accepted such a definition of their role. And most would subscribe to the idea that the university should be the locus of their work and the object of their loyalty.

All the statements prior to World War II emphasized these responsibilities. There was no overt denial of these duties, obligations, loyalties, but practice had begun to erode their reality. It was true to a greater extent in the United States than in Canada or England, but everywhere the recognition given to research, the satisfaction of work with graduate students, and the attractions of supplementary work and pay outside the university were changing the professors' own conception of their role. They accepted, and perhaps believed in, the rhetoric of the day, but by 1950 increasing numbers of their colleagues were denying it in practice.

Professional Associations

As university professors gained more recognition and status, particularly after the turn of the century, they became more self-conscious, that is, more conscious of themselves as a professional group with distinctive interests and concerns. This led to professionalization.[11]

Professionalization, however, took two forms in academic life. One was the profession of specialists—physicists, psychologists, philosophers, etc.—who had common interests in a specialized subject. The second was the profession of university teachers who shared similar responsibilities in the university and had presumably the same rights and obligations in that institution.[12] As the decades of the twentieth century passed, almost all university professors became members of two professional organizations: (1) with colleagues from in or outside the university who were specialists in a similar discipline and (2) with colleagues in all disciplines who taught in university. The gradual development, formalization, and increasing influence of these professional organizations profoundly affected the character of the university and the role of the professor in it.

Profession by specialization: The first profession—that of specialists—was given initial impetus by the German concept of research, by the expansion of the curriculum and the beginning of specialized teaching, and particularly in the United States by the organization of departments, the expansion of graduate schools, and the highly specialized research training provided for the Ph.D. degree. Professional organizations of specialists developed and multiplied on a national and international scale, as new disciplines and subjects emerged, with each profession establishing machinery for promoting its common interests: regional, national, and world meetings; national and international journals; and subtle systems of job placement and replacement.[13]

While the interest of academic men and women in England in professional associations grew in the twentieth century, it did not become the absorbing passion that it appeared to be in the United States. The strong tradition of the academic profession as a guild of resident teachers united by their clearly defined relation to students persisted. It was a link which up to 1950 resisted the pressures toward specialization to the exclusion of all else.[14] But the specialists' examinations initiated early in the century were the countervailing trend of the future, "for these are associated with the expert, with discipline, and ultimately with professionalism." [15]

In Canada professionalization came much later. This related to the slower development of Canadian universities and the influence of the British model. Canada had a Royal Society (founded in 1882),[16] which, as in Britain, developed a pattern of annual meetings at which men of broad interests came together. Later annual meetings of the Royal Society combined with meetings of learned societies that were made up of groups of specialists. Thus the practice of holding joint and separate meetings during the same week on one campus permitted specialists to pay deference to the idea of the unity of knowledge and the unity of the university. But as the proportion of teaching staff with Ph.D.'s from the United States increased and as competition for staff and for prestige mounted, Canada's professors became drawn to the American marketplace and many became deeply involved in North American professional associations.

The teaching profession: The second kind of professional group to which professors gave allegiance was an association of university teachers—of all those with teaching appointments in the university regardless of specialization. The American Association of University Professors (AAUP) was organized in 1915,[17] the Association of University Teachers (AUT) was founded in Britain in 1919,[18] but significantly the Canadian Association of University Teachers (CAUT) was not established until 1951.[19] That these associations were valued by professors is attested to by the fact that in 1970 some 91,316 professors in the United States belonged to the AAUP,[20] that some 60 percent of British professors belonged to the AUT in 1968,[21] and that in Canada in 1970, "about 80 percent of university professors belonged to the CAUT." [22] Since all members paid fees, these associations were not only large but sufficiently well financed to develop central offices, a full-time secretariat, and a regular news journal. They thus became powerful influences in university life in their respective countries.

The purpose of these associations, in general terms, was to promote "the interests of teachers and researchers in universities—and to advance the standards of the profession." [23] Specifically, they exercised great pressure in the United States for academic freedom and tenure and for a greater degree of self-government in universities, particularly for control of academic programs and appointments by professors. In Britain pressure was for a more democratic form of university government and for a formal position in the determination of national policies of higher education, such as the degree and rate of expansion. In Canada academic freedom and tenure and university government were central concerns.[24] All the associations were concerned with academic salaries and working conditions; all published detailed analyses of comparative salaries; and all were influential in gradually improving the status of professors both in material terms and in terms of their position in the university and in society.

Largely through these associations professors gradually achieved a high degree of control of universities during the twentieth century—formal in Britain and Canada, by tacit approval in the United States.

> They control education for and entrance to their profession; selection, retention and promotion of their members; the curriculum of work schedules; and evaluation of their own performance. The individual faculty member's independence is enhanced by the principles of academic freedom and tenure. With increasing professionalization, he has attained a substantial degree of personal autonomy. Consequently, says Bundy, "when it comes to a crunch, in a first-class university it is the faculty which decides." [25]

Both these types of professional associations exerted strong influence on the professors: the one toward achievement and recognition by peers in their field of specialization; the other toward attainment of freedom, security, and adequate pay in university employment. In a sense both associations drew professors away from their universities and their students. It was assumed the latter were important, but the major thrust of the professional associations was to isolate professors as a separate group in the total life of the university. Even the local campus association was concerned primarily with the "rights" of the professor, and the university became less one's home than an agency with which one bargained for these rights.

The dual professional membership led to another important schism in university life. For those prolific in research and the dissemination of their findings and ideas, the profession of specialist was of prior importance. The specialists tended to be less interested in local campus affairs, including the local campus association, than professors of lesser scholarly achievement. The latter tended to run the local campus association, while the specialists participated only when there was a crisis or an issue of great importance.[26]

Priorities in roles became differentiated. The well-known author or researcher, if not on the faculty of a prestigious university, was seeking to get there, and whatever success had been achieved encouraged the professor to consider research and publication as responsible and ultimately leading toward further achievement. Professors less successful in these endeavors tended to focus more on the local campus and to justify their positions by stressing the importance of committee work, good teaching, and a strong local faculty association.

The two kinds of professional associations lived together, and most professors belonged to both forms of organization. But their importance in total was probably to lessen ties with the local university community and to accentuate differences in priorities in the professor's role in academic life.

Formal Statements of the Professor's Obligations

Throughout the history of the university, and perhaps no more so than in the twentieth century, the professor was conscious of his responsibilities and sought to define them so that his priorities and obligations were clear. Prior to 1950, "one could feel the sense of honor throughout the academic world." [27] Relative to 1975, the university before the Second World War was a small enterprise in which, despite changing practices, there was a large degree of agreement about essentials: worthy scholarship; the importance of teaching; indifference to material goods; the need for civilized relations on campus; the necessity of the neutrality of the university on political issues; the importance of character, tradition, tolerance. Lord Robbins, writing about his early teaching days at Oxford in the 1920s, stated:

> This was the Oxford which, after lengthy and portentous debate in Congregation, imposed a *numerus clausus* on the proportionate entry of women; the Oxford which refused to elect Roger Fry to the Slade Professorship because, his wife having been incurably insane for many years in spite of his pathetic devoted care, he had latterly formed an affectionate relationship with another woman; the Oxford which, in conspicuous contrast to Cambridge, had shown itself totally unable to decide how to use a magnificent Rockefeller offer of money for a new University Library. . . . Of course it would be foolish and wrong to indict a whole generation; there were splendid rebels in those days and fine scholars. But little suspicion of any sort of inadequacy disturbed the serene self-confidence of the dominant majority; although in fact there was much both in organization and in intellectual tradition that was open to criticism.[28]

But in spite of such examples, and there are many of them, there were clearly accepted standards of behavior and responsibilities for the university professor. Most of those who write about their experience as teachers in the 1900–1950 period speak with some nostalgia of the academic community with its clearly defined standards, responsibilities, and goals. For example, the rationale for academic freedom rested on the professor's devotion to certain values implicit in widely accepted standards of scholarly and scientific activity:

> Such values as tolerance and honesty, publicity and testifiability, individuality and co-operativeness, have been part of the scientific bequest. Two other values deserve particular emphasis. The scientific criterion of reliability—the dis-

sociation of a scientific work from the beliefs and associations of its author—has bestowed on academic freedom the value of universalism. By universalism is meant the elimination of particularistic criteria—credal, racial, or national—in judging the merits of a work, and the elimination of unearned advantages—connections, rank, and caste—in considering the merits of a man. The second value is that of neutrality, an interest in disinterestedness that is deeply ingrained in science. By assimilating the value of universalism, academic freedom has come to signify the brotherhood of man in science that is akin in aspiration to the brotherhood of man in God.[29]

The many statements of the professor's responsibilities prepared by individuals and by committees suggest both the sensitivity to these obligations and certain common themes of professional conduct. As early as 1915 the American Association of University Professors was stating its opposition to dogmatic teaching, and advising teachers to guard against

. . . taking unfair advantage of the student's immaturity by indoctrinating him with the teacher's own opinions before the student has had an opportunity fairly to examine other opinions upon the matters in question, and before he has sufficient knowledge and ripeness of judgment to be entitled to form any definitive opinion of his own.[30]

Throughout the years, this association secured consensus on policy in respect of such issues, and as late as 1966 had developed and approved the following statement on professional ethics:

The professor, guided by a deep conviction of the worth and dignity of the advancement of knowledge, recognizes the special responsibilities placed upon him. His primary responsibility to his subject is to seek and to state the truth as he sees it. To this end he devotes his energies to developing and improving his scholarly competence. He accepts the obligation to exercise critical self-discipline and judgment in using, extending, and transmitting knowledge. He practices intellectual honesty. Although he may follow subsidiary interests, these interests must never seriously hamper or compromise his freedom of inquiry.

As a teacher, the professor encourages the free pursuit of learning in his students. He holds before them the best scholarly standards of his discipline. He demonstrates respect for the student as an individual, and adheres to his proper role as intellectual guide and counsellor. He makes every reasonable effort to foster honest academic conduct and to assure that his evaluation of students reflects their true merit. He respects the confidential nature of the relationship between professor and student. He avoids any exploitation of students for his private advantage and acknowledges significant assistance from them. He protects their academic freedom.[31]

Until recent years British academics were more prolific in writing about the responsibilities of the university and its academic staff [32] than their counterparts in the United States or Canada. There was among them an unusual degree of agreement regarding the role of the university as a center of intellectual and character development and the close identification of the professor with this function. It was clear that the priority of the academic staff was high standards of scholarship. One example of a rather typical statement of responsibility may be briefly summarized:

(1) a devotion to the preservation and advancement of intellectual values;

(2) the obligation to be meticulously accurate in dealing with empirical evidence;

(3) the attempt to eliminate personal predilection in judging controversial matters;

(4) the freedom to think and the responsibility to publish; and

(5) the conviction that the university has a social responsibility, but this is first and foremost a responsibility for focusing the community's intellectual conscience.[33]

A close examination of the literature on the role and the responsibility of the university professor during the first fifty years of this century suggests considerable agreement. This may well have been, as indicated earlier, rhetoric describing a role whose nature had already begun to change. But this agreement represented values which members of the academic staff accepted, shared with each other, and found reassuring. It mattered little that these values were by 1950—particularly in the United States—somewhat inconsistent with what was actually happening. For the moment they provided a secure framework in which to live and work.

The Professor in the Postwar World

The relatively stable and comfortable world of the professor was to be severely tested in the decades following the war. The neat package which contained the traditional concepts of role, ethics, and loyalties had been damaged in previous decades; it was opened now in the postwar period to expose somewhat tarnished ideals which to many were seen to be irrelevant, if not completely obsolete. The major shifts from the traditional were the following:

In the locus of loyalty: The university was considered to have "first call" on the time, energy, and loyalty of professors. It became increasingly clear in the postwar period that this was not true. A small study by Wilensky in 1964[34] was suggestive of this reality. To the question "Whose judgment should count most when your overall professional performance is assessed?" the replies from professors in two large American universities were:

Students	9%
The administration	2%
The department chairman	6%
Colleagues in one's own department	24%
Colleagues in one's discipline, whatever their affiliation	56%
Community leaders	0%
College faculty as a whole	1%

This relative modest study—suggesting as it does that professors think that colleagues and other specialists are the proper source of evaluation of professional worth—confirms the view of most students of higher education that the compelling attraction of the specialist's profession dulled the interest of professors in their own universities, reduced in their minds the importance of that institution in evaluating their worth, and altered their priorities among the various traditional roles that they played in their institutions. By mid-century the typical professor was less identified with the university than with the discipline.[35] Thus one analyst states:

> The "knowledge explosion" has meant the fragmentation of knowledge, the triumph of specialization under the guise of professionalism. . . . It has turned the academics away from the university, made them over into men of affairs and entrepreneurs for whom the university is merely a base, a part-time employer, and a focus of partial allegiance.[36]

Institutional loyalty of any kind was a declining force in the sixties, and there was little doubt that this affected both students and teachers in the universities. But for professors there was a powerful counterattraction: their specialties which bound them closer to their peers in professional life and gave them new opportunities and rewards beyond the local campus.

> One could be a distinguished professor . . . in the old professionalism, and never leave campus, never seek a grant or directorship in foundation or on-campus institute, never hire a technician, never engage a teaching or research assistant, never even attend meetings of the American Bar Association. To think of trying to become a distinguished—let us say successful—professor of sociology or physics or biology during the period 1945–60 and *not* do all of these things was patently absurd.[37]

In the balance of teaching and research: The concept of "teacher-scholar" had meant a dual obligation which professors were assumed to balance in a manner that permitted neither responsibility to suffer. But it was increasingly apparent that for many professors teaching was a lesser attraction and a neglected responsibility. One careful and revealing study of the priorities of American professors indicated a very high rating for academic freedom and pure research, but

. . . only one [goal] in any way involves students. Even this
one refers to training students for research or other creative
endeavors which is, after all, closely associated with what professors consider to be important and represents a possible
output to them or to the academic field. . . .[38]

It would be impossible to conceive in the early part of the
century, even when there was great enthusiasm for research,
that professors would not consider their obligation to students as very important. But there was now no question that
"the new single source of prestige was research."[39] In the
postwar period, even at a time when universities were expanding rapidly and needed extra help from their senior professors, most resisted extraneous duties or more student contact.

Today . . . few well-known scholars teach more than six
hours a week, and in leading universities many bargain for
less. Even fewer read undergraduate examinations and pa-
pers.[40]

William Arrowsmith put the case bluntly in the 1966 key-
note address to the American Council on Education:

Scholars, to be sure, are unprecedentedly powerful, but their
power is professional and technocratic; as educators they
have been eagerly disqualifying themselves for more than a
century, and their disqualification is now nearly total. The
scholar has disowned the student—that is, the student who is
not a potential scholar—and the student has reasonably retali-
ated by abandoning the scholar.[41]

While most pronounced in the United States, the pull of
the professional (specialist) associations was everywhere felt.
They were the source of new ideas, information, and inspiration in the area of specialized interests. Their attraction
shifted the professor's concern away from his students,
courses, and teaching competence to many, and more exciting, fields.

In the relation of teacher to student: The value orientation of
the scientist-scholar, which emphasized neutral, objective,

and skeptical attitudes, encouraged an apprentice-scholar role for the student. It is not, and was not, an attitude congenial to large classes in which there might be many marginal, uninterested students.[42] It was inevitable that the scientist-scholar would look with favor on a few bright apprentices and neglect the role of Mr. Chips. There developed therefore a considerable gap between many of the leading scholars and many of the students in the rapidly expanding universities.

On the other hand, the egalitarian spirit thriving in the late sixties led to quite a different teacher-student relationship. At many of the "teach-ins" during the student revolt, students and professors shared the platform. Almost anyone, regardless of qualification, was allowed to teach: what one felt was as important as what one knew. This egalitarian posture had the effect of breaking down the boundaries between teacher and student, and was frequently carried over into the classroom. A number of professors took pains to emphasize that they were in no way different from their students and wished to have no more say about, or influence in, university affairs than their students.[43] This attitude supported the student drive for participation, and parity with professors, in university councils and shifted perhaps irreversibly the traditional student-professor relationship.[44]

It could well be said in 1975 that faculty members were confused about their role and their relation with students. The tradition of *in loco parentis* had disappeared; their interest in scholarship focused their concern to those students who shared this interest; the "democratic" and egalitarian move of the sixties forced them to be more considerate of students as "equals" and to surrender some of their professional priorities to their customers—the students. These conflicting pressures made for confusion: each professor sought his own *modus operandi*; there was no clear consensus about the relation of student and professor.

In professional values: For generations the academic had claimed freedom from involvement in indoctrination and had sought to be neutral and nonevaluative in teaching and "value free" in research. The sixties brought challenges to all these concepts. As we have seen, faculty members were both initiators and positive reactors to many campus disruptions. Professors became increasingly involved in politics, some as party activists, some as intellectual commentators on political events, some as advisers or commentators on relevant policy matters.[45]

A number of professors were becoming politicalized, a role inconsistent with the traditional nonpartisan concept of the university teacher.

> There are many academics now in almost all the advanced countries of the West who do not look upon universities and research institutes as places where the first charge is the pursuit of truth about important problems, and who do not believe that they should be left alone to make their own decisions in academic affairs. They have fallen victim, in one form or another, to the view that the universities are, for better or for worse, the instruments of contemporary politics. They believe that the university should be the instrument of society, i.e., of whichever part of society they purport to admire, or that the universities are the corrupt and soulless servants of an evil society and nothing but that—and should accordingly be overpowered. They think the first obligation of the universities is to be open to every kind of changing doctrine, rather than to work steadily on the path of understanding and to convey to their pupils the best possible understanding of the universe, or nature, of society, of man and his works. . . .[46]

The clash of ideologies among academics disrupted not only the university but many professional societies in which the validity of the traditional values of the scholar were hotly disputed. The confrontation tactics of the new radicals left many senior faculty members aghast: ". . . one felt in the presence of some wild irrational force. . . . It was at once tragic and comical. One felt indignant, then sad, then embarrassed . . . and yet (no one said the obvious) it does not make any sense."[47]

In the rise of the "new scholarship":   Many of the theories, insights, methods, and ideologies involved in the "new scholarship" had little support before the student revolution, but after 1970 they appeared, often in association with the radical left as part of an attack on traditional scholarship, and of sufficient attraction to young faculty members and students to create a school designated the "new scholars." [48] The field of history was the locus of perhaps the greatest ferment. Radical historians were reexamining conventional views of slavery, of the labor movement, of the lives of working-class people; "psychohistorians" were using techniques of psycho-analysis to explain the public behavior of major historical figures; some, believing that traditional history had too long been absorbed with "leaders," were focusing their study on "followers"; others were using computers to collect data from city directories, tax lists, and parish registers that would provide fresh insights into population movement and character. Frequently these pursuits became associated with professors who held radical political positions, and their work was often affected by, or at least identified with, political ideologies. As a result criticism by established scholars tended to blur their differences with (1) the quality of scholarship and (2) the political position of the "new scholars." In any case, there was little doubt that a serious chasm among scholars existed, that attack and counterattack led to much bitterness, and that many of the older scholars, like Oscar Handlin, longed "for the days of the 30's when historians had a sense of being a member of one community . . . together working its way toward the truth." [49]

In the movement toward faculty unions: Another issue that threatened to divide professors and to alter further their role in the university was that of collective bargaining. The traditional posture of professors was that of a professional who wanted an association to represent them with restraint, negotiate with respect, and resist when necessary with calm deportment.[50] Now came a surge of militant interest in unions and in collective bargaining. In 1972, 43 percent of a sample of university teachers in the United States agreed that "the recent growth of unionization of college and university faculty is beneficial and should be extended." [51] A report in

1974 listed 338 colleges and universities in the United States in which faculty had chosen collective bargaining agents.[52] In Canada in the early seventies, collective bargaining was initiated at several French-speaking universities and at least one major English university.[53] There were many professors who resisted this movement and decried the loss of professionalism,[54] but this served only to widen divisions within the ranks of academic men and women.

The movement to collective bargaining struck at a number of areas of great importance to professors and their role in the university. These may be briefly summarized as follows:

(i) A union is organized for the purposes of collective bargaining under the jurisdiction of the labor laws of the state or province, and such laws are usually enacted to regulate the relationship between management and employees.[55] Professors have traditionally resisted the designation "employees" and have sought to be "members" of the university. Once a member of an "academic union," the professor found the name "employee" and its connotation difficult to reject.

(ii) A profession involves a set of symbols of work which are ends in themselves and not a means to some end of individual self-interest.[56] A union involved in collective bargaining is frankly seeking material and other benefits for its individual members. The shift to collective bargaining goes some way to destroy the image many academics have of their status.

(iii) A union tends to shift the locus of decision making in respect of appointment, promotion, and tenure outside the university. While many agree that there have been arbitrary decisions in respect of these matters by the administration, nonetheless the principle of peer evaluation was generally established, and the power of administration limited to action which might upgrade weak departments. But the thrust of the union was to protect junior candidates who did an adequate job (even if better candidates appeared later), to promote on the basis of seniority, and to reduce the power of management. In terms of rewards it was suggested that "a levelling process has occurred," that "most benefits have gone to lower level institutions," [57] and that

. . . the introduction of procedures that can be defended before an arbitrator or a judge will incur a cost in quality. The
pressures toward egalitarianism from both inside and outside
the university are strong and to date academic unionism
seems to have worked to reinforce them.[58]

(iv) The principle of a "self-governing community" so dear
to the hearts of many academic men and women seems
threatened by collective bargaining procedures, since some
of the policy matters previously determined by faculty senate
(policy regarding appointments, research, and teaching
loads) may gradually be shifted to the negotiating table
where management and union meet.

It is difficult to avoid the conclusion that, as bargaining
agents become firmly established, other faculty mechanisms
will find themselves restricted to a relatively narrow range of
internal "academic" functions.[59]

(v) The organization of unions may cause further deteriora-
tion of faculty-student relations. Many observers believed
that bargaining in the university would be a tripartite (rather
than a bilateral) arrangement in which student unions would
be "the third party." [60] And it was predicted that "in this dispute students will usually line up with the administration
against the faculty." [61] Whether this has been the case or not,
the organization of unions tended to eliminate students from
some share in university decision making just at the time
when they had achieved recognition and status in this area.

While unionism appeared in 1975 as the most pressing issue, the changes in role and conflicts about that role described earlier were of equal import. For all were bound together in the creation of a confusing picture which reflected
not only internal strife but also the changing society in which
the academic was required to find an appropriate role.

Notwithstanding the above, the university professor had
secured for himself a rare position in the professional and social hierarchy of the day. Salaries, which often reflect the
value which society places on an occupation, rose appre-
ciably. In England a normal salary for a professor before the

war was about £1,000. By 1975 it was above the £5,000 range for many university teachers.[62] In Canada and the United States similar increases in salaries prevailed. By 1975 the average salary for full professors in universities was close to $25,000,[63] but senior professors in prestigious universities frequently were paid $35,000 or more per annum. In these three countries salary increases outpaced increases in the cost of living throughout the 1960s. Many professors earned additional income through research, consulting, or writing, and there was no question that academics had improved their income status relative to other occupations and professions. Financial restrictions in 1975 threatened to reverse this trend, but this reversal was far from certain.

There were other emoluments for academics as well. There were in most universities in the countries considered here policies of sabbatical leave, which, depending on the university, provided a professor a paid leave of absence for six months to a year after five, six, or seven years of service. There were substantial research funds available in these countries, and research assistants and secretarial help could be funded through such grants. There were favorable pension plans and insurance schemes to help. And there was tenure, a secure position for life in an institution as long as one behaved with reasonable decorum.

Above all there was freedom. Freedom to pursue one's own studies, to pursue one's own research, to work out one's own schedule—even to determine one's own commitments outside the university.[64] And in those areas of institutional life that might affect one's work, there was a machinery for government which permitted one to have a say and a vote.

> Indeed, it is hard to imagine a more privileged life of freedom than that enjoyed by the average British university teacher from these two points of view [academic freedom and self-government].[65]

With minor exceptions this was equally true in Canada and the United States.

A study in the United States in the 1960s suggests that professors recognized and appreciated their special position.

Workers in thirteen categories of occupations and professions were asked, "What type of work would you try to get into if you could start again?" The assumption behind the question was that those who selected the same occupation tended to be satisfied with this occupation. Urban professors headed the list, 93 percent indicating satisfaction with their present position, compared to 43 percent of all white-collar workers and 24 percent of blue-collar workers.[66] The essentials for work satisfaction ranked in order are said by this study to be "interesting work, enough help and equipment to get the job done, enough information, enough authority, good pay, opportunity to develop special abilities, job security, and seeing the results of one's work."[67] For most professors, it could probably be said in 1960 that these conditions were present in their daily life and work. To be a professor then, appeared to be one of the most satisfying positions available to anyone.

In the early 1970s this bright picture began to darken. Funds for all purposes including research were being restricted. The great period of expanding enrollments was past. University teachers were no longer in short supply. Some of the conflicts and tension described above within the academic profession affected adversely both the public's respect for the academic and the latter's own image of his work. There was evidence that conservative forces within the faculty were seeking to gain control of senates and councils, but there were other forces pressing for unions and bargaining rights. The radical left, perhaps small in number, could neither be ignored nor denied.

There was a feeling in Canada, England, and the United States—the extent and intensity of which was difficult to gauge—which appeared skeptical if not hostile to the academic profession. A government commission in Canada in the early 1970s reported that while sabbaticals should be retained, tenure should be abolished, suggesting instead limited terms and renewable appointments with a strict code of ethics to guide the conduct of staff. "Without strong external intervention in the years ahead, entrenchment of mindless professionalism will likely curtail the introduction of any sig-

nificant changes in the process of education."[68] Similar senti-
ments, followed in some cases by action, had been expressed
in state legislatures in the United States.[69] The Ohio legislature, for example, passed a series of measures to reduce the
state subsidy for Ohio students and to terminate sabbatical
and research leaves for professors. It also considered an on-
the-job equivalent of a forty-hour work week for all academic staff members.[70] These were but symptoms of a rising
tide of sentiment which questioned—if not threatened—the
privileged position of the professor.

It was clear that the profession's own confusion about its
role and responsibility was creating a vacuum which some
public authority would fill. Perhaps never had the university's teachers been so divided. What may have been at the
heart of the problem was a decline in respect for, and loyalty
to, the university as an institution. Many professors may have
lost perspective by their generally high status and popularity
in society. In the rush of public acclaim, perhaps the university with its multiple traditional demands on the professor
seemed unreasonable. And yet ". . . academic men have
come to occupy a position at the apex of teaching and research *mainly* through the development of universities."[71]
The internal attacks on the university and the lack of loyalty
to and support of that institution by professors was often interpreted as a "death wish" on the part of academics. For
without the university and public support of the university
the security and freedom of the professor would cease. This
was the problem in 1975.

Conclusion

The first university teachers were clergymen "called to service." Even when science and research became dominant,
the academic man felt the "call" to a special field of en-
deavor. It was not one which demanded devotion to poverty,
but it was one largely indifferent to material gain and given
to a quiet, genteel, and civilized way of life. All the values inherent in such a community were understood and protected.

The ideology of this way of life became part of the mythology of the university as the latter became more practical, more research-oriented, and more professionalized. The "academic man" left his retreat to become a "man of the world." But it was not until the 1950s and the 1960s that the myth was fully exposed and professors were seen as well-paid citizens, with special privileges but with obligations which they did not seem to be fulfilling very well. The outcome of the conflicts and tensions that followed as professors sought to define a new role for themselves could not be clearly seen in 1975. It appeared that the struggle was not over a single simple issue but involved a complex of issues, each with many ramifications. There was, for example, the question of the professor's role as a "member" of the university, as a relatively independent professional person, as a member of a separate collective—a union; the question of whether the professor's work should be organized on the professional or bureaucratic model; the question of whether the teacher's work should be restricted to value-free cognitive learning or whether expressing "value-positions" on a wide variety of matters was permissible; the question of whether university teaching was to be restricted to talented students or available to all. These and other issues confronted the academic world; on them professors divided in different ways so that an odd configuration emerged in which, except for a small solid "left" and a solid "right," one could not expect any large number of professors to have the same opinion on such a series of issues. But out of the arguments that attracted various scholars to various positions on the above spectra may come some resolution of what the purpose of the university is and what the role of a professor in it is to be.

NOTES

1. Scott, 1966, pp. 265–275.

2. N. Gross, 1963, pp. 61–62.

3. Lyte, 1886, p. 216.

4. Ulich, 1965, p. 49.

5. Ibid., p. 49.

6. Jencks and Riesman, 1968, p. 38.

7. Smyth, 1972, p. 284.

8. Ben-David and Zloczower, 1962, p. 62.

9. Ashby, 1971, pp. 44–45.

10. In 1960 the author attempted to obtain data on the number of Canadian students doing graduate work in the United States and in Great Britain. The best estimate that could be obtained was that there were about 7,000 Canadians doing graduate work in the United States and probably fewer than 1,000 in Great Britain.

11. "Professionalization represents an *indigenous* effort to introduce *order* into areas of vocational life which are prey to the free-playing and disorganizing tendencies of a vast, mobile, and differentiated society undergoing continuous change. Professionalization seeks to clothe a given area with standards of excellence, to establish rules of conduct, to develop a sense of responsibility, to set criteria for recruitment and training, to ensure a measure of protection for members, to establish collective control over the area, and to elevate it to a position of dignity and social standing in the society" (Blumer, 1966, p. xi).

12. There are some who argue that an association of university teachers is not strictly speaking "a profession," for it does not meet all criteria developed by some authorities. For our purposes, however, it is sufficiently included in Blumer's definition above.

13. Jencks and Riesman, 1968, pp. 13–14. ". . . the first important one was the American Chemical Society, founded in 1876. It was followed in 1883 by the Modern Language Association of America, and in 1884, by the American Historical Association. The social sciences were the last to organize (the American Anthropological Association in 1902, the American Political Science Association in 1903, and last, the American Sociological Association in 1905). Simultaneously, scientific journals were founded, beginning in 1878 with the American Journal of Mathematics" (Touraine, 1974, pp. 156–157).

14. Halsey and Trow, 1971, p. 238.

15. Ibid., p. 50.

16. Mackintosh, 1958, pp. 12–22.

17. Veysey, 1965, p. 356.

18. Halsey and Trow, 1971, p. 185.

19. Harris, 1973, chap. 30, p. 6.

20. This figure is provided by Tom Truss, Associate Secretary of the AAUP, who in a letter dated March 28, 1974, says, "I know of no way to factor out a percentage which would be useful in terms of eligibility for membership in the Association."

21. Halsey and Trow, 1971, p. 184.

22. Harris, 1973, chap. 35, p. 54.

23. See Hofstadter and Metzger, 1955; Veysey, 1965; Ben-David, 1972 (re U.S.); Halsey and Trow, 1971 (re Britain); Harris, 1973 (re Canada).

24. Harris, 1973, chap. 30, p. 6.

25. McConnell, 1971, p. 99.

26. Lipset, 1970, pp. 85-118.

27. Nisbet, 1971a, pp. 52-53.

28. Robbins, 1971, p. 110.

29. Hofstadter and Metzger, 1955, pp. 365–366.

30. *AAUP Bulletin,* 1915, p. 35.

31. Joughin, 1967, pp. 88–89.

32. It was only after the student crises in the sixties that American professors focused on the problem of which they were part and, with their usual enthusiasm for any new need or demand, produced a spate of books which more than made up for the paucity of such material in the United States in the early part of the century.

33. Moberly, 1949, pp. 122-127.

34. Wilensky, 1964, p. 152.

35. Ben-David, 1968-69, p. 24.

36. Hoffman, 1970, p. 187.

37. Nisbet, 1971a, pp. 108-109.

38. E. Gross, 1968, p. 530.

39. Ben-David, 1972, p. 167.

40. Jencks and Riesman, 1968, p. 40.

41. Quoted in Powell, 1971, p. 71; see also Arrowsmith, 1968, p. 118; and Touraine, 1974, pp. 160-165.

42. Lipset, 1970, p. 114.

43. Riesman and Grant, 1973, p. 301.

44. Sanders, 1973, p. 67.

45. Touraine, 1974, p. 224.

46. Shils, 1973*b*, p. 288.

47. Ulam, 1972, p. 22.

48. "The 'New' Scholars," 1973, pp. 9-10.

49. Ibid., p. 10.

50. Hofstadter and Metzger, 1955, p. 470.

51. Riesman and Grant, 1973, p. 307.

52. "Where College Faculties Have Chosen or Rejected Collective Bargaining Agents," 1974, p. 24.

53. Bigelow, 1973, pp. 18-19.

54. *Report of the General Secretary, AAUP,* 1973, pp. 146-149.

55. George, 1974, p. 8.

56. Ladd and Lipset, 1973, p. 2.

57. Ibid., p. 81.

58. Garbarino, 1972, p. 17.

59. Ibid., p. 11.

60. Ladd and Lipset, 1973, p. 89.

61. Ibid., p. 89.

62. Caine, 1969, p. 12.

63. "Characteristics of 42,345 College Teachers," 1973, p. 4; see also Caine, 1969, p. 12.

64. "AAUP Statement on Professional Ethics," 1966, sec. 4, p. 57-58.

65. Halsey and Trow, 1971, p. 47.

66. "Urban University Professors Happiest Workers in U.S.," 1973, p. 6.

67. Ibid.

68. "A Future of Choices, A Choice of Futures," 1972, p. 13.

69. Mortimer, 1972, p. 17.

70. Rejai and Stupak, 1972, p. 8.

71. Halsey and Trow, 1971, p. 33.

chapter five

●

THE PEOPLE'S REVOLT

The great uprising which took place in colleges and universities throughout the world during the 1960s cannot be called a successful revolution in the sense that the existing governments of universities were overthrown. But the result was nonetheless profound: the power structure of the university was substantially altered, the established roles and hierarchical arrangements were changed, and the traditional normative order was challenged in a manner that created division and conflict in university councils. The university of the seventies appeared relatively calm and concerned with new problems of financing and state control. But internally the university was far from tranquil, and there remained unresolved many of the issues which first came to light in the student demonstration at Berkeley in 1964.

The Background of Revolt

Potentially, there had always been the threat of rebellion on the university campus. There had always existed the "generation gap"—between adults and youths, with the former exercising authority over the latter. The gap represented a break in communication, and the authority that bridged the gap was often resisted and always resented by the young. There had always been, also, some alienated youth who rejected current values and practices and who wished to separate themselves from accepted ways of doing things. There was probably always such a group in the university. Then, too, the university ideally was, and had been in varying degrees, a "free community" in which new ideas were consid-

119

ered, eccentric behavior encouraged, a degree of anarchy tolerated. These conditions of university life, present since its beginning, were always touchstones to revolt.

In the 1950s new elements were added to this continuing situation. One was the return of war veterans to the campus. They came in great numbers, older and more serious than the usual student, accustomed to authoritarian life and discipline, many married and some with children. On the whole they had little interest in, or time for, participation in the student culture of the campus. If the Hollywood version of the campus was dying, the new serious, highly motivated veteran dealt it a death blow. A new campus ethos existed: it was less concerned with fun and frolic than with grades and graduation. But the demise of many aspects of the student "fun culture" left the less serious students with little to occupy their time and probably more discontent with campus life than was the case before the war.

In the postwar period there emerged two further developments that combined to change existing university practices. The first was the enlarged youth population, which in terms of percentage of the total population was probably the largest in world history.[1] The second was the "extension of full citizenship" to many youth who had been excluded in the past from the mainstream of education, particularly at the university level.[2] These two developments combined to force the universities to admit a much larger percentage of a much larger youth population,[3] and enrollments escalated at an extremely rapid pace. In Canada, England, and the United States college and university enrollment more than doubled in the sixties.

The result of this was inevitably disruption, as universities struggled to provide sufficient classrooms, enough teachers, and a semblance of order for ever-increasing numbers of students. Some of the latter were disenchanted with the confusion, the unresponsive bureaucracy, the impersonal processing. But the student population was not only larger, it was much less homogeneous than before 1950, when it was not easy to be admitted to university if one was black, female, a Jew or a Catholic, or from a working- or lower-class family.[4] The new heterogeneous population on the campus was less knowledgeable about, and less accepting of, long-standing academic traditions than the relatively close-knit student body in the early decades of the twentieth century. One could no longer assume acceptance of old standards.

As attendance at university increased, the pressure to go to college became almost irresistible to many youth and their parents. The result was the movement toward "universal higher education" and the presence on campus of many "involuntary students" so that "in some strata and places, colleges began to resemble elementary and secondary schools, where it has long been recognized that compulsory attendance increases problems of student motivation, boredom and the maintenance of order." [5] The involuntary student was a new problem for the university, for inevitably this student felt some resentment about the pressures that forced him to attend university, and he often reacted with hostility and anger at the situation in which he found himself.

Thus, in the early sixties new problems confronted universities in Canada, England, and the United States. All required rapid internal adjustments. But the university was unaccustomed to quick change or fast decision making. In terms of tradition, habit, and structure, the university was ill-equipped to deal with a dynamic new situation with very limited time parameters.

The vastly increased and now much more heterogeneous student body seemed to justify experimentation and development of new techniques by which the learning process might be more effectively stimulated. But the evidence suggests that "institutions had not developed new educational techniques to accommodate the newer kinds of students." [6] There seemed few substitutes for huge classes, little flexibility to accommodate minority group students, no means of dealing quickly with mounting administrative problems. Enrollments increased, but so did dropout and failure rates.[7] Fissures in the success record of higher education began to appear. And student discontent was not the least of these fissures.

Some of the trends, to which reference has been made in

previous chapters, did little to ease this discontent. World War II had given impetus to the growth of research and graduate schools. Focused on these exciting fields, many universities tended to overlook the needs of large numbers of new kinds of undergraduates.[8] Often research assistants or doctoral students, not themselves "socialized" in university habits or practices, were assigned to teach these undergraduates.[9] Universities were thereby themselves giving up any idea of seriously acting *in loco parentis* to undergraduates. Even Oxford and Cambridge had to modify their views, as college halls could not accommodate increased enrollments and more students were "living out" than were "living in." [10] The universities were in effect giving up their traditional relationship with the undergraduate and forcing a new role on him. But no one—except students—stopped to consider what the new role should be.

All these matters lay in the background, and in quite different configurations in different universities and in different countries. They cannot be said to have caused the student revolt; they were simply problems not adequately resolved. The existence of unresolved problems was not new to the university, and given time it may well have made the necessary institutional adaptations to deal with these problems. But time was not to be had. For new ideas were to fan the breeze of discontent.

The New Elements of Revolt

There emerged in the 1960s one of the most remarkable youth movements in history. It had always been assumed by adults that young people would have a "wild period"; indeed, some societies encouraged and made provision for youth "to sow their wild oats," but it was always assumed by both young and old that after this experience youth would be assimilated into, and accept the values and practices of, the adult culture. What was remarkable about the revolt of the 1960s was that the values and habits of the youth culture had a profound impact on adults and that many of the ideas and practices of the youth culture were adopted by adults.[11] Even adults who rejected the new ideas were forced to reconsider their old values, and many emerged from this experience with a good deal less confidence in their previous assumptions. It is perhaps the first time in history that youth seemed to have reversed the traditional practice—to have forced the adult world to accept and adopt, in part at least, youth's definition of that which is good and what is to be valued.

It is not our purpose here to examine in detail the complexities of the new ideologies, but a brief reference to these is essential. There were, on the one hand, increasingly strident demands on the part of the disadvantaged (the blacks, the lower-income groups, etc.) to be counted as full members of society, and on the other hand, growing support for such rights by middle-class youth from well-educated, professional, liberal families.[12] Many of the latter were in universities where their preexisting attitudes and disposition to change the social order were nourished by liberal or leftist faculty members. Indeed, Lipset goes so far as to say:

> . . . a significant section of the faculty in the institutions which have been the largest centers of student radicalism have encouraged the political values underlying such protest.[13]

In any case there was among the student body in the sixties the basis for a new activist movement disposed to remedy many of the social evils of the day.

A different, but not unrelated, ideology—more psychocultural than sociopolitical [14]—emerged at this time also. It had to do with the quality of life in postindustrial society and rejected the human and ecological price being paid for technological advance. It encompassed ideas of personal identity and fulfillment and new forms of intimacy, awareness, and community.[15]

There were events in society to stimulate these movements: the Vietnam war, the treatment of blacks in South Africa and in the United States, and the apparent compromise or indifference of officials to these and other issues such as nuclear disarmament.[16] There were perhaps other forces at play. But to the long-standing student-university frictions were added new problems of overcrowding and impersonality. New ideologies emerging in the sixties and seeking change in the world around them could easily find in the university a locus of discontent, a center for organization, and a focus for attack.

The New Ideologies

There were two basic trends in the revolt: cultural and political. While the two interpenetrated and supported each other, it is necessary here to examine them separately.

The cultural revolt both opposed aspects of the current adult culture and sought a new free, natural way of life. It represented what Paul Goodman called a "crisis of belief." [17] Its basic tenets were best described by Daniel Yankelovich:

> To push the Darwinian version of nature as "survival of the fittest" into the background, and to emphasize instead the interdependence of all things and species in nature.
>
> To place sensory experience ahead of conceptual knowledge.
>
> To live physically close to nature, in the open, off the land.
>
> To live in groups (tribes, communes) rather than in such "artificial" social units as the nuclear family.
>
> To reject hypocrisy, "white lies," and other social artifices.
>
> To de-emphasize aspects of nature illuminated by science; instead, to celebrate all the unknown, the mystical, and the mysterious elements of nature.
>
> To stress cooperation rather than competition.
>
> To embrace the existentialist emphasis on *being* rather than doing or planning.
>
> To devalue detachment, objectivity, and non-involvement as methods for finding truth; to arrive at truth, instead, by direct experience, participation and involvement.

To look and feel natural, hence rejecting makeup, bras, suits, ties, artificially groomed hairstyles.

To express oneself nonverbally; to avoid literary and stylized forms of expression as artificial and unnatural; to rely on exclamations as well as silences, vibrations, and other nonverbal modes of communication.

To reject "official" and hence artificial forms of authority; authority is to be won, it is not a matter of automatic entitlement by virtue of postion or official standing.

To reject mastery over nature.

To dispense with organization, rationalization, and cost-effectiveness.

To embrace self-knowledge, introspection, discovery of one's natural self.

To emphasize the community rather than the individual.

To reject mores and rules that interfere with natural expression and function (e.g., conventional sexual morality).

To preserve the environment at the expense of economic growth and technology.[18]

The expression of this philosophy in the university struck at some of the fundamental principles of that institution, where knowledge, empirical investigation, intellectual analysis, and cognate learning were of supreme import. The challenge to authority, the demand for greater freedom, the desire for cooperative living were, of course, not new and could be handled with a good deal of understanding and sympathy by the academic staff. But to "devalue detachment, objectivity, and non-involvement as methods of finding truth . . ." was to challenge the foundation on which the university was based. One would expect that professors would rise to this challenge to speak with vigor, to defend unanimously and with their lives if need be the validity of the principles of their professional work. But as we have indicated, professors were themselves divided on this issue. Many "new scholars"

125

accepted or sympathized with this new philosophy. The assumed consensus about purpose and method in the academic staff did not exist.

Perhaps a defense of the traditional position would have been forthcoming had this view of life been the only issue or if it had been in clear focus. But it was clouded and confused by rapid politicalization of the campus as radical groups exploited obvious practical problems in the university.

The political movement often described as the "New Left" was composed of numerous and different political philosophies, including Marxism and anarchism. It was able to bring these various ideologies together in a temporary coalition and to gain the support of many politically unsophisticated students because it was able to focus on a few broad underlying themes about which there was a high degree of student dissatisfaction or discomfort. These common problems helped create an approximation of a united front on campus and created a movement of great power.[19]

The tactics used in the civil rights movement in the United States and the guerrilla war tactics in Cuba provided the means or methods for the implementation of the New Left's objectives. This was the utilization of the mass demonstration, the protest march, the sit-in, the surprise attack on some person, building, or idea that seemed particularly vulnerable. There was often less argeement about means than about ends, but even extreme measures were supported, or had the sympathy of, students who would not themselves participate in immoderate actions.

If the movement had been less diverse in philosophy it would perhaps have been more effective. As long as it concentrated on campus issues on which all could agree, it was united and effective. When disagreements arose about tactics, about wider issues, about fundamental goals for individuals and for society, divisions arose and the movement floundered.

The thrust of the political movement was directed at two objectives: campus reform and the reform of the wider society. The first related to a host of current practices in the university: the right of professors to teach when they are "more interested in writing books and articles than in spending time with individual students, more interested in the esteem with which their colleagues hold them than in respect from their students";[20] overcrowding; courses out of touch with modern-day reality; inadequate student participation in the decision-making process in the university; examinations, grades, the lecture system; and all those practices many students thought adversely affected the quality of their education.[21]

Mario Savio, the leader of the first student revolt at Berkeley, said:

> . . . the schools have become training camps—and proving grounds—rather than places where people acquire education. They become factories to produce technicians rather than places to live student lives. And this perversion develops great resentment on the part of the students. Resentment against being subjected to standard production techniques of speedup and regimentation; against a tendency to quantify education—virtually a contradiction in terms. Education is measured in units, in numbers of lectures attended, in numbers of pages devoted to papers, number of pages read. This mirrors the gross and vulgar quantification in the society at large—the *real* world—where everything must be reduced to a lowest common denominator, the dollar bill. In our campus playworld we use play money, course units.[22]

The transformation of the university seemed to many students to require democratic control, and although views differed on how this was to be achieved, there was probably considerable agreement on the general proposition of one student leader whose moderate position was stated as follows:

> . . . the university views itself much like a consummate welfare state, deciding for the students the important questions of mind as well as body . . . but *always deciding for the student,* with his best interest in mind. This suggests that if we are serious about self-development as a primary goal of higher education, we must immediately confront the question of university governance. . . . If, on the other hand, we are aiming at the self-development of the students, and are trying

to develop in them a capacity to take responsibility for their own learning, their own decisions, and their own work, then we must begin to move toward a more democratic university.[23]

The second major threat of the politicized students on campus was to relate the university to the evils and corruption of society:

> . . . authority figures in all the major institutions of American society were perceived by growing numbers of students as inextricably linked together to maintain the status quo and oppress the "have-nots" of society.[24]

Thus there appeared "the Establishment": the rulers of business, industry, the military, and the university who joined hands to make a technocratic, inhuman, unjust society—to make all of us, as Herbert Marcuse said, "victims of the technological *a priori.*"[25] The association of university leaders with corruption in society was constantly emphasized to the extent that some came to believe that "to distinguish, say, the Vice-Chancellor of the University of Warwick from the Commander of the U.S. forces in Vietnam is to make a false and probably deliberately deceptive distinction."[26]

It was not difficult to place the university in this context: the research carried on in university for the military, for business and industry, for government; the preparation of students in universities to take positions in these same institutions; the posture of the universities in relation to the major social injustices of the day, for example, discrimination against minority groups; the influence and control of businessmen on university boards or councils. Thus the university, so long surrounded by mystique and prestige, was exposed and shamed. For some radical groups it was considered to be an evil institution supporting the forces of technology and injustice in society.

> . . . Authority in the university is discredited, partly because it is seen as being hand-in-glove with these external sources of power, and partly because the special claim of an academic authority dissolves when the work of universities is felt to be

directed solely to serving the interests of a corrupt and exploitative society.[27]

The attack on the university as a symbol of the Establishment found students with rather different views and motives. A great many were simply not interested in broad political questions; they were content if they were freed from many existing constraints and allowed to "do their own thing." Some were interested only in immediate practical reform: in democratizing the university by giving students greater power in the operation of the university, by opening up the universities to blacks and other minority groups, by making the university "a true community" responsive to the needs of its members, of whom the students constituted the greater part. Others wanted the university to play a new role in society by speaking and striking out against the injustices of the Vietnam war, colonialism, capitalism, racial discrimination—to become an instrument for the reform of society. Still others wanted to destroy the university; they saw it as an evil institution and felt that forcing it to terminate its operations would represent a symbolic act of great importance—perhaps the first step in a great social revolution.

What made the situation explosive was that on many issues all these students, the political and the less political, the radical and the moderate, were able to join together and were supported by the new campus culture and value system to which almost all students subscribed. The degree of political sophistication varied widely. The number of knowledgeable and politically informed radical students was probably not great. But they were one with the vast number of less sophisticated students who saw and felt only the need for change and reform. It was a new phenomenon: "Elvis Presley's and C. Wright Mills' constituencies were quite separate. Can one truly say the same about those of Bob Dylan and Herbert Marcuse?" [28] It was the decade of the sixties in which all youth joined to force their views on society.

Support for the student protest came from two additional sources. The first was a considerable number of faculty members, some of whom were themselves members of the

New Left and some of whom were liberals who were generally sympathetic to students' objectives and not opposed to mild demonstrations to achieve these ends. A survey by the American Council on Education of 281 colleges and universities in 1967–68 indicated that "of the 181 schools in which there were demonstrations, faculty were involved in the planning of more than half of the protests and in 11 per cent they were among the leaders. In close to two-thirds of the demonstrations the faculty passed resolutions approving of them." [29] The second group supporting the student protest movement was drawn from "communities of marginal intellectuals and bohemians. . . ." [30] These communities usually contained many bright nonconformists, attracted by the university environment, sometimes employed in university research enterprises, and almost always "ready to act as a class that sets itself against those in power." [31] The formation of such communities around almost all major universities in the sixties made for a politically volatile situation which favored the student radical movement.

Thus were many of the elements of conflict present in an unusual way on the campus in the 1960s. Discontent and hostility were present in abundance, as were idealism, new values, desire for change. What usually started a serious disturbance was an issue on which most students would have a common view: recruiting on campus by firms making materials for war, the presence of reserve officers training corps, censorship of a student newspaper, the breakup of a student march. On almost all such issues the groups mentioned above were united in opposition to the university, its officers, and a relatively small number of conservative faculty members. The universities had little knowledge of how to deal with such wide and intense hostility, and as David Astor said in an article in the London *Observer:*

> The university officials find it just as hard to act in an adult manner with their students as parents do with their teenage children. They are either too strict or too permissive.[32]

Certainly, in perspective, it is clear that university officials were often inept in handling the new confrontation politics of the students[33] and that this very ineffectiveness widened the base of support for student revolt.[34]

In any case serious disruptions occurred on most campuses in Britain, Canada, and the United States. The movement was most conspicuous and disruptive in the United States, less so in Canada, and was relatively mild and restrained in England. The reason for the difference may relate to the traditonally close student-professor relationship in England and the smallness of the English universities. To a lesser extent this would be true of Canadian universities compared to those in the United States. Then, too, both Britain and Canada had reputable "third parties" in politics well left of center and, perhaps, therefore an object for identification for reform minded but less radical and less militant students. In any case it seems clear that in terms of the spread and intensity of the student protest movement the United States was more affected than Canada or England. But this is not to say that in these three countries disruption was not general: everywhere revolt or potential revolt was present. Conflict and tension were to be found in all colleges and universities in the sixties.

By 1970 the fire in the student revolt had largely disappeared. Why it had started so quickly, burned so brightly, then seemed to extinguish itself so rapidly, no one can adequately explain. It may be, as a study by the Carnegie Commission in 1970 showed, that most undergraduates were satisfied with the education they were getting.[35] Perhaps, basically, most students in Britain and Canada shared this view. Or it may have been as Professor Keniston put it in a speech in 1971:

> . . . the . . . movement and new culture dedicated above all to peace, justice, democracy and equality was moving toward the systematic violation of these various principles.[36]

Or it may have been that what some described as "a spreading mass neurosis" [37] had run its course and more moderate and more mature minds had come to dominate the situation. More likely the primary reason related to the increasing difficulty of keeping the New Left coalition intact and its problem of discovering new issues that would galvanize student dissent into strong action.[38] Of great importance also was the gradual loss of faculty support. Many faculty members who in the early years of the sixties strongly agreed with demonstrators' demands had shifted by 1970 to support more conservative policies and turned against the student movement and the faculty left.[39] In any case the belligerence, the deep hostility, the mass demonstration, the tactic of direct confrontation all but disappeared in the early seventies. To a considerable degree the student had new freedom on the campus, and this freedom may well have been the fundamental drive behind the revolt. By 1972 it could be said:

. . . today, only two or three years since what we labeled the "counterculture" indisputably dominated the campus, it has lost social momentum. The counterculture has become an ill-defined thing, increasingly more difficult to discern from what it supposedly "counters." It has gained some concessions and made some, and in this manner its former polar relationship to the old culture is being synthesized, gradually, into a new, single culture.

A wound in healing. Students are more flexible socially than they were a decade ago. Individual freedom is this generation's proclaimed common value, and it has necessitated a general increase in social tolerance. Consequently, society's authority over the individual has decreased and, so too, has the individual's concern with the standards of society.

In the college community the results of increased individuality are visible. Student activities are fewer and less ambitious. Involvement in the campus community has dwindled and student organization is dissolving. . . . People seem more relaxed (much more than they were just two years ago) and lend themselves less to being stereotyped.[40]

Results of the Revolution

It was obvious in the seventies that student protest had altered the ethos of the campus in many significant ways. There was, for example, the relaxation of admission requirements, the adoption of pass-fail grading in many courses, the increasing provisions for independent study, the emphasis on creative arts, the growth of work-study programs, the free choice of a wide variety of subjects—the movement toward a "cafeteria" as opposed to a "set meal" curriculum. All in a sense may be said to "break the lock-step and give the student greater control over the decisions that affect his life." [41]

It has been suggested that perhaps the most profound outcome of student activism was the lowering of the legal age for adulthood to eighteen in Britain, Canada, and the United States.[42] This may well be so, for it established the fact that, in effect, all students are adults and are to be treated as such. It put to rest forever the concept of *in loco parentis* and gave the student new status in the university and presumably a new role to play in that institution. Restrictions on the behavior and activities of students outside the classroom all but disappeared, and even in the classroom a new relationship was apparent.

Perhaps the most critical factor in defining the new role of students related to their participation in the governing or power structure of the university. In this respect there could be no doubt that students made significant gain. This we will describe in Chapter 7, on university government. Suffice it to say here that while experience in Canada, England, and the United States differed, it could be said that in these three countries students secured recognition as legitimate participants in some of the university's senior decision-making bodies. The student body was a "party with rights," entitled to have its voice heard and its influence felt in university committees and councils.

The academic community was, however, deeply divided in Britain, Canada, and the United States about the degree of participation students should have.[43] There was now no argument: students did share the power. The vital question was to what extent and in what areas? [44] Particularly sensitive was the issue of student representation on committees dealing with selection, promotion, and tenure of academic staff.[45] Many of the faculty members who accepted the idea of student participation in many university areas resisted the pressure of student representation on such sensitive committees.

But in respect of the student's role in the university, a significant point in the history of the university was turned. Students could no longer be considered children, wards, or merely customers. They had a new relationship to the university: they were adults with responsibility for their own behavior and conduct; they were franchised members of the university with voting rights on some issues and potentially on all issues within the university community; their relationship to their professors in some areas was that of equals, and even in the classroom a number of teachers shared responsibility for their courses with their students.

The student movement had great impact on social and political attitudes in the wider community as well. It is not our purpose to pursue this influence, but it should be noted in passing that the civil rights movement; the "peace" signed with the hope of ending the Vietnam war; the increased opportunities for blacks, women, and minority groups—all were affected by student attitudes and actions. There has seldom been a time in history when students throughout the world united spontaneously to press their views on society and to act together to change traditional thought.

Within the university the thrust of the student protest was to create a new environment in which many of the old assumptions no longer seemed tenable. The fire of revolution had died by 1975, but it had, at the very least, raised, both within the university and in the wider society, fundamental questions about the purpose of higher education; how it should be organized, governed, and directed; how much, if any, freedom and autonomy there should be for universities. All of these we will discuss in detail in later chapters. But, however one may regard some of the student leaders and the response of some authorities to their activities, one must acknowledge the value of the self-examination which the student protest movement forced on the university.

NOTES

1. Moynihan, 1973, p. 11.

2. Keniston, 1970, p. 48.

3. Fleming, 1958*a*, p. 26; see also Fleming, 1958*b*, p. iii; *Higher Education for American Democracy*, 1947, vol. 1, p. 27; Kuhn and Poole, 1972, p. 13.

4. Keniston, 1970, p. 48.

5. Trow, 1970, p. 25.

6. Mayhew, 1972, p. 48.

7. Ashby, 1971, p. 18.

8. Friedenberg, 1970, pp. 72–73.

9. Jencks and Riesman, 1968, p. 40.

10. Kneller, 1955, p. 51.

11. Ross, 1971, p. 17.

12. Flacks, 1967, pp. 52–75.

13. Lipset, 1970, p. 86.

14. Keniston, 1970, p. 49.

15. Ibid.

16. Crouch, 1972, p. 206.

17. Goodman, 1969, pp. 142–147.

18. Yankelovich, 1972. p. 35.

19. Perhaps the single most effective organization was the Students for a Democratic Society (SDS), formed in 1962 under the leadership of Tom Hayden and Al Haber. It gave national leadership to local units and kept constant emphasis on the involvement of the university in a corrupt society (Touraine, 1974, pp. 230–231).

20. Califano, 1970, p. 68.

21. Woodring, 1966, p. 150.

22. Savio, 1966, pp. 87–88.

23. Powell, 1971, p. 68.

24. Knott, 1971, p. 5.

25. For example, Lionel Rubinoff in *Tradition and Revolution* says: "Buildings crowd into the air, not because their occupants have any particular desire to live that way, but because the invention of electric elevators and new methods of steel and glass construction makes these ziggurats possible and the

possibility presents itself as economic compulsion. Wildness and silence disappear from the countryside, sweetness and serenity vanish from the air not because the disappearance or elimination of these qualities serves any human purpose, but because highways are required to bury nature in asphalt and cement in order to carry the automobiles without whose production our technology and economy would grind to a halt" (Rubinoff, 1971, pp. 19–20).

26. Crouch, 1972, p. 203.

27. Ibid., p. 205. See also Jerome, 1972, p. 200.

28. Ulam, 1972, p. 93.

29. Lipset, 1970, p. 86.

30. Ben-David, 1972, p. 109.

31. Ibid.

32. Quoted in Califano, 1970, p. 50.

33. One reason for the ineffectiveness of the university was that it was what Etzioni calls "a normative organization" in which loyalty to the institution and its values is the basis of motivation for membership and in which conflict is resolved by rational means and reference to the common values of the institution. The student revolt destroyed this image of the university (see Etzioni, 1961, p. 366; Archer, 1972, pp. 1–35).

34. Fashing and Deutsch, 1971, p. 243.

35. "Faculty-Student Views on Colleges," 1971, p. 262.

36. Quoted in Schick, 1972, p. 94.

37. Ulam, 1972, p. 144.

38. Crouch, 1972, p. 199.

39. Lipset, 1970, p. 105.

40. Campbell, 1972, p. 12.

41. Mayhew, 1972, p. 56.

42. Bressler, 1972, p. 189.

43. See McGrath, 1970; Ross, 1972.

44. McGrath, 1970, pp. 60–70.

45. Thompson, 1972, pp. 166–167.

part three

THE
ISSUES

chapter six

●

GOALS

One of the major contributions of the revolt of the sixties
was to expose the widely divergent conceptions of the
university held by academic people. The university was under attack; it was unable to respond because it was very soon
discovered there was lacking the common front, the shared
values, the agreed-upon purpose assumed to exist within it.
The university had grown up based on century-old norms
that, however binding in the past, no longer seemed realistic
or relevant to many in the universities in the 1960s.

"The gravest single problem facing American higher education is this alarming disintegration of consensus about purpose. . . .[1] To say there is no consensus on . . . goals is an
understatement: there is dangerous discord," [2] wrote Sir Eric
Ashby after his survey of universities in the United States in
1970. And in England, where tradition has played a more
significant role, it was suggested in 1972:

> One major theme is likely to dominate the debate of British
> academics and administrators in the new academic year and
> it devolves on the most fundamental question of them all:
> What are the purposes of the contemporary university? [3]

There was evidence to suggest that while the differences of
view among academics in England on this question were not
as wide nor as sharp as in the United States or Canada, consensus in respect of this issue was clearly lacking;[4] evidently,
determining the purpose of the university was a major and
serious problem for the English academic system.

There are several well-known hypotheses in sociology that

have relevance for our discussion of university goals; briefly summarized, they may be stated as follows: (1) if the goals individual members of the university (students, professors, administration) have for the institution differ markedly from the formally established goals of the university, there will be some disharmony in the organization; (2) if there is not consistency between "means and ends," that is, if there are not acceptable means of achieving the formal goals of the university, there will be disorganization and aberrant behavior; and (3) if there is considerable inconsistency between the stated goals of the university and its real or operational goals, the organization may well be dysfunctional.[5] In all organizations there are probably some deviations in one or more of these areas. The important issue is the degree: if the gap becomes substantial and recognizable, the result is often frustration, despair, anomie, or perhaps as the record of the 1960s suggests, revolution.[6] The status of goals, norms, and functions is then of great importance for an organization like the university, for these are indexes of the state of health of the institution.

Idealized Values and Goals

University people deal with ideas and words. It is to be expected then that over the centuries there would be a great outpouring of articles, addresses, and books about the university: its purposes and goals. This is, indeed, the case. But while there have been differences of view in respect of these matters, the differences had, up to 1950, been within a framework about which there has been a remarkable degree of agreement about what the university was and should be doing. The profile that emerged over the centuries and from a surfeit of words and ideas is approximately the following: the university is a small community of intellectually talented people separated from the larger society and united internally by a respect for knowledge and a love of learning that is involved in a search for truth and the perpetuation of high culture and civilized living. It is worth examining some of the views about the concepts involved in this definition.

140

The university community is for an intellectual elite: "It must be a select and therefore a very small community with a capacity for developing an organic life." [7] "Indiscriminate admission of unqualified students is historically a road to educational and societal disaster." [8] "Democracy is a social and political, not an intellectual possibility." [9] "We must not allow ourselves to be deceived by the inevitable demands of those who oppose the idea of an intellectual hierarchy." [10] "Enrollments should be proportionate to the number of good teachers available." [11]

The university is separate from society: The university is an independent and largely autonomous community. "Like the church it derives its autonomy . . . from an imperishable idea of supranational, world-wide character: academic freedom." [12] "The state [must] respect the university and protect it against all other forms of interference." [13] "Universities [are] places insulated from society to pursue knowledge disengaged from its social implications." [14] "The university stands outside the society, and contains within itself all varieties of creeds and beliefs and all kinds of persons subject to the one qualification . . . competence in the world of learning and scholarship." [15] "The university is more than a physical structure, it is a spiritual being." [16] "Is there any more promising hallmark for a civilized society than its willingness to support a class of persons whose principal business is to think, to arrive at knowledge, and to induct others in this principal business?" [17]

The university community is united by, and devoted to, knowledge and learning: "To be permeated by the idea of the university is part of a way of life. It is the will to search and seek without limitation, to allow reason to develop unrestrictedly, to have an open mind, to leave nothing unquestioned, to maintain truth unconditionally, yet recognizing the dangers of *sapere aude* [dare to know]." [18] "The function of a university is, then, the search for truth and its communication to succeeding generations." [19] "The university's main and honorable function is to transmit knowledge. . . . [It] cannot be expected to fulfill . . . religious cravings of many." [20] "What is the dogma that the university is built on? *Knowledge is important.* Just that. Not 'relevant' knowledge; not 'practical' knowledge; not the kind of knowledge that enables one to wield power, achieve success, or influence others. *'Knowledge.'* " [21]

The university's responsibility to students is not only to awaken them intellectually but to provide them with the qualities that will perpetuate culture and provide leadership to society: "Now the great End for which the College was founded, was a Learned, and pious Education of Youth, their Instruction in Languages, Arts, and Sciences, and having their minds and manners form'd aright." [22] "A university education . . . gives a man a clear conscious view of his own opinions and judgments, a truth in developing them, an eloquence in expressing them and a force in urging them. It gives him, too, a certain *savoir faire,* enabling him to find common ground with his fellows in every class and to conduct his social life with skill and grace. Liberal education . . . makes not the Christian, not the Catholic, but the gentleman." [23] "Students, by rubbing shoulders with one another especially, but also with faculty at least to some extent, would . . . sharpen moral and social aptitudes. Both the intellectual and the moral development of the individual student were, in other words, aspects of the traditional academic community." [24] "At the heart of the traditional university is its commitment to the transmission of the high culture, the possession of which has been thought to make men truly civilized." [25] And with the intention of placing "the administration of human affairs . . . in the hands of educated men," [26] "a real university instills in its students . . . not only intellectual skills, but intellectual curiosity which is the best antidote to that boredom and despair incorrectly called alienation." [27]

Two other ideas, fundamental in the medieval universities and revived again after 1850, have been incorporated into this concept of the ideal university, albeit somewhat reluctantly by some and with limiting conditions by others.

These are concerned with research and professional education.

There are obligations and conditions of research which exist in the university: Cardinal Newman's idea of the university did not include research. In his *Discourses on University Education* he wrote:

> The nature of the case and the history of philosophy combine to recommend to us this division of intellectual labour between Academies and Universities. To discover and to teach are distinct functions; they are also distinct gifts, and are not commonly found united in the same person. He too who spends his time in dispensing his existing knowledge to all comers is unlikely to have either leisure or energy to acquire new. The common sense of mankind has associated the search for truth with seclusion and quiet. The greatest thinkers have been too interested in their subject to admit of interruption; they have been of absent minds and idiosyncratic habits, and have, more or less, shunned the lecture room and the public school.[28]

This idea, while hostile to developments in society and in the university, had a profound and lasting effect on thinking about universities, and even in recent years there have been a few outbursts against research.

> For God's sake, stop researching for a while and begin to think. We need . . . not only discoverers of facts . . . but explorers of ideas and rethinkers of values. . . .[29]

But scholarship and the search for truth were research by other names, and these were central purposes of the university. "The combination of research and teaching is the lofty . . . basic principle of the university." [30] Hence, in spite of some reservations, there was after 1850, even among the most traditional, acceptance of research as a central goal of the university. There were, and are, however, in the traditional view of research, certain guidelines that distinguished "university research" from other kinds of research. One was that research in the university must be scholarly research

based on cumulative scholarship. This differs from in-
spirational or intuitive research. It

> . . . does not disparage reason, intuition, or common sense.
> Like the first, it aims at wisdom, truth, and enlightenment.
> But it differs from the first in the monumental emphasis that
> is placed on cumulative knowledge, corporate knowledge; the
> kind of knowledge that is gained by men working in terms of
> the works of others; the kind of knowledge that declares the
> indispensability of texts, of sources, of the *ipsissima verba,* but
> also the indispensability of profound learning regarding what
> *others* have said about these texts, sources, and words.[31]

This view stresses the traditional role of the university in the
scholarly enterprise: to build step by step the knowledge required for insight and understanding. It implies that innovations without this scholarly approach may not belong in
the university.

A second condition guiding and limiting university research was that it should be carried on "wholly irrespective
of utilitarian application," [32] or potential social gain. In other
words, the search for truth was not to be influenced or directed by social needs, offers of grants, promises of material
reward. The true scholar's research was directed solely by his
own inner curiosity and drive, his desire to know. The third
general principle guiding university research was that research time and interest must always be balanced by the professor's obligation to his students and to this teaching. Fundamental in this view was the university's duty to help,
guide, and teach students and to be forever "conscious of our
responsibilities to students." [33]

***There is a place for professional education in the university, al-
though some would limit its extent:*** The ideal university
came to be described in the early twentieth century as primarily an arts and science faculty. Its ends were mainly nonvocational. This view was difficult to sustain in light of the
popularity of professional schools in medieval days, the
status of the established professions of law and medicine, the
growth of "practical studies" in the universities after 1850,

and society's need for trained manpower. There was thus some acceptance of the inevitability of certain professional schools, particularly the traditional ones, but reluctance to accept, and even hostility toward, many new professional and semiprofessional schools seeking status in the university.

Flexner was shocked at the "incredible absurdities" and the "host of inconsequential things" found in universities in the United States in the 1930s. "It is clear" he wrote, "that of Harvard's total expenditures not more than one-eighth is devoted to the *central* university disciplines at the level at which it ought to be conducted." [34] He wanted Harvard to disown the graduate school of business and let it become, if it had to survive, the "Boston School of Business." He would banish all schools or faculties of journalism, home economics, and much else that made the universities "service stations" for the general public.

The emphasis was on arts and science, as the central and clearly superior part of the university. While unrealistic, it was argued that from the very beginning:

> . . . it had been tacitly recognised that the University was "founded in Arts," or, in other words, that its primary duty was rather to provide students with a liberal education than to instruct them in the distinctive elements of any particular profession.[35]

And this view persisted, was expanded, and justified with a wide variety of arguments through the centuries.

The aims of university education suggested in the president's commission on higher education in 1947 are almost all related to concepts to be found in arts faculties or colleges.[36] Ulam, writing *The Fall of the American University,* suggested that the modern university may be attempting to be "excessively practical" and asks, "Can a modern university prosper unless its ideals and the focus of its activities be 'those purer speculations'? . . . studies . . . in which the only doubt can be whether the beauty and grandeur of the subjects explored, or the precision and cogency of the methods and means of proof, most deserve our admiration." [37]

The conception of the university that emerged over the

centuries and that prevailed up to World War II thus was that of a selective small, autonomous, self-contained community devoted to the preservation and advancement of knowledge, exercising something like pastoral care over its students, focusing on the great humanistic issues in life, and providing a place for the more prestigious professions in its midst. This was the "idealized university"—or college.[38] There was little disagreement about its purpose or form and none about its virtues. By 1950, of course, the multiversity had already begun to take shape; science was in the ascendancy; utilitarian programs of study and research were prominent. The vision of the idealized university persisted nonetheless. The movement for change had already begun and was soon to overwhelm the dominant concept of the university. But until 1950 the idealized university was the dominant theme in university rhetoric. It was achieved to a degree in the prestigious colleges and universities in New England, in Oxford and Cambridge, and in the better Canadian universities. But it was somewhat removed from reality even before World War II, and completely unrealistic after it. What is important about this conception of the university, however, is that it represented an agreed-on purpose for the university. If there was not unanimity and if there was practice to the contrary, there were few voices to dispute the value of the "idealized university." It represented a consensus about form and function which provided a secure and stable fortress; it was the object of loyalty by faculty and students and of admiration and respect by society.

It is not difficult to see in retrospect the problem that lay on the horizon. These idealized goals did not exist simply because their virtues were endlessly extolled by respected scholars and university presidents. For many students the purpose of the university was training for a job; for many professors it was to provide a base for their research activities; for society it was to feed a growing industrial machine. None of these was consistent with the aspirations of the idealized university. Further, the activities of the university were increasingly separating it from its idealized position: the swelling enrollments; the acceptance of large grants from

146

outside bodies, which reduced its independence; the multiplication of vocational schools; the abandonment of *in loco parentis* were only some of the aberrations. Indeed the very means of achieving the ends of the idealized university were disappearing as professors were appointed or promoted because of their research competence and not because of their loyalty to "the idea" of the university or for their interest in students or for their capacity for teaching. The gap between the ideal and the real was widening. The consequences of the separation of means and goals delineated by Robert Merton[39] were all evident in the postwar university. It was inevitable that the crisis of goals would arise.

Goals In the Postwar Period

Reformulation of traditional goals: The reality of the crisis described above could not be avoided, and many attempts were made to come to grips with the issue by formulating new statements of university goals. On the whole these formulations sought to restate traditional objectives and to add some ideas to describe more realistically what, in fact, the university was doing.

Daniel Bell, for example, described the four functions of the university as: (1) "the keeping of the traditions of Western culture . . . ," (2) "the search for truth through inquiry and scholarship . . . ," (3) "the training of a large number of professionals in specific fields . . . ," and, significantly, (4) "the application of knowledge to social use. This task included, in earlier years, aid to agriculture; more recently it has been of service to technology and to planning." [40]

The aims of higher education enunciated in the Robbins report were consistent with those above, but it is of considerable importance to note that the report stated that the first purpose of the university was:

> (1) instruction in skills suitable to play a part in the general division of labor. We put this first, not because we regard it as the most important but because we think it is sometimes ignored or undervalued. . . . We deceive ourselves if we claim that more than a small fraction of students in institutions of

higher education would be where they are if there were no significance for their future careers in what they hear and read. . . . Progress . . . depends to a much greater extent than ever before on skills demanding special training; a good general education, valuable though it may be, is frequently less than we need to solve many of our most pressing problems.[41]

A bold attempt to rationalize the multiplying functions of the university was made by Parsons and Platt. They saw the many functions of the university as bound together in a "cognitive complex," in which devotion to "knowledge, rationality, learning, competence, and intelligence" were the dominant values.[42] They recognized various divisions in, and services of, the university, but these were all related to the cognitive function. Thus they pictured the structure of the university as diagrammed below: [43]

	Knowledge "for its own sake"	Knowledge for "problem-solving"
Institution-alization of cognitive complex	The core of cognitive primacy (research and graduate training by and of "specialists")	Contributions to societal definitions of the situation (by "intellectuals" as "generalists")
Utilization of cognitive resources	General education of "citizenry" (especially undergraduates as "generalists")	Training for applied professions (as "specialists")

It is clear that Parsons and Platt saw many new functions for the university; it is not confined to "knowledge for its own sake," but knowledge is to be applied both in the training of manpower and to problem solving in society. Neither is it to be confined (in spite of many affirmations to the contrary) to purely intellectual affairs, for training for citizenship and the socialization process require other considerations having to do with "the nature of the academic community and the combinations of cognitive, moral and affective concerns. A special contribution can be made by an educated citizenry but only if there is a close articulation of the moral and affective components of socialization with the cognitive component." [44] The university must be a community concerned with moral and affective issues about which it is assumed there is, within the university, a large degree of agreement.

While the university is "institutionalized" as a cognitive complex in society and renders various services as such to society, it is a closed, largely autonomous, system. "The preservation of autonomy is necessary if the society of the future is to continue making available the contributions of the cognitive complex to its many different values and interests." [45]

The difficulty with these and many other definitions of goals and descriptions of functions was the assumption that many almost irreconcilable aims could be merged in a single institution with a common intellectual and moral base. The new definitions went some way to enlarge former concepts of "the idea of the university," but they were not sufficiently catholic to encompass the many varied activities of the modern university. Further, these definitions assumed a large degree of autonomy for the university to determine its own ends. They recognized that higher education must go some way to serve social needs, but the university was clearly not to be the servant of society. Most of these definitions assumed the value of traditional goals, amended slightly, in a society which was questioning these values and asking for new and expanded services in the whole educational system. The great virtues of "learning, freedom, excellence, community, and humanity," [46] which had inspired so many commencement speakers and which were presumably the basis of the university idea, seemed restrictive, elitist, and irrelevant to many in the era of revolt. The newer formulations of aims went some way to meet these criticisms, but they were insufficient for the day.

The multiversity: It was Clark Kerr in his widely read God-kin Lectures in 1963 who defined the postwar university most realistically and forced new concepts on the academic world. The very title of his lectures, *The Uses of the University,* was in itself a deviation; the implication was that the university should be useful in many practical ways to the society in which it existed. His description of the multiversity, although precise and accurate, moved far away from traditional concepts.

It was painful for many people to see in cold print an outline, not of what the university should be, but what it was. Kerr compared it to a large city, in which

> . . . there is less sense of community than in a village but also less sense of confinement. There is less sense of purpose than within the town but there are more ways to excel. . . . As against the village and the town the "city" is more like the totality of civilization as it has evolved and more an integral part of it; and movement to and from the surrounding society has been greatly accelerated. As in a city, there are many separate endeavors under a single rule of law.[47]

What Kerr foresaw was a huge, comprehensive, and diversified system of higher education that would interact with society to the end that both would grow and develop in mutual support of each other to produce one of the world's great civilizations. The core of the university was the intellect and the application of it to all areas of life. But he used new words, strange in the rhetoric of academics, such as "the knowledge industry"; and ideas foreign to the idealized university. "The university as producer, wholesaler, and retailer of knowledge cannot escape service. Knowledge today is for everybody's sake." [48] While he accepted the fact that a community should have a soul, he believed that "the multiversity has several—some of them quite good, although there is much debate on which souls really deserve salvation." [49]

Kerr described in some detail the comprehensive and multifunctional character of the University of California, which

> . . . had operating expenditures from all sources of nearly half a billion dollars, with almost another 100 million for con-

struction; a total employment of over 40,000 people, more than IBM and in a far greater variety of endeavors; operations in over a hundred locations, counting campuses, experiment stations, agricultural and urban extension centers, and projects abroad involving more than fifty countries; nearly 10,000 courses in its catalogues; some form of contact with nearly every industry, nearly every level of government, nearly every person in its region. Vast amounts of expensive equipment were serviced and maintained. Over 4,000 babies were born in its hospitals. It is the world's largest purveyor of white mice. It will soon have the world's largest primate colony. It will soon also have 100,000 students—30,000 of them at the graduate level; yet much less than one-third of its expenditures are directly related to teaching. It already has nearly 200,000 students in extension courses—including one out of every three lawyers and one out of every six doctors in the state. And Harvard and California are illustrative of many more.[50]

Kerr's description of the new university was far removed from the prewar concept of the idealized university. It was large and growing; it was service-oriented, seeking to meet the needs of humans everywhere; it was multifunctional, performing many functions, some of which seemed strange in an institution of higher learning; it was composed of a number of separate and largely unrelated communities; its activities and programs were influenced, if not determined by, social needs. Yet he saw this new institution dominated by traditional goals, including "the preservation of eternal truths, the creation of new knowledge, the improvement of service wherever truth and knowledge of high order may serve the needs of man." [51] To some readers it seemed that Kerr had simply described a huge conglomerate with many varied corporate interests to which he gave the name multiversity and, quite inappropriately, ascribed to it the ancient purposes of the university.

Whatever may be said of these lectures, they represented a major breakthrough in thinking about university goals. There was, of course, resistance and hostility: a rejection of Kerr's analysis by some, a denial of its relevance for many colleges and universities, a demand that the "evils" of the multiversity be remedied. But the thrust of the argument—

that universities performed many varied and even unrelated functions and were an integral part of society—could hardly be refuted.

The importance of Kerr's analysis was that it described a system that was successful when judged by many of the criteria that one might apply to the measurement of a university's quality. Some would ask where was "the single, recognized, and inspiring function that gives it [the university] its character, that supplies cement for human allegiances?" [52] But the fact was that these large universities produced a higher proportion of Nobel Prize winners and doctoral students than other universities in the United States[53] and that the American institutions of higher education as a whole became "the principal centre for advanced study and research for students and scientists from all over the world." [54] One might quarrel with some aspects of the system, but one could hardly deny its achievements.

It was inevitable that both Canada and England would be influenced by the successful American model. As the movement to mass higher education gained acceptance in all parts of the Western world, many more universities in Canada took on the appearance of the great state universities in the United States. The English universities sought to remain relatively small and to retain emphasis on undergraduate teaching, but even here it was obvious that it would be increasingly difficult to maintain elite universities, to ignore the needs of society for manpower trained in practical skills, to give anything but support for expanded opportunities for graduate training. As with universities in Canada and the United States, the state-supported English universities "are forced into a less rigid emphasis on high or traditional academic requirements for admission. They have to acquire a vocational and service emphasis. They have to recruit their staff more widely. They have to submit to a lesser degree of autonomy in relation to the government agencies which provide funds." [55] For those devoted to the traditional university, Kerr's picture of the changing university had poignancy in Canada, England, and the United States.

The radical position: For the New Left none of the above definitions of functions or aims were adequate; indeed, Clark Kerr's analysis only served to support their contention that the university had become an institution of corruption.

The radicals had two major criticisms of the university. First, the university had become caught up in the technological processes of society so that it was indistinguishable from the community around it, insensitive to human values, indifferent to the human condition, involved in the mindless destruction of the human personality. So deeply committed had the university become to society's way of life that it made "no distinction between the glories of modern medicine and the horrors of modern war." [56] And second, the university had become an integral part of the great industrial-military complex, which provided the university and its researchers with funds, projects, and policies that inevitably enslaved the university in unwholesome enterprises.[57]

In the radicals' view, the remedy was a clean break with these involvements and a redirection of the energies of the university to solving the great human problems of the day. The university had used the idea of detachment and disinterested inquiry as a means of evading responsibility; it was time now to drop the pose of neutrality, and to give not merely intellectual leadership but a moral commitment to human values and the building of "the good society." [58] A necessary condition for this was internal reforms in the university: self-government, the abolition of research grants for military purposes, a break with symbols of the authoritarian society (exams and grades), concentration on the "here and now" issues while discarding the university's obsession with the culture of the past. Cognitive learning was less important than sentiment, feeling, sincerity, conviction.[59]

The radical thrust had considerable impact on the university, and particularly on the debate about means and ends. For one, it raised questions about university purposes and activity that had not been considered heretofore. There were many moderates in the university who were shocked to discover how, probably without conscious thought, the univer-

153

sity had become involved in a variety of what appeared to be
unhealthy enterprises and how far it had strayed from its traditional goals. Entirely new issues emerged for debate on the
floor of university councils. Further, it created a radical bloc
in the university which rejected compromise in favor of confrontation. It widened the gap between conservative and
radical in internal deliberations, and it made more difficult
the definition of common aims.

Summary: In the period 1950–1975 there were many attempts to define the purpose of the university in terms appropriate to the times. Almost all of these fell into one of the
three categories described above. There were some who argued for a return to the "idealized university" [60] or even to
the ideas of Cardinal Newman. But strong as nostalgia for
the past might be, these views appeared highly unrealistic in
the postwar world; "like the perfume of an empty vase" they
stirred old memories but did little to change what seemed to
be the inevitable link of the university with a rapidly changing society. What was involved for the university was not a
choice between three or four positions on purposes, but a
resolution of a number of fundamental issues, each of which
seemed to require its own resolution.

The Issues

A statement of objective usually precedes the establishment
of policy and practice in an organization. In the university
changes both in policy and practice had occurred with little
reference to goals. There was therefore, as suggested, a considerable effort in the period 1950–1975, when this inconsistency became apparent, to reformulate realistic goals that
would define, limit, and structure accelerating changes taking place in ideology and activity in the university. A major
difficulty was that much discussion focused on various immediate policies, and it appeared that the resolution of these issues would in cumulative form constitute the new goals of
the university. Thus, again, the conventional process might

be reversed: pragmatic definition of policy and practice would determine ideological aims.

The policy questions of the day all touched on fundamental aspects of university life, but they were fragmented to such an extent that an overriding philosophy or solution seemed difficult to achieve. Very briefly, these issues may be summarized as follows:

(1) *Constituency:* Is the university for the "talented few," or for all those who meet minimum academic standards; or should it be "open" to all adults regardless of their capacity and previous academic record? Should the university be an instrument of social justice, providing special opportunities, even if a quota system is necessary, for those disadvantaged persons in lower income or minority groups?

(2) *Functions:* Should the university restrict itself to its traditional task of higher learning in the arts and sciences and some professions, or to these together with new professional and semi-professional faculties; or should it follow the path of the multiversity, expanding its operations and functions comparable to the huge multinational corporation?

(3) *Ethos:* Should the dominant character of the university be cognitive—intellectual, rational, scientific—or should this feature be merged with affective and moral concerns, or even move aside to give priority to personal and social issues and to feeling and sentiment about such issues?

(4) *Standards:* Should the university rely on the standards of scholarship established over the centuries to measure and appraise the work of masters and students, or should less objective and more personal standards be introduced that would encourage growth and achievement on an individual basis?

(5) *Autonomy:* Should the university seek to achieve substantial autonomy, or fight for freedom in certain critical areas, such as the appointment of academic staff and the determination of curriculum; or should it accept the fact that it is now "in the public domain" and must simply be one of many participants in society's planning of a system of higher education?

(6) *Political posture:* Should the university seek to retain its traditional posture of neutrality in respect of great social and political issues, or should it become actively engaged both inter-

nally and externally with political questions that seem important and relevant to the day?

(7) *Curriculum:* Should the core of the university be "the spectrum of intellectual disciplines represented in the faculty of arts and sciences," which have national and international status; [61] or should the spectrum be broader, more relevant to current issues (such as ecology, human relations, racial tension, etc.), and more practical to provide training for new professions and occupations in the health, welfare, educational, and industrial fields?

(8) *Community:* Should the university seek to achieve a sense of community, of oneness of purpose, of loyalty to colleagues, common ideas, and to community; or should the concept of the large city with its diverse interests, activities, and civil service be the accepted model?

These and other issues strained for resolution in the university in 1975. Time might ease internal tensions and permit a new consensus to emerge. Or external forces, primarily governments and their agencies, might exert pressure to force policies which would give the university a new form and character.

In the meantime, the university stood in danger of disintegration—or at least of mindless drift. For as Merton suggests,[62] if an organization is without clear objectives, if its members have widely different goals for it, if its "means" and methods appear confused because they are not related to any definitive agreed-upon goal, the inevitable result is a variety of organizational maladies, not the least of which is to sink into a state of anomie.

The prospect of merging traditional and revolutionary goals appeared remote. There was nonetheless in 1975 evidence on all sides of some softening of positions which had been rigidly held ten years earlier. Traditionalists were recognizing the necessity of dealing with social change; the values and the problems of the multiversity were more apparent; some of the reforms urged by the New Left seemed less radical. With time a reconciliation and a new agreed-upon purpose might be achieved. But the bothersome question was: was such time available?

156

NOTES

1. Ashby, 1971, p. 104.

2. Ibid., p. 92.

3. MacArthur, 1972b, p. 6.

4. See Halsey and Trow, 1971, pp. 456–459; Britain, Committee on Higher Education, 1963; MacArthur, 1972a, p. 5; "Oxford Discussions on Higher Education," 1972, pp. 295–318.

5. Merton, 1957, pp. 121–138.

6. Ibid.

7. Bayley, 1972, p. 86.

8. Califano, 1970, p. 81.

9. Flexner, 1968, p. 338.

10. Jaspers, 1965, p. 110.

11. Sir Ernest Barker, quoted in Kneller, 1955, pp. 146–147.

12. Jaspers, 1965, p. 19.

13. Ibid., p. 132.

14. Ashby, 1971, p. 104.

15. Bell, 1971, p. 165.

16. Kneller, 1955, p. 224.

17. Nisbet, 1971a, p. 208.

18. Jaspers, 1965, p. 81.

19. Stevenson, 1956, p. 179.

20. Ulam, 1972, p. 10.

21. Nisbet, 1971a, p. 24.

22. Morison, 1965, pp. 22–23.

23. Quoted in Zangwill, 1965, p. 9; see also J. H. Newman, 1959, pp. 144, 191–192.

24. Nisbet, 1971a, pp. 116–117.

25. Trow, 1970, p. 2.

26. Ashby, 1971, p. 38.

27. Ulam, 1972, p. 217.

28. J. H. Newman, 1959, p. 10.

29. Moberly, 1949, pp. 183–184.

30. Jaspers, 1965, p. 58.

31. Nisbet, 1971*a*, pp. 31–32.

32. Hofstadter and Metzger, 1955, p. 376.

33. Nisbet, 1971*b*, p. 68.

34. Flexner, 1968, p. 197.

35. Lyte, 1886, p. 52.

36. *Higher Education for American Democracy*, 1947, vol. 1, pp. 50–57.

37. Ulam, 1972, p. 80.

38. Millett, 1952, p. 28.

39. Merton, 1957, pp. 121–138.

40. Bell, 1971, pp. 163–164.

41. Britain, Committee on Higher Education, 1963, pp. 6–7.

42. Parsons and Platt, 1973, chap. II.

43. Ibid., p. 106.

44. Ibid., p. 364.

45. Ibid., p. 363.

46. Bundy, 1970, pp. 531–567.

47. Kerr, 1963, p. 41.

48. Ibid., p. 114.

49. Ibid., p. 19.

50. Ibid., pp. 7–8.

51. Ibid., p. 38.

52. Nisbet, 1971*a*, pp. 201–202.

53. Kerr, 1963, pp. 91–92.

54. Ben-David, 1972, p. 2.

55. Halsey and Trow, 1971, p. 464; see also "Education; A Framework for Expansion," 1972, sec. 106.

56. Rubinoff, 1971, pp. 23–24.

57. Fashing and Deutsch, 1971, p. 285.

58. Ibid., p. 284.

59. Bell, 1971, pp. 153–172.

60. Nisbet, 1971*a*; Ulam 1972.

61. Parsons and Platt, 1973, p. 363.

62. Merton, 1957, pp. 121–138.

chapter seven

●

GOVERNANCE

The university is one of the most complex of modern organizations, and therefore one of the most difficult to administer. But in the postwar period of increased demand for participation and of democratization, the problem of how to administer efficiently, operate fairly, and govern wisely became acute. The university was going through a period of transition, experimenting with new methods and techniques of governance, but to many observers these new forms of government seemed absurd and the university to be in chaos. Indeed, the failure to establish stable government in the university by the 1970s led numerous competent writers to conclude that "perhaps higher education had become ungovernable and was well on its way to obsolescence." [1]

Over the centuries in the Western world there had been a process of "civilization of authority," in which authority gradually became more sensitive, more restrained, and more responsible in practice.[2] But this process was much too slow for the radical thrust of the 1960s when "university authority" was not only accused of being arbitrary but lacking legitimacy as well.

The result was immense pressure for change in university government to include "all estates" in decision making in the university. During this very time, of course, the institution was facing many unfamiliar problems: rapidly increasing enrollments, new types of students, uncertainty about space and finance, demands for expanded services. It was a most difficult time to accommodate a shift in power. It was inevitable that there would be confusion and conflict—that the university would appear to some to be unmanageable.

The problem of governance was, then, one of the most serious the university faced in the 1970s, and it can only be understood in terms of the long traditions in respect of it, and the new demands about it, that collided at that time.

II

One cannot speak of university government as if there were a form or pattern common to universities in Britain, Canada, and the United States. Each country developed distinctive forms of governance which provide interesting and significant contrasts. But all emerged from the medieval universities, and one must turn back to them to find the roots of certain conceptions of governance which persist in the university tradition in all countries. The fundamental theme which emerged at this time was that of a self-governing community. There would be a head, but he would be "first among equals." Essentially the university was a self-governing community of colleagues bound together by loyalty to each other and to the institution.

The idea of such a community probably came from the monastery and the guild. One of the influential figures in monastic development was Saint Benedict of Nursia, who in A.D. 530 effected a rule stating that when important matters in the monastery were to be decided upon, the head of the monastery was to call together the whole community of monks in a meeting at which the questions at hand would be discussed. The head of the monastery would, in light of the discussion, make a decision and initiate action. The importance of consultation, on both large and minor matters, with all colleagues, both old and young, became standard practice in the monastery during the Middle Ages.[3] It was from this period that there emerged the belief that "all legitimate authority [is] derived from consent of the governed." [4]

The university adopted this idea and practice. But consultation, with the exception of the Italian universities, was with the masters, and "consultation" came to mean formal councils in which binding votes were taken to limit the freedom and the authority of the rector or chancellor. It was the teachers who developed effective control of the medieval university at Paris and Oxford, electing the head, determining the curriculum, deciding who should be permitted to teach, making its rules and regulations. The practice, recognized and admired by Canadian, American, and English academies, was that of Oxford:

> The government of the University lay of course in the hands of the Masters. Strictly speaking, they were its only members. At Oxford, it is true, the Non-Regents, the Masters who had ceased to lecture, had an authority denied to them elsewhere. They took part in the making of Statutes and in other important University affairs. But the regular business of the University was largely in the hands of the Regent Masters, and among these the Masters of Arts . . . took the lead.[5]

Thus the idea of self-government by the masters or teachers emerged as the proper form of university organization. But if this structure was to be effective, loyalty to the enterprise was essential. Very early the university adopted the practice that masters should take "an oath of obedience to statutes of a university." [6] The oath was of considerable importance, because fundamental to the concept of self-government was acceptance of the corporate authority and allegiance to it.

Over the centuries there have been a few key words and phrases to which academic men have been consistently devoted. One of these is "self-government," and it is impossible to understand the persistent efforts of university teachers to achieve this ideal unless one recognizes that it is a part of that matrix of ideas which academic men believe to be their legitimate heritage.

England

Two forms of university government emerged in England, one at Oxford and Cambridge, and a second at the Redbrick and the new universities: but both, over the years, have moved toward a very considerable degree of control over the internal affairs of the institution by the senior academic members of those universities.

The Oxford-Cambridge form of government is an extremely complicated one that need not be described in detail here. The supreme legislative body[7] is very large, consisting of the masters of arts and holders of degrees in divinity, medicine, and civil law who have paid the required dues. The actual power of initiating proposals rests with a smaller council [8] composed of the senior officers of the university, the heads of colleges, and a small number (four or six) of professors and an equally small number of members elected by the senior legislative body. The councils "were the central governing bodies of their respective universities." [9] But a good deal of freedom and autonomy was given to each college, to be controlled by fellows of the college, and there was thus "a balance of power" between the colleges and the university but one in which the colleges, in many instances, appeared to dominate the affairs of the university.[10]

> Within the overall legislation governing their affairs, the senior members of Oxford and Cambridge had control of, and were responsible for the government of their universities. In accordance with the provisions of the parliamentary acts concerned, the senior members of Oxford and Cambridge established, implemented and revised their own policies concerning who would teach, what would be taught, and how funds would be allocated within their universities. They participated also in the establishment of policies and procedures regulating all aspects of the internal government of their respective university and colleges. Thus they enjoyed, in full measure, the privilege of being members of self-governing academic communities.[11]

The early Redbrick universities were started by laymen—civic authorities and leading citizens in the local community. These universities were at first almost completely under the domination of lay governors. Professors had little to say about university policy or finances or even, in the early days, about appointments or curriculum,[12] and indeed, in some cases, were not permitted by statute to sit on the governing council. " 'When a professor walks into the Council Room,' said a member of the governing body in the early days of University College, London, 'I shall walk out.' " [13]

There was, therefore, in the nineteenth century, a long and often bitter battle by academic men to gain a place in the affairs of the new universities. Gradually, perhaps beginning with the Parliamentary Act of 1870 [14] incorporating the new University of Manchester, a mixing of teachers and laymen on the senior council of the university was introduced and a movement toward a new form of governance began. What emerged for the new English universities in the early twentieth century was a three-level form of government: (1) a *court* consisting of representative graduates of the university and important citizens with an interest in the university; (2) a *council* made up of administrative heads of the university, lay representatives appointed by the court, members of the faculty nominated by the senate, and a few members at large; and (3) a *senate* composed entirely of faculty members to act as adviser to council and with authority over academic affairs. While the Oxford-Cambridge government was often referred to as a "direct democracy," the style of the newer universities was referred to as "a combination of an oligarchy and a representative democracy." [15]

In this form of government the council became the effective decision-making body in the university. And in the council, perhaps because of its more extensive and intimate knowledge of the university, the faculty voice came to be dominant.[16] The senior officers of the university were of influence but not dominant in council affairs, for the British had made such officers the servants rather than the masters of the faculty. "There is no administrative estate in British universities" said Sir Eric Ashby.[17] And Sir Sydney Caine, an experienced academic administrator, admits:

> Administrators can in the end only go as far as the teachers with whom they work are willing to go . . . and [their role] is likely to remain a mediatory and subordinate role.[18]

As the decades of the twentieth century passed, it was clear that the senior university teachers gained complete authority in respect of academic affairs and that they had a solid and influential position on the council in the development of all other university policies. On the whole there seemed to be satisfaction with this result:

> Its defects are obvious; but let me recite its virtues. The teaching staff spend dreary hours in faculty board meetings: but they are involved in and committed to the policies they create. These policies are untidy, sometimes wasteful; but they are generally determined on educational grounds and not on grounds of expediency or misconceived efficiency. The administration is controlled by amateurs; but the happy consequence of this is that tension between faculty and administration is practically unknown. To this extent, therefore, our British tradition, which almost eliminates the administration as a "power point" in the university, is a good one. It promotes cohesion in the academic community and it simplifies the community structure.[19]

The Robbins report in the early sixties found only two criticisms of current practices considered sufficiently serious to require extended discussion: (1) the predominance of lay membership on council and (2) the excessive power of the professoriat (the senior members of the academic staff) in senate affairs.[20]

In respect of lay representation on the council, the commission rejected the criticism it met.

> More than 85 percent of university finance comes from public sources and in our judgment it is in general neither practicable nor justifiable that the spending of university funds should be wholly in the hands of the users. Academic autonomy is more likely to be safe-guarded where the public has a guarantee that there is independent lay advice and criticism within the university. . . . Where men and women of wide experience and high standing in the world of affairs can spare time to associate themselves with university activities, the universities gain from the partnership strength and sagacity in their dealings with the outside world. And, even where academic affairs are concerned, lay arbitration is a valuable resource in case of conflict.[21]

On the second point the commission was sympathetic to the feeling of younger staff members that they had an inadequate share in decision making in the university. Some suggestions for improvement were made, but the commission was not inclined to alter the status quo dramatically and its recommendations were not designed to please the more radical members of staff. The commission suggested (1) some sharing of routing duties by younger staff members but rejected the idea that these duties can be

> . . . sensibly discharged by a democratic committee or by someone elected "democratically.". . . There must be someone to take decisions; and we have heard nothing that leads us to question the appropriateness of the head or chairman of the department being the person responsible.[22]

The commission also recommended (2) that decisions on such matters as appointments, promotions, and recommendations on individual salaries should be left in the hands of senior professors:

> . . . otherwise the door is open to interested combinations and bargains—the junior who is on a promotion or appointment board may be in a position of acute embarrassment.[23]

The commission stated its general position on many other matters:

> . . . from broad questions of policy and general method of instruction to questions of syllabuses—we think there is strong reason to afford all members of the permanent staff an effective and satisfactory representation on the senate and its committees. . . .[24]

All this reflected the dominant view prior to the student uprisings in the late sixties. It is significant that, in spite of early Scottish student activity and the position of the National Union of Students, the Robbins report made no suggestion of a role for students in university government.

The "revolt" altered thinking about this. By 1970 it was apparent that some minor alteration in the system of government must be made: the role of laymen, for the reasons Robbins suggested, should be protected; junior members should have greater representation on the senate and its committees;

and students should have some role in the governance of the university. This last was, perhaps, the only radical suggestion that appeared, and it was accepted with obvious reluctance and not as fully as students desired.[25] "In 1968 of 47 universities and colleges only 6 had students on Council and the same number admitted students to Senate." [26] But in that year "an historic concordant" between the Committee of Vice-Chancellors and the National Union of Students was reached that provided that students should be allowed to participate on university decision-making committees.[27] At its conference four years later there was obvious dissatisfaction among members of the national students' union with what they considered to be their minority position on committees and their exclusion from "real power." The union at this meeting pressed for representation "equal to other interests" and proposed that even on academic selection committees "representation should be equally composed of academic staff, non-academic staff, and students." [28] An indication that students were making progress toward such goals was suggested by a major study of the governing structure of the University of London in 1972 (the Murray report) [29] which provided for student representation on important committees. A vice-chancellor's consultative committee to study this report, composed of thirty-four members, six of them student-elected representatives, is symbolic of the kind of representation the Murray report envisioned for students. Provision for lay representation was, of course, also made. To some, the whole structure seemed, by giving students and laymen representation on necessarily small boards and committees, to diminish the crucial role of the academic in the life of the university:

. . . they have missed a golden opportunity to make of London a university governed by its academics, responsive to their opinions, and arousing their loyalties in support.
What can one say of a system in which a student politician of three years' standing with no commitment whatever to the ideals and future of the university, can aspire to membership of Senate, if not of Court, while a senior lecturer of 15 years' service has to remain so insufficiently trusted for the oligarchy

to fear that it would be unsafe to allow him and his colleagues any real voice in the running of his university? [30]

It was clear that England was not to change traditional
forms of government without resistance, but the pressure to
accept new ideas, particularly to accept students on councils
and committees, was great. By 1975 a limited role for students was being provided, but this did not include membership on the more important committees, which the students
had sought.[31]

Canada

Most of the early Canadian universities were denominational
colleges, under the control of their respective churches, and
directed by a group of laypersons (a majority of whom were
often clergymen) appointed by the churches.[32] The two early
nondenominational universities—Dalhousie and McGill—
were, like the Scottish universities, started by important citizens. In the governing structure of all these colleges the role
of the layman was dominant and that of the teacher minimal.
Perhaps the most liberal charter[33] of these days was that of
King's College (1827), the Anglican institution that was the
forerunner of the University of Toronto.

> The Visitor, to whom was entrusted the supreme judicial con-
> trol of the College, was the Anglican Bishop of the Diocese.
> . . . The College . . . was governed by a Council. The Coun-
> cil, according to the charter, was to consist of the Chancellor,
> the President and seven professors, all of whom were re-
> quired to subscribe to the Thirty-Nine Articles of religion as
> set forth in the Anglican Book of Common Prayer.[34]

There was thus a disposition to give members of the academic staff some authority—providing they were sufficiently
committed to the Thirty-nine Articles—as members of council. It was a major step, undoubtedly influenced by the Oxford-Cambridge model, which, unlike the structure that orig-
inated in Scotland and was adopted by most of the early
universities in Canada, gave academicians a share in direct-

ing and shaping the university. It was not likely that the Visitor—the supreme authority—at King's College would permit any unorthodox behavior to develop at the college, but it was also unlikely that he would interest himself in details of academic affairs or administration, therefore allowing some degree of control over these matters by professors. It was a first but important step in implanting the idea in Canada of participation by academic men in policy-determination in the university.

The second major step in Canada was also taken at the University of Toronto (the successor of King's College). A royal commission on the University of Toronto was appointed in 1905 and, after wide and detailed study of the governance of universities in the United States and Britain, reported in April 1906. Included in the report was a draft act (or constitution), which with minor modification became the University of Toronto Act 1906. It was a significant document in many respects but primarily because it clearly established the "two-tier" system of government, which was soon to be adopted by other universities in Canada and which gave specific control of the academic program to the academics. It states:

> The plan . . . aims at dividing the administration of the University between the Governors, who will possess the general oversight and financial control now vested in the State, and the Senate, with the Faculty Councils, which will direct the academic work and policy. Upon these two executive branches and whatever dependent machinery may be set up to carry out their authority, the whole administration should rest. They are designed to be the permanent agencies in the system of government, with their spheres of operation clearly defined and the functions of each duly prescribed. . . .[35]

Thus there were to be two executive branches, and while the board of governors was the senior body with ultimate authority and responsibility, nonetheless the senate (the academic body) was to have clearly defined jurisdiction over the academic program of the university. Faculty members were not to be members of the board, nor were graduates to be permitted to elect members to the board.

. . . no steps should be taken to lessen the responsibility of the legislature for the efficient management and support of the institution. To confer upon the graduates the power to elect some of their number to the Board would divest the State of its full control of the governing body. This, in our opinion, would be unwise.[36]

It was clear also that the president was to assume a major role in the administration of the university and that his office was to be a more significant one than the vice-chancellor of a British university.

The connecting bond between the Governors and the Senate should be the President. His identification with the academic side of the University life makes him the natural channel of communication between the two. His powers should be sufficiently defined to constitute him the general executive officer, subject to the Governors, and the representative of those special University interests which are under the guardianship of the Senate.[37]

As already suggested, this form of government was adopted in Toronto and in ensuing years by almost all major universities in Canada. While the board had final authority, it was understood and accepted, with very few exceptions, that it (the board) should not interfere in the affairs of senate but, indeed, should be highly tolerant of its eccentricities and ambitions. The president was placed in an unusually critical position, for he was in most instances the sole communication link between these two executive bodies. Because of this his position was an extremely influential and powerful one.

This system of government prevailed in Canadian universities until the 1960s—with relatively few difficulties. On the whole the system worked, although:

There was by the nature of things, always tension between these two bodies [the Board and the Senate]. The senate was concerned about effectiveness; the board with efficiency. The difference was that the senate was primarily interested in scholarship and in developing students of scholarly bent, whereas the board was concerned that this work be carried on in as orderly and economical a fashion as possible.

The tension between the two groups was not without value; it provided a nice balance of power between the practical and the academic worlds, it provided a useful check on rash action by either group, it meant a divided government which kept administrative officers from dominating the university. But there was constant dissatisfaction, particularly among members of the academic staff who argued, with some justification, that it was not possible to separate financial and academic planning and demanded that academics should be represented on the board of governors. More recently students have sought—successfully in some universities—representation on both senate and the board.[38]

In 1961 the Canadian Association of University Teachers joined with the National Conference of Canadian Universities and Colleges to sponsor a study of university government in Canada. The study was conducted by Sir James Duff, formerly vice-chancellor of University of Durham, and Professor Robert Berdahl of San Francisco State College, whose report *University Government in Canada* was published in 1966. The report recommended much closer liaison between the senate and the board and urged that the latter should include some faculty members. Like the Robbins commission in Britain before it, the Duff-Berdahl report failed to understand or to anticipate the changing mood of students and made no provision for students in the governing structure of the university. Nonetheless the Duff-Berdahl report stirred great interest in the subject of university governance, caused many universities to set up special committees to study the problem, and led to the kind of flexible attitude and policy that made it possible for Canadian universities to adapt their governing structures gradually to include students on the senate and on important committees and to change the composition of the board to include faculty members and in some cases students.[39]

The most dramatic change was made at the University of Toronto.[40] Here the local committee composed of four faculty members, four students, and the president (but with the board and alumni each allowed two observers) recommended that the board and the senate be abolished and a new governing council of equal numbers of faculty, students, and laymen be established with authority over both administrative and academic affairs in the university. "Parity," i.e., equal representation of faculty and students in all university councils and departmental committees, was a principle endorsed by the commission and one which caused great debate on the campus. This principle was not approved by a universitywide committee of 150 members called to study the report nor by the provincial legislature. But the idea of the unicameral system of a single governing council was agreed to by all parties. The final arrangement incorporated in the University of Toronto Act 1971 called for a governing council with fifty members: the chancellor and the president; sixteen members appointed by the government; two members appointed by the president; and by election of their constituent bodies twelve members of the academic staff, eight students, eight alumni members, and two of the administrative staff. A rather critical appraisal of the new act suggested:

> What the new act seems to call for is a cooperative enterprise: all those in the university (teachers, non-academic staff and students) must join with those outside (government appointees and alumni members) in planning and developing the course of what is now a great public corporation. Gone completely are the old concepts of the university as "a community of self-governing scholars"; as a community in which authority is based on knowledge and acquired wisdom; as an independent, largely autonomous institution; as an organisation which exists within but apart from (rather than as part of) the larger community in which it is located. The new idea of the university is a great democratic enterprise in the direction of which all interested parties should have a voice. The interested parties are not, of course, "equal," but it is clear that in the determination of policy in the university the academic members are unlikely to be the primary or dominant party.[41]

The new act was significant in numerous ways but not more so than in legally establishing the position of students as members of the governing structure of the university. Parity, a principle dear to the early commission, was not attained, but by securing eight seats (to twelve for faculty) on the supreme governing council—a representation enacted in law—students for the first time in Canada were made "members" of the university with rights to participate in the government of the institution. The 8 to 12 (2 to 3) ratio adopted for student-faculty representation on the governing council was generally accepted as the proper one for all university councils and committees.

When the question of council membership was raised formally again in 1974, the governing council agreed to recommend to the government that the total membership of council should be fifty-seven, consisting of sixteen government appointees, thirteen teaching staff, eleven students, ten alumni, three administrative staff, two presidential appointees, as well as the president and the chancellor. If this recommendation is approved by the legislature, it will be a gain of three seats for students compared to one for the faculty and one for the administrative staff. Clearly the influence of the academic staff would diminish relative to these other groups.[42]

Because the University of Toronto was one of the largest and most prestigious universities in Canada, it was believed that this form of government would be quickly adopted by others. Three years after the passing of the new act this was not the case, but there was little doubt that the new act gave encouragement to experimentation with various forms of government and to the inclusion of students at all levels of university policy making.

By 1975 the traditional two-tier system was present in form in most Canadian universities, but its original purpose—to divide responsibility by giving laypeople authority over administrative matters and the academic staff authority in academic affairs—was greatly changed. Boards in most universities were likely to include faculty members and students, and the senate to include substantial student representation.

United States

The constitutional history of the American university is the history of the devolution of authority in intellectual and academic matters from the board of trustees and the president to the department and its individual members. This, coupled with the vigour of strong presidents, is the source of the unequalled adaptiveness and innovativeness of the American university and the social structure of scientific research in America.[43]

In capsule form this quotation may give the story of governance in American universities, but it does little justice to the intensity of efforts made over three centuries to decentralize authority in the university and to secure a role for faculty members in the determination of university policy. Even in 1975 there were many academics in the United States who felt that they did not have the degree of freedom and self-government enjoyed by their colleagues in England and Canada. One of the reasons for relatively strong faculty sympathy in the United States with the student uprisings in the 1960s was its own long and often frustrating struggle to secure a place for itself in the governing structure of the university.[44]

The governing structure of the first American colleges (Harvard, William and Mary) was influenced by the Oxford-Cambridge model, as both were formed with governing councils composed of internal members (the president and teaching fellows) in tandem with external supervising boards that held final approval powers and the right of visitation.[45] This type of organization was not to prevail, however; the more common pattern was that at Yale, where in 1701 a charter was provided which authorized a group of ministers to "erect, form, direct, order, establish, improve and at all times in all suitable ways for the future to encourage the said school." [46] In place of immediate control of the private colleges by the teachers or professors, the practice, adopted at Yale, involved granting complete power to governing boards composed of external members,[47] and the state universities developed "not as agencies of state government under ministers of education in the continental tradition . . . but . . . took the form of public corporations parallel in their general organization to the private colleges." [48] It gradually became

173

the practice of legislatures to delegate governing power over state institutions to boards of control. In both private and public universities, then, the governing structure was essentially a board of trustees or management composed of external lay members with authority to control "property, contracts, finances, and relationships with students, faculty members, and administrative personnel." [49]

Harvard was perhaps unique in its form of organization. It changed from its original form by acquiring a new charter in 1650 which created a board of overseers and a corporation. The board of overseers, composed of laymen, was "to safeguard the interests of the Commonwealth and churches, and to prevent the President and Fellows from doing anything unwise." [50] The corporation, made up of the president, the treasurer, and fellows intimately acquainted with the College, was expected to be the governing body of the college, although all its actions were subject to approval by the board of overseers.[51] Later an informal body known as the "immediate government," consisting of the president and the teaching members of the college, was established to handle detailed matters of management, student discipline, and expulsions. In the early nineteenth century this was superseded by "the faculty," and while it did not have formal legal power, it developed substantial authority within the college.[52]

But prior to the Civil War, few colleges or universities followed Harvard's lead: the pattern was that of a highly authoritarian board of laypeople which interested itself in the most minute details of life in the college—even to such matters as the way members of faculty kept their minute book, arrangement of hours of recitation, the ringing of the college bell, any absences of faculty from the campus. And, of course, classroom visitation by trustees was a regular practice.[53]

It was undoubtedly these practices which caused deep resentment among faculty members, still remembered today, which led to insistence on change. President Barnard of the University of Mississippi wrote:

You have appointed us because we are professional teachers and you believe we understand our business; you have prescribed the broad outlines of our work, and we have undertaken to do the work on those lines. Now, if you are to direct the details of the work at every step, you will succeed no better than you would succeed if you were to direct the engineers of the Mississippi Central in the same way. Our professional knowledge and experience will be set aside and rendered useless, and our whole work will probably be badly botched.[54]

This led, in part, to revisions of the statutes of this university in 1856 in a manner designed to give faculty some control over educational policy.

In the post-Civil War period, as universities expanded and as the status of professors rose, it became obvious that the latter could not be treated like junior-level schoolteachers but must be given freedom and a voice in decisions related to their professional competence. At Yale great powers were yielded to faculty, not only in making curriculum changes and in discipline, but including the right to approve all new appointments. In 1871 Yale's president was to say:

. . . with scarcely an exception, no law has been passed, no officer appointed, unless after full consultation and exchange of views between the boards of control and of instruction.[55]

Gradually policies that were formulated by faculty found their way to the board for approval; there were fewer arbitrary regulations made by the board.

But this change came slowly and very unevenly. Whatever power the faculty had, it had de facto; it was seldom incorporated in legislation in the statutes of the university. The university remained in its formal structure a highly centralized authoritarian organization. For many faculty members it was a great indignity to be tossed "crumbs of power" by an unenlightened board. As late as 1917 Charles Beard, in resigning from Columbia University, wrote:

Having observed closely the inner life of Columbia for many years, I have been driven to the conclusion that the University is really under the control of a small and active group of trustees who have no standing in the world of education, who are reactionary and visionless in politics, narrow and medieval in religion. . . .[56]

In that same year a study showed that Cornell was the only institution of 100 public and private colleges surveyed that allowed for faculty representation on the board of trustees, was one of ten institutions that provided for faculty nomination of deans, was one of seventeen institutions that gave professors the formal right to participate in the determination of educational policy.[57] In terms of faculty recognition and control of such matters as educational policy, admissions, appointments of academic staff, the American universities lagged far behind those in England and Canada.

One of the reasons for this was the dominance in American life of business and the entrepreneurial spirit. As society and education became increasingly secularized, membership on university boards shifted from clergymen to businessmen. The latter were accustomed to holding and exercising power; they shared authority reluctantly and then only with a person or persons with similar views. Employees were not to share this power—and in the view of most board members professors were employees!

The most vehement but by no means the only academic critic of the businesslike operation of the universities in the United States was Thorstein Veblen, who believed that there was being created in the university an atmosphere antithetic to higher education:

The final discretion in the affairs of the seats of learning is entrusted to men who have proved their capacity for work that has nothing in common with the higher learning. . . . In point of fact these businesslike governing boards . . . control the budget of expenditures; which comes to saying that they exercise a pecuniary discretion in the case mainly in the way of deciding what the body of academic men that constitutes the university may or may not do with the means in hand; that is to say, their pecuniary surveillance comes in the main to an interference with the academic work, the merits of which these men of affairs on the governing board are in no special degree qualified to judge.[58]

The pattern frequently followed by a board was to seek out and to employ a strong man to head the university and to give him guidance and support. The "head man" was "the key man," and boards sought "great presidents" who, like themselves, were effective organizers, entrepreneurs, administrators.[59] The board would decide policy, but the president was responsible for the day-to-day operation of the university, including the welfare and discipline of both staff and students. Thus emerged a new type of university president, less scholarly than his predecessor but with a new style, new skills, new ambitions:

> Their aggressiveness, their concern for budgets and public relations, their interest, for example, in the statistics of their establishments, set what was then an entirely new standard. . . .[60]

With a new type of leader came a new form of organization in university life: the administration. This was usually the president, deans, business staff, and often a few senior professors.[61] This small group was presumably advisory to the president, but it formed a power bloc of the greatest importance not only because of its proximity to the highest authority in the university but also because it tended to represent those people who characteristically thought in terms of institutional management and of organizational planning [62] rather than of educational values. Thus while faculty members were gradually achieving some control over the academic program of the university, they were subject to another indignity and another arbitrary authority: the administration. The reaction of some faculty members is revealed in the following, published in 1907:

> There is set up, within the university an "administration" to which I am held closely accountable. They steer the vessel, and I am one of the crew. I am not allowed on the bridge except when summoned; and the councils in which I participate uniformly begin at the point at which policy is already determined. I am not part OF the "administration," but am used BY the "administration" in virtue of qualities that I may possess apart from my academic proficiencies. In authority, in

dignity, in salary, the "administration" are over me, and I am under them.[63]

But all was not lost. The period from 1890 to 1920 was one of great university development. Ambitious presidents recognized that the great universities they sought to build could be accomplished only with great scholars, who must be provided with rights and privileges consistent with their status. Thus it was that in the highly competitive academic marketplace concessions were made, reforms instituted, and authority exercised in a less arbitrary way. But the reforms and changes were uneven, not consistent throughout the country, and seldom enacted in law. The power of the board and of the president continued to exist de jure.

After 1920 the trend toward decentralization of authority continued. Major shifts in the power structure of the university were obvious: (1) to the faculty over educational policies affecting the entire university, (2) from the president as educational leader to administrator of finance and public relations, (3) from the board of trustees over internal operations of the university,[64] and (4) to students via their inclusion in discussions of university policy.

More fundamental, perhaps, was the devolution of authority to subunits of the organization, particularly to the academic department and to the great professor and his research institute or enterprise. Although neither had formal power and their decisions were subject to review by deans, the president, and the board,

> . . . the departments and the schools, have, as a rule, complete self-government, within the limits of their budgets and the general administrative procedures.[65]

And the most prestigious professor was free "to run his own shop" since he was

> . . . a sort of academic baron, commanding his own sources of money, selecting and commanding (and sometimes paying) his own staff, and able to migrate to a more accommodating university if his departmental autonomy is infringed.[66]

The academic man (and the same applies to the academic woman), particularly if he had status in his field of specialization, could in the 1950s operate with freedom and security in his department; he could ignore universitywide issues, for few of them would affect him or his work; and he could leave to others the task of "keeping the university democratic." Many senior scholars did just that. Willingness to serve on committees or on the senate was minimal, and even if membership was accepted, attendance was often infrequent.[67] Further, membership in committees, councils, and senates was usually confined to "the less research-oriented faculty [who] tend to be more politically conservative and locally oriented to campus affairs. . . . [These] are the people who staff the committee system."[68] With the increase in staff-student committees, this conservative faculty representation tended to be extended, for only those most devoted to local affairs could endure the many long meetings the new democracy required.

Nonetheless the trend was to establish a universitywide body—usually a senate—including student representatives, to advise on, if not direct, university policy. A 1972 study showed that of 1,700 institutes surveyed, 620 had established such bodies.[69] Of these, two models should be identified.

The Columbia University Senate was formally established in 1969 with a membership of 101. Of these forty-two were elected from tenured faculty, fifteen from nontenured faculty, twenty-one from the student body, and nine from the ranks of senior administrators. The remaining fourteen seats were awarded to a variety of employee groups, none having more than two seats. The statutes provide that "the Senate shall be a policy-making body which may consider all matters of University-wide concern, all matters affecting more than one Faculty or School, and all matters pertaining to the implementation and execution of agreements with the other educational institutions that are now or may hereafter become affiliated with the University."[70]

The Cornell Senate, organized in 1970, had one hundred and thirty-two members, sixty chosen by the faculty, sixty by the students, and the others from a variety of positions from the provost to representatives of nonacademic employees. The responsibility of the senate was that of policy review and formulation of university affairs "which are non-academic in nature and are of direct and joint concern to students, faculty members, and other employees of the university. . . ." [71]

It was obvious that the organization of such bodies moved a good way toward the concept of community self-government, for even if legal authority remained with the board of trustees, the recommendations of such powerful bodies in respect of internal policy could hardly be ignored. As in Canada, however, the role of the academic seemed to be of diminishing importance. While academic policy was usually left to faculty councils, it was often subject to review by the senate, on which the faculty shared power with many other groups. For example, the Cornell Senate was charged with study of education and research policy and had the power "to require the reconsideration of any vote taken by the University Faculty and to suspend new University Faculty legislation. . . ." [72]

The long struggle for academic self-government in the United States was won slowly and by 1950 was almost complete. No sooner was this achieved, however, than new forces came into play that required this authority to be shared with students and others. In the broad context of policy making in the university as a whole, many watchers felt that the professor was in a more vulnerable position than he had been for many decades. It was undoubtedly one reason for the growth of interest in unions for university teachers in the United States.

Summary

The type of government established early in the life of Oxford and Cambridge was the goal of most academics in other universities. It was never achieved, because in all other universities in Canada, England, and the United States a degree of lay participation in the governing structure was involved. Nonetheless by 1950 university teachers had almost complete control of the academic program in universities in these three countries and had the determining voice in the appointment and promotion of their peers.

While the universities in the United States undoubtedly benefited by the wealth and business acumen of lay boards of trustees, by the enthusiasm and drive of able presidents, and perhaps by the large administrative structure that evolved, these were all negative factors in the struggle for self-government. Professors in Canadian and English universities by the early years of this century had established themselves as members of the university with jurisdiction over the academic program and, in England, a voice in the determination of all university policies. The professor in the United States had to fight the business orientation of the university, which, subtly or otherwise, classified him as an employee. The struggle for self-government was particularly difficult in the United States, and while it was achieved in practice, final authority in most American universities remained legally in the hands of boards of trustees.

But even before the turbulent sixties, forces were at work to erode the structure of self-government that was emerging. The early medieval concept of self-government was one of a relatively small community in which all masters were involved and loyal to the institution. As specialization and professionalism developed, professors were less interested in universitywide issues than in the concerns they shared with their peers in their own discipline. The senior professorship in England, the department in Canada and in the United States became the locus of interest on the campus for many professors. And the attraction of national and international professional meetings made local campus issues appear relatively unimportant. There was a tendency, particularly for the research-oriented professor, to be less interested and less active in—and perhaps less loyal to—his or her own university. The conditions for self-government in the medieval universities—loyalty and participation—were being destroyed by the growth of professionalism, increased mobility, and by the assimilation of the university into the larger community.

Thus, when the thrust for reform came in the sixties, it

could not be said that there was a strong, competent form of government able to adapt and adjust to the new forces. This was less the case in many of the smaller universities and at Oxford and Cambridge, where the medieval ideas of loyalty and participation were very much alive. But generally speaking, and in the larger universities particularly, the concept of self-government, for which professors had fought vigorously and consistently, was being eroded by neglect. Power was being diverted to the administration, to the senior professor, to the department. The inevitable result of lack of concern by the teaching staff with the welfare of the university as a whole was a weakened central government.

The rationale for self-government by masters was that they possessed the knowledge, experience, and expertise to govern. The reform movement of the sixties was based on a different philosophy. It assumed that students and employees of the university possessed a kind of "organizational citizenship" [73] that entitled them to representation in decision making. The movement in the seventies was to develop new forms of government to provide for such participation, and it appeared, as indicated in this chapter, that the new philosophy would prevail and be widely implemented. Many unanswered questions, however, about the new form remained, and new issues in respect of it arose.

The Issues

Many of the early arguments for the democratization of the university were the same as those used for participation in a democratic state: John Stuart Mill's principle that "the rights and interests of every or any person are only secure from being disregarded when the person is himself able . . . to stand up for them";[74] John Locke's statement that "the liberty of Man, in Society, is to be under no other Legislative Power, but that established by consent . . .";[75] and, Aristotle's remark that "there are a number of arts in which the creative artist is not the only, or even the best judge. Just as the diner—not the cook—will be the best judge, of a feast." [76] These were all compelling reasons for citizen participation in the affairs of the state. But were they equally applicable to participation in university government? In one of the most thought-provoking statements on this issue, Dennis Thompson argues that they are not:

> Whatever plausibility these arguments may have for the governing of a state, they have considerably less for the governing of a university. Because the range of activities of the state is so great, and so many decisions cover much of this range, expertise in one or another activity does not justify a right to exclusive participation in politics. However, in a university, with its more limited and specific purposes, expertise or competence in some of its activities can be a more appropriate basis on which to grant authority. This difference between a university and a state does not establish the desirability of exclusive faculty or administrative government in a university . . . but it does suggest that the argument from the competence of citizens, even if it is valid for a state, cannot without qualification justify equal rights to participate in the governing of a university.[77]

Patently the comparison of state and university was unrealistic, for carried to its logical conclusion it would mean "one person—one vote" which would allow students to dominate and control a huge, extremely expensive, and complex organization. This would not be tolerated by the public, whose taxes are required to finance such institutions. The experience of "student-controlled" operations, such as Rochdale College in Toronto, indicates that these are not feasible models for the future.

The problem, therefore, was to determine the extent to which the university could be "democratized." There were many who believed that the democratic model, implying as it did a political process, was not a proper one for the university. This case was put forcefully by Adam Ulam:

> It is a virtue of democracy that it is responsive to pressures and passions of the moment, that only its basic principles remain free from the processes of bargaining and compromise. But not so with education; it must adhere to basic rules which remain free from the excitements of a season, and which find their source in the rational argument alone. We have seen in

the past and in other societies what has happened to schools which have allowed extraneous considerations, no matter how tempting in their alleged solicitude for the general welfare, to affect their educational policies and processes. They have allowed themselves to become seats of obscurantism, of political and philosophical partisanship rather than of learning, sources of national weakness and cultural and scientific backwardness rather than of strength.[78]

By 1975 universities in Canada, England, and the United States had moved to a point where Ulam's thesis, convincing as it was, was irrelevant. Students and employees were already participants in some decision-making bodies in almost all universities in these countries. There was now no turning back. There was indeed, a good deal of support for the new democracy, for it was recognized that the university had been insensitive to changes in society, to the needs of students, to its own traditions. Wider participation seemed not only relevant to the day, but a possible means of revitalizing the university.

Thompson, in stating the moderate position which supported "participatory democracy," gave three reasons for its potential for revitalization. (1) It could improve the quality of decision making: "Decisions are likely to be made more wisely if the diverse perspectives of members who contribute in various ways to the university's aims are brought to bear on the issues. . . ." (2) It would aid in securing willing and informed acceptance of decisions: "As Aristotle wrote there is 'serious risk in not letting [the general body of citizens] have some share in the enjoyment of power; for a state with a body of disfranchised citizens . . . must necessarily be a state which is full of enemies.' " (3) Participation is in itself educational: "Political activity expands an individual's range of ideas, encourages him to consider the public interest . . . and makes him a more active and creative person." [79]

While there was not, as suggested, unanimity about these views, they did nonetheless prevail. The university was deeply involved in the seventies in developing new governing structures that encouraged representation by students, professors, employees of the university, and laymen. These new structures created many new issues, among which the following were perhaps the most difficult:

(1) The size of the central representative body constituted something of a dilemma. If it had a membership of 100 or 200 to give "all estates" proper representation, the problem of efficient and effective operation arose. If the central body was small, say fewer than fifty members, could representation be meaningful? That is, could ten students reflect the views of their 20,000 fellow students or two employees the attitudes of 2,000 colleagues? Experience by 1975 was not encouraging: the large groups became useful public forums, without getting essential work accomplished; the small groups became elitist and something less than adequately representative.

(2) The administrative staff required to operate a "democratized university" appeared to be very large. Indeed a whole new bureaucratic structure comparable to the civil service in government seemed to be necessary on the campus, for all involved in "governance"—students, laymen, faculty—were engaged in other work and could not be expected to handle the details of meetings and management. The Murray report, for example, recommended that an annual budget of £250,000 be provided for the new senate at the University of London.[80]

(3) The question of the areas of the university that were to be "democratized" remained unsolved. "A university where the mathematics syllabus would be fixed by majority vote is unthinkable," said the leftist Touraine.[81] But it was not inconceivable to some. Similarly, appointments, promotions, and the granting of tenure were held by some to be the prerogative of the academic staff, but in some universities students already had representatives on committees to decide such matters. A resolution of the areas in which experience and competence should have priority over "representation" had not been made. Nor had the issue been adequately explored or its implications fully comprehended.

(4) There are long-established goals and traditions in the university. However much they may be in dispute, there remained a heritage understood by faculty and older members of the university. Were these goals to be reformulated by heterogeneous groups, some of whose members had little understanding or appreciation of these traditions? "If academic excellence is an objective of the university, is this compatible with democratic processes of decision-making? Or, if you prefer it, if democratic

processes of academic decision-making are intrinsic to a university, are these compatible with scholarly integrity?" [82]

(5) Finally, it is probable that a university teaching staff will work effectively or "be managed" only with a high level of voluntary cooperation and professional responsibility. In the new structures of university government the role of the professor was considerably diminished. In some situations his status and number were no greater than those of students. Could the level of cooperation required to make the university operate effectively be maintained in this new situation? This was perhaps the fundamental question. Traditionally, major decisions in the university reflected faculty views. This may not be true in the future. Can a university survive without a dominant role in it for its best professional teachers and researchers?

NOTES

1. Mayhew, 1972, p. 48.

2. Shils, 1972*a*, p. 6.

3. Smyth, 1972, pp. 13–14.

4. McNeill, 1971, p. 259.

5. Mallett, 1924, vol. 1, pp. 176–177.

6. Smyth, 1972, p. 48.

7. The Great Congregation at Oxford and the Senate at Cambridge.

8. The Hebdomadal Council at Oxford and the Council of the Senate at Cambridge.

9. Smyth, 1972, pp. 195.

10. New statutes in 1926 increased the educational authority of the university over the colleges. See Kneller, 1955, p. 21; Caine, 1969, p. 155.

11. Smyth, 1972, p. 196.

12. Ashby, 1970, p. 8; Smyth, 1972, pp. 72–73.

13. Ashby, 1970, p. 8.

14. Smyth, 1972, p. 216.

15. Kneller, 1955, pp. 38–39.

16. Caine, 1969, pp. 155–157.

17. Ashby, 1971, p. 67.

18. Caine, 1969, p. 166.

19. Ashby, 1970, p. 11.

20. Britain, Committee on Higher Education, 1963, pp. 217–218.

21. Ibid., pp. 217–218.

22. Ibid., p. 219.

23. Ibid., p. 220.

24. Ibid.

25. Caine, 1969, p. 157.

26. Halsey and Trow, 1971, p. 112.

27. MacArthur, 1972*c*, p. 6.

28. Ibid.

29. "The Murray Report and Recommendations," 1972, pp. i–iii.

30. Watt, 1973, p. 14.

31. MacArthur, 1972*c*, p. 6.

32. Smyth, 1972, pp. 400–450.

33. Ibid., p. 421.

34. Ibid., pp. 419–420.

35. Harris, 1973, chap. 14, p. 23; see also *Report of the Royal Commission on the University of Toronto,* 1906, p. xxi.

36. Ibid., p. xxiii.

37. Ibid., p. xxi.

38. Ross, 1972, pp. 242–243.

39. Ibid., pp. 242–258.

40. For a full account of this, see ibid.

41. Ross, 1972, p. 255.

42. "Parity on Governing Council Voted Down," 1974, p. 16.

43. Ben-David, 1968–69, p. 24.

44. Trow, 1968, pp. 14–21.

45. Duryea, 1973, p. 18.

46. Dexter, 1887, p. 10.

47. Duryea, 1973, p. 18.

48. Ibid., p. 20.

49. Ibid., p. 20.

50. Morison, 1936, vol. 1, pp. 12–13.

51. Smyth, 1972, pp. 103–104.

52. Ibid., pp. 103–108.

53. Hofstadter and Metzger, 1955, pp. 303–304.

54. Fulton, 1896, pp. 204–205.

55. Pierson, 1955, p. 134.

56. Hofstadter and Metzger, 1955, p. 502; Letter of Beard to Butler, 1917, pp. 89–90.

57. Hofstadter and Metzger, 1955, p. 456.

58. Veblen, 1965, pp. 65–69.

59. See for example Veysey, 1965, p. 379: "Because it came into being in the 1890's and in the American midwest, and because Harper's genius ran in the direction of efficiency, the University of Chicago was indeed rather like a factory in many respects."

60. Ibid., pp. 305–306.

61. Ibid., p. 305.

62. Ibid.

63. Ibid., p. 389.

64. N. Gross, 1963, p. 64.

65. Corson, 1960, pp. 43–44, 85–87.

66. Ashby, 1971, p. 68.

67. See Thompson, 1972, p. 168; McConnell, 1971, p. 101.

68. Lipset, 1970, p. 110.

69. Thompson, 1972, p. 164.

70. Garbarino, 1972, p. 9.

71. Ibid.

72. Ibid.

73. Ibid., p. 10.

74. Thompson, 1972, p. 158.

75. Ibid.

76. Ibid., p. 159.

77. Ibid.

78. Ulam, 1972, p. viii.

79. Thompson, 1972, pp. 160-162.

80. Annan, 1972, p. III.

81. Touraine, 1974, p. 186.

82. Parr, 1974, p. 41.

chapter eight

●

ACADEMIC FREEDOM

In spite of the fact that academic freedom is considered fundamental in university life, it is a concept that is subject to a wide range of interpretations and has had rather different emphases in England, Canada, and the United States.

There are two main areas of import: (1) the freedom of the institution to function without undue control or influence by external forces or agencies and (2) the freedom of the individual in the university to pursue study and to teach without restraint or inhibition. The former aspect—institutional freedom—we will deal with in the chapter that follows; in this chapter we will focus on academic freedom as it relates to individuals in the university.

Whenever the university has housed people of great intelligence, curiosity, and creativity, it has inevitably explored ideas that were in advance of, contrary to, or unpopular with those prevailing in society, particularly the ideas and beliefs of the formal leaders of society, were they heads of church or of state. There has been, therefore, throughout the centuries pressure by external authorities to limit the freedom of expression of leading scholars in the most vital universities. There is a long history of repression of free thought and expression in the university, sometimes accepted with calm submissiveness and at other times resisted with vigor. It is not our purpose here to review in detail this struggle, but some brief account of the development of the concept of academic freedom may suggest the great importance professors and others in the university attach to this phrase.

II

The medieval universities were for a short period robust, aggressive institutions where masters, by using guile and flattery, "cessation" and "migration," and sometimes their fists and clubs, won a large measure of philosophical freedom not given or permitted to others in society at that time.[1] There were masters of "enormous independence and self-confidence" such as Abelard and Roger Bacon, who were not inclined to intellectual restraint; they often attracted the largest body of students, and they created a climate of intellectual ferment that was to be the envy of scholars for centuries thereafter. There were, of course, pressures to conform, which many obeyed. But there were powerful voices speaking out for honest and frank exposition:

> Masters should be diligently aware lest, frightened where there is nothing to be feared, they think they have good reason for being silent when there is none; few are to be found who can be blamed for excess in speaking truth, but many indeed for silence.[2]

As we suggested in earlier chapters, means were soon found to curb inventive and resistant masters. Government and the church, seeking stability, could not readily tolerate institutions in which ideas and practices contrary to their own were approved. Gradually but forcefully the universities were brought under control: that which was taught was carefully censored, those who taught were supervised diligently. The long years between the bright days of the medieval university and the nineteenth century were not ones in which free expression of new ideas flourished in the university. Religious conformity was insisted upon in the colleges and universities in England, Canada, and the United States.

Early in the nineteenth century the German concept of *Lehrfreiheit*—the freedom of the professor to investigate and to teach the results of his research without interference—became known in England and in North America. It was an idea which gave both freedom and status to the teacher as a professional person and it was warmly embraced by many in the universities. But its interpretation and its implementation were quite different in England, in Canada, and in the United States.

The differences that emerged related to the social climate in these three countries but also, and equally important, to the form of university government developed in each country.

England: The long struggle in England for parliamentary democracy, for civil rights, and for freedom of the press; the record of the dissenting academics; and the rise of the Labour Party as a major political force all helped to create an atmosphere in which the idea of academic freedom was acceptable. Then, too, English universities were elitist institutions which fitted neatly into a predominantly elitist society. The Oxbridge-London axis, to which reference has already been made, persisted well into the 1960s. It was an informal association of elites. And the elite could trust the elite. Some eccentric behavior and unorthodox ideas were part of this tradition and could be tolerated—always with the expectation that things would be kept under control. There was fertile soil in England for the growth of a sound tradition of academic people teaching, studying, and speaking in public "unfettered."

The degree of self-government achieved in English universities was a decisive factor. The English professor made, or was influential in making, "the rules of the game," the ethos of the community, the character of the university. He was instrumental in creating the kind of environment in which he could most effectively work. This was a community in which freedom for scholarly study and teaching was essential. It was inevitable that a largely self-governing organization of scholars would favor conditions highly tolerant of intellectual dispute, new ideas, eccentricities of mind and character. These parts of the trade or the profession were accepted with grace and protected with vigor.

In any case it was in England that there emerged again the medieval concept of a self-governing community which was free to teach the subjects it chose and in which the teachers were free to express their views on all topics, however controversial these latter might be. The result was that academic freedom for the individual in the twentieth century was not an issue in Britain. It was established and accepted—both in the university and in society.

> As regards freedom to follow and express political and social views in opposition to government or convention there has never been any serious question. Nor is there any formal obstacle to a pursuit of research and intellectual interests determined by the individual university teacher for himself.[3]

On the large canvass the freedom of English universities and professors was everywhere admired. But in respect of some details, which could best be observed by those involved, there were grounds for some discontent. The Council for Academic Freedom and Democracy in Britain consistently found abuses of what it considered academic freedom. It saw the senior professors in British universities as very powerful "establishment figures" who manipulated appointments and promotions in a way that supported their own position and the status quo. The Council found the 1970 British university "mundane and unexciting." At its meeting in 1972, the retiring chairman of the Council referred to a letter from the head of a prestigious college seeking a reference for a junior appointment and asking "if the applicant was in any way radical?" [4] This the Council considered a serious abuse of academic freedom. Relative to abuses of academic freedom elsewhere, this incident did not seem to be a matter of the greatest import; but the efforts of the council, in spite of exaggerated statements by some of its more radical members, were probably to keep British universities as free as any in the world. In the late 1960s, however, there arose a much more serious threat to this long and established tradition of academic freedom in England. It was to arise similarly in Canada and the United States and was to require rethinking and redefinition of all that was to be implied by the term "academic freedom." To this we will return in the concluding section of this chapter.

Canada: Canada was in the British tradition but perhaps less liberal in social thought, less elitist in character, and, in the universities, permitting somewhat less authority for the professor in policy making. Still, the Communist party was formally founded in 1921 and legally established in 1922.[5] Professors from the University of Toronto and McGill University formed the League for Social Reconstruction in 1932, and this provided the intellectual left-wing support for the development of a socialist party (the CCF) in the same year.[6] This party, with support from some labor unions and from some farm organizations, won a number of seats in Parliament and later gained power in some of the provincial legislatures. It was a force to be reckoned with, in spite of the fact that it seldom had support from more than 20 percent of the Canadian people. It could not be said that Canadians were without knowledge of or tolerance for liberal and even left-wing political ideas.

And in the universities Canadian professors had authority in respect of the academic program. They were not full members of the university as were their colleagues in England (for they could not be members of the board of governors), but neither were they regarded as mere employees, as was often the case in the United States. The Canadian professor was in this respect a hybrid—both a member and an employee—but in the fullest meaning of these terms he was neither. Nonetheless he was in a position, which he frequently used, to defend the concept of academic freedom. In the thirties and afterward there were attacks on the universities for harboring radicals and those "speaking disparagingly of the British Empire," and boards of governors were urged to "weed out men who poison the minds of [our] finest young men and women," [7] but on the whole there was stout defense of free speech in the universities and in society. Perhaps the most famous case was that of Professor Frank Underhill, who, on the basis of a speech which seemed to be inadequately reported but was in any case far from irresponsible, was asked to resign by the president and board of governors of the University of Toronto. This he refused to do. There was a groundswell of opinion supporting his position.

In one account:

> A large deputation of his colleagues, headed by the Dean of
> Arts, waited on President Cody to protest against the unwar-
> ranted action. A voluntary petition from his former students
> testified to the notable part he had played in their intellectual
> development, the inspiring nature of his teaching, and his
> moderation and tolerance where controversial matters were
> involved. His present students sponsored a similar testi-
> monial. Graduates of the university, recent and of long stand-
> ing and in many walks of life, joined in the protest.[8]

Professor Underhill remained at his post until his formal re-
tirement some years later.

On the whole it can be said that up to 1960 there was a
healthy degree of freedom in Canadian universities but that
there did not seem to be many professors in Canada who
were inclined to test the degree that would be tolerated. After 1960 the situation changed, as it did in England, and to
this we will return in later sections of this chapter.

United States: The situation in the United States was quite
different. The social climate here seemed less hospitable to
unorthodox thought. The long religion-versus-science controversy, characterized by the famous Scopes trial in 1925
(the debate about these issues seemed to have peaked at Oxford in 1860), the resistance to the development of a third
party in the political life of the country, and the generally
hostile attitude to radical political thought made for an atmosphere in which academic freedom for the individual professor was an uncertain proposition. Then, too, the form of
government in which, to a significant degree, conservative
businessmen held power in the university was not one which
would encourage the adventurous or radical political thinker
in that institution. But it was in the United States that the
battle for academic freedom was most vigorously fought and
the issues most dramatically revealed. There was progress
toward freedom for professors in the 1960s when the then
short supply of university teachers gave them a preferred
bargaining position and perhaps a more secure posture in the

university than ever before. But the course was not one of steady progress; rather it was erratic and inconsistent. A victory was followed by a defeat; one university would provide greater freedom only to have several others deny it. Sometimes the restrictions were overt and harsh, at other times subtle but nonetheless inhibiting. In the prestigious universities in the early part of the twentieth century, there was a condition of academic freedom very close to that which prevailed in England, but in the decades that followed it was to come under severe attack. It is useful, perhaps, to illustrate a number of these engagements.

In 1894 Richard T. Ely, a distinguished economist at the University of Wisconsin, was accused of believing in "strikes and boycotts, justifying and encouraging the one while practicing the other." [9] He was tried by a committee of regents, and the expectation, given the conservatism of the day, was that he would be dismissed. To the contrary, the trial resulted not only in Ely's exoneration but in a declaration that some refer to as the "Wisconsin Magna Charta," a famous document which was at the same time a notable achievement. It read in part:

> As Regents of a university with over a hundred instructors supported by nearly two millions of people who hold a vast diversity of views regarding the great questions which at present agitate the human mind, we could not for a moment think of recommending the dismissal or even the criticism of a teacher even if some of his opinions should, in some quarters, be regarded as visionary. Such a course would be equivalent to saying that no professor should teach anything which is not accepted by everybody as true. This would cut our curriculum down to very small proportions. We cannot for a moment believe that knowledge has reached its final goal or that the present condition of society is perfect. We must therefore welcome from our teachers such discussions as shall suggest the means and prepare the way by which knowledge may be extended, present evils be removed and others prevented. We feel we would be unworthy of the position we hold if we did not believe in progress in all departments of knowledge. In all lines of academic investigation it is of the utmost importance that the investigator should be absolutely free to follow the indications of truth wherever they may lead.

> Whatever may be the limitations which trammel inquiry elsewhere we believe the great State University of Wisconsin should ever encourage that continual and fearless sifting and winnowing by which alone the truth can be found.[10]

Quite a different outcome resulted a few years later at Stanford University when another distinguished professor, E. A. Ross, spoke and wrote in a manner that offended Mrs. Leland Stanford, the widow of the founder of the university which bore his name and then the single wealthy sponsor of the university. Ross was an alert, able scholar with wide interests and a tendency to speak frequently in public on controversial issues. It is clear that the president of the university, David Starr Jordan, sought to protect Ross, but he was under great pressure from Mrs. Stanford to dismiss him. After long and difficult discussions with Mrs. Stanford, he bowed to her wishes and in 1900 asked for and secured Ross's resignation.[11]

This was a cause célèbre and one which might have been expected to encourage an uprising among Ross's colleagues, at Stanford and elsewhere. Indeed, this was partly the case, for Ross's dismissal was headlined in newspapers throughout the nation; seven members of the faculty at Stanford resigned in protest; and the American Economic Association voted in 1900 to investigate the case. For a time it seemed that there would be a revolt of sufficient proportions to force Stanford to reverse its position. But a majority of the Stanford faculty supported President Jordan, the investigation by the Economic Association did not prove fruitful, and Ross was not taken back at Stanford.[12] This particular battle was clearly lost. But the case for academic freedom was nonetheless advanced, as wide discussion in the university and in the press focused on the meaning of freedom in academia. It was the most famous of many cases at the turn of the century, and it undoubtedly strengthened the determination of numerous professors to secure for themselves and their colleagues freedom to investigate, teach, write, and speak consistent with their learning.

During the First World War emotions ran high and pressures for loyalty and conformity in university ranks were great. Yet the leading universities resisted these. One of the first cases was that of Professor Munsterberg, an eminent and popular academic at Harvard. He had tried, before the United States became engaged directly in the war, to present the German case to the American public, and "this he did with dignity and good taste." There were, nonetheless, wide public demands that he be dismissed as "a poisonous pro-German influence on students." This the corporation refused to do, and Munsterberg died a professor at Harvard in December 1916.[13]

Through these and other controversies that stirred considerable public interest, the question of academic freedom received increasing attention, and there was unquestionably a movement, certainly among the prestigious universities, in the early twentieth century to provide freedom and security for members of their faculties. Thus:

> Mr. Lowell and the deans and Governing Boards, at a time when discussion was being muzzled and the free expression of opinion stifled in many American universities, acted so as to make every member of the teaching faculties feel that he could teach, write, and say what he believed to be the truth, with due regard to decency in utterance, and appropriateness in occasion. No reasonable man could breathe the air of Harvard at this time and not feel free.[14]

This condition prevailed at Harvard and other leading universities. But even here the situation was not supported by an understanding society, and outspoken professors were often under attack. In universities in which the concept of academic freedom was most firmly established, there was always the threat that external groups would force a change. In other colleges and universities academic freedom was precarious at best.

The precarious position of academic freedom in the American university was well illustrated by two events in mid-century. One of these was the famous "oath controversy" at the University of California that continued over a period of years in the late forties and early fifties.[15] The board of regents, reacting to the prevailing mood of anticommunism, suggested to the university senate that members of faculty be required to take an oath (reworded at various times) that said in effect:

> I do not believe in, and I am not a member of, nor do I support any party or organization that believes in, advocates, or teaches the overthrow of the United States Government, by force or by any illegal or unconstitutional methods; that I will support the Constitution of the United States and the Constitution of the State of California, and that I will faithfully discharge the duties of my office according to the best of my ability.[16]

The early reaction of faculty members seemed to accept this requirement, but as the implications of taking such an oath became more obvious, many questions about it were raised, and a small group of overt dissenters was organized. The arguments for and against taking the oath were revealing. On the one hand it was asserted by faculty supporters of the oath that the Soviet Union and the Communist party were opposed to freedom of speech:

> No one, therefore, who desires to maintain academic freedom in America can consistently favor that movement, or give indirect assistance to it by accepting as fit members of the faculties of universities, persons who have voluntarily adhered to an organization one of whose aims is to abolish academic freedom.[17]

On the other hand, it was said by faculty opposing the requirement of an oath:

> If a teacher, as an individual, should advocate the forcible overthrow of the government or should incite others to do so; if he should use his classes as a forum for communism, or otherwise abuse his relationship with his students for that purpose; if his thinking should show more than normal bias or be so uncritical as to evidence professional unfitness, these are the charges that should be brought against him. If these charges should be established by evidence adduced at a hearing, the teacher should be dismissed because of his acts of disloyalty or because of professional unfitness, and not because

200

he is a Communist. *So long as the Communist Party in the United States is a legal party, affiliation with that party in and of itself should not be regarded as a justifiable reason for exclusion from the academic profession.*[18] [Italics added]

The debate continued with vigor. The state of California finally introduced a bill which required all employees of the state, including members of the university staff, to sign an oath much as that stated above. As a result thirty-two members of the faculty who refused to sign the oath were dismissed. An appeal for an investigation by the American Association of University Professors was made, and Professors Quincy Wright of the University of Chicago and R. F. Aaragon of Reed College were charged with this responsibility. Their report was sent to the AAUP in December of 1951. The long-expected censure of the university's administration did not materialize until over four years later—in April 1956! [19] It was a shocking lack of decisive action by the association in respect of a fundamental issue of academic freedom in the United States. Equally surprising, perhaps, was the indifference to the whole controversy by some of the most famous professors at California.[20]

Some saw the fundamental issue as one by which the board was seeking to exert its authority over faculty, but however one may regard the matter, in perspective it seemed that members of faculty opposed with less vigor than would seem appropriate for a group "united and devoted" to the course of academic freedom. The issue had been clearly stated and fully debated, and adequate time for reflection had been provided. There was no decisive faculty reaction. The irony of the situation is seen in the following comment:

As far as the faculty of the University of California was concerned, the AAUP had not voted to censure when the action would have helped (1950-1952) but had censured when it hindered the rapprochement between the faculty and the Regents. Censure was lifted in 1958; and in 1964 the association's seventh annual Alexander Meiklejohn award was made to Clark Kerr, President of the University since 1958, and to the Board of Regents for contributions to the cause of academic freedom.[21]

The second event was the attack of the U.S. Senate committee to investigate un-American activities, under the chairmanship of Senator Joseph McCarthy, on people who were accused of having been members of the Communist party or having had association with it. It mattered not that some of the accusations were false, that some were of people with quite conservative political affiliations, or that very few persons were clearly shown to be "un-American." The accusations and innuendos were hurled relentlessly, perhaps particularly at academics; fears and suspicions were aroused and spread throughout the country.

It is useful to take Harvard as an example here, for it had great prestige, friends in high places, and apparent stability. But on November 5, 1953, Senator McCarthy charged that there was a "smelly mess" at Harvard and that its students "were threatened with indoctrination by Communist professors." [22] In May 1954 President Pusey made a major speech on "Freedom, Loyalty and the American University," [23] in which he sought to speak not only for Harvard but for other American universities as well. He accepted as fact that a Communist could not teach in a free university.

> We need feel no uncertainty about Harvard's, nor any other university's attitude toward communism. Harvard wants no part of it. Nor do the others. Inasmuch as communism seeks to control and dictate to men's minds, communism is any true university's inevitable enemy. The Harvard Corporation has stated that Harvard wants no one who has given up his conscience to Communist discipline. Such a man lacks the necessary independence of thought and action.[24]

The speech detailed the contribution of Harvard and other universities to the public welfare and to the war effort. It sought to reassure America that its universities were loyal, indeed engaged in the fight against communism, for "in addition to our knowledge of Russian communism we should seek to prevent its outbreak in this country by attacking it at the roots. One way is to turn out well-balanced, intelligent citizens, which Harvard aims to do. Another is to stamp out the germs of communism bred in ignorance, ill health, economic stress and social unrest." [25] Pusey concluded his statement with the following:

> If there is anything I should like to say to the American people about the current situation in education it would be to urge them not to be misled by those who would exploit a few very exceptional and quite atypical examples for personal advantage. Educators at every level have shown themselves well aware of the Communist problem and have demonstrated their ability to cope with it.[26]

Pusey's formal reply to "the communist scare" is significant for a number of reasons: (1) it represented the university's—at least the university establishment's—formal position on communism; (2) it accepted the proposition that a Communist could not be neutral, fair, and objective in the classroom as could presumably a devotee of any other political party or religious cult; and (3) it asked only that universities themselves be allowed to discover and dismiss any Communists found in their midst.

It is not an exaggeration, we believe, to say that neither the oath controversy nor the McCarthy attack could have happened in England or perhaps even in Canada.[27] There would have been a much more determined opposition by faculty members and probably more public support for that (faculty) position. Not only were these serious blows to academic freedom in the United States, but they blurred again the meaning of academic freedom, for now the phrase seemed to mean that qualified academics should be free, but only if their speech and behavior were within what seemed to be ill-defined parameters. In neither case was there a clear and convincing differentiation made between (1) a professor's personal beliefs and (2) a professor's professional conduct.

If one were to judge by the situation in the leading universities in the United States, one would be tempted to say that they had resisted the most vicious attacks on their integrity but that they had to some extent, and perhaps necessarily, compromised the traditional concept of academic freedom. But the situation as a whole in the United States was even less reassuring, as was shown in a careful assessment by Lazarsfeld and Thielens:

> Our interviews contain reports of abrupt dismissals for such things as taking the Fifth Amendment, for "speaking too freely in class on the subjects of race and sex," for "having too liberal politics," and so on. Professors also described a number of instances in which they themselves had been directly threatened with firing. Still others were convinced that opposition to the wishes of the president of their school could readily result in their dismissal. Teachers who said they would like to protest strongly against a ban by the president of a debate on the admission of Red China to the United Nations or of an invitation to a controversial guest speaker, sometimes added that such a move would probably bring them instant dismissal. . . .
>
> Promotions and tenure, too, are often arbitrarily withheld by administrations. . . .
>
> At some schools presidents and administrative officials take it upon themselves to monitor the research produced by their faculty. Our interviews contain instances in which research reports had been significantly delayed for publication. . . . Some school presidents do not hesitate to request that certain research topics be completely avoided, that important passages be deleted, etc. Sometimes, in fact, research reports are edited in advance by teachers, in anticipation of adverse administration reactions. . . .[28]

By the 1960s new kinds of problems were arising that suggested that the United States had not yet resolved clearly what academic freedom meant or how it should be applied in these new and complex situations. We will refer later to some of these issues, but to continue the sequence of illustrative incidents we refer here to another type of problem. In 1972 H. Bruce Franklin, a tenured associate professor of English at Stanford University, was dismissed after a long hearing by a faculty advisory committee, which by majority vote recommended such dismissal. Franklin was accused of disrupting a speech and of inciting three other demonstrations on campus.[29] The majority of his colleagues on the advisory committee, while affirming the advantage of having on the faculty "active representatives of political views that while they may be considered extreme or dissenting here, are held by large numbers of people in the world," believed that:

> The code of the institution does, however, demand that the speech and conduct of a professor stay behind the line of inciting or physically causing the impairment of the institution's functions, especially its function as a forum in which various *other* points of view can also be heard. . . .[30]

The minority view on the faculty advisory board agreed that the violation was a serious one but did not agree with the proposal for dismissal. In fact it said:

> Because we live in a society in which there are increasing public pressures to curb dissident speech and action, the university has a special responsibility to insulate its procedures from such influences. That need is magnified by the special significance of tenure, which historically protects the institution's faculty from social trends toward political conformity. We should therefore be scrupulous in protecting violators of university rules against excessive penalties imposed by collective judgment, especially when those violators espouse uncomfortably heterodox views.[31]

This brought into sharp focus a new conflict. The traditional posture of the professor was that of scientist-scholar: neutral, objective, disinterested in political activity—indeed it was on the basis of this position that he justified his right to academic freedom. Now this posture was being challenged by the political activist on campus who had a commitment to political ideas and activities which he would claim were as compelling—and more relevant—than the scientist's commitment "to search for truth." The narrow majority vote in the advisory faculty committee and the tolerance of the statements both for and against the dismissal of Franklin clearly indicated sympathy for the new radicalism. It underlined also the depth of the dilemma this posed for those devoted to traditional concepts of academic freedom. We will return to this issue in the concluding section of this chapter.

Tenure

The 1915 statement of the American Association of University Professors contained two revolutionary recommendations: for tenure appointments and for faculty trials before dismissal. The aim clearly was to diminish the arbitrary power of trustees to discipline or dismiss a teacher, to provide security for the teacher in his profession, and to make academic freedom a reality. In respect of tenure (permanent or continuous appointment), it recognized wide differences of practice but insisted that the length of the term of each appointment should be agreed upon and that this agreement be morally, if not legally, binding. Teachers could be removed from office only for "just cause." [32] In respect of trials, the statement read:

> Every university or college teacher (at the rank of associate professor or above) should be entitled, before dismissal or demotion, to have the charges against him stated in writing in specific terms and to have a fair trial on those charges before a special or permanent judicial committee chosen by the faculty senate or council, or by the faculty at large.
>
> At such trial the teacher accused should have full opportunity to present evidence, and if the charge is one of professional incompetence, a formal report upon his work should be first made in writing by the teachers of his own department and of cognate departments in the university, and if the teacher concerned so desires, by a committee of his fellow specialists from other institutions appointed by some competent authority.[33]

The statement was the first bold declaration by professors to define the conditions essential for academic freedom. In effect, it said, "Academic freedom is necessary in a university, we wish to utilize such freedom fully and responsibly, but to do so there must prevail conditions that assure security and fair play for us." What was being suggested was a form of contract with the university. The professor was to have freedom and security, but in turn he was to be considerate of the whole academic community and responsible as a professional person to his students, to his university, to his profession, and to society.

Thus, in the United States—and later in Canada—academic freedom and tenure became inextricably linked, to the extent that one was seldom mentioned without reference to the other. The raison d'être of tenure was academic freedom; full academic freedom was possible only with tenure. This was clearly the basic position of the association.

In 1940 the AAUP issued another statement on tenure which stated:

> Tenure is a means to certain ends; specifically: (1) Freedom of teaching and research and of extra-mural activities, and (2) A sufficient degree of economic security to make the profession attractive to men and women of ability. Freedom and economic security, hence tenure, are indispensable to its obligations to its students and to society.[34]

But while tenure was to be provided for all who successfully completed a probationary period of service, a clause which later became known as the "up and out" practice was introduced. Briefly this meant that if after six years of probationary full-time service a teacher was not to be continued, he or she should be given notice that one year hence his or her appointment would terminate. This was designed, presumably, to remove the incompetent and gradually to improve the quality of the academic staff. Thus, if a teacher was not considered adequate after seven years, he or she was, in effect, separated from the university and required to look elsewhere for work.

The statements nourished two important developments. First, they established a standard that all universities were urged to accept and against which performance could be measured. In the United States, with its vast array of postsecondary institutions, practice varied tremendously; the standard set was not accepted by many. But the weight of opinion was toward acceptance of the idea of tenure, and gradually it became a major factor in the hiring and recruiting of faculty in North America.

Second, there was the beginning of an investigative function by the AAUP in the United States and the CAUT in Canada. The purpose was to identify cases of abuse of academic freedom and tenure, to prepare a factual report, and to recommend action. In many respects neither of these bodies was capable of fulfilling these obligations in vast countries that necessitated expensive travel by an investigative team required, often in a brief time, to study complex issues on a strange campus. "The investigator needed the talents of a psychologist, a lawyer, and a philosopher—and an abundance of common sense." [35] There were always men ready for the job: those who thought all administrators malevolent and those susceptible to the administrative ethos. Neither was suitable. Thus it was not easy to form effective investigative teams. Nonetheless, this work proceeded. Undoubtedly, the threat or possibility of investigation and the publication of the results of investigation mitigated against abuses of academic freedom. In many cases resolutions of conflicts were achieved by simple mediation initiated by the teacher's organization.

The most serious cases, in the view of the AAUP, were reported in its *Bulletin.* There were 124 of these in 1953.

> The reported cases . . . justify the assumption that academic freedom is dependent upon academic tenure and due process. In fully 63 of the 94 cases in which the administration was held to blame, guarantees of tenure were absent and dismissal on short notice was permitted by the institution.[36]

In Canada the CAUT, organized in 1951, became involved in its first investigation of academic freedom in 1958. This was the famous "Crowe case," in which Professor Harry Crowe was dismissed because the contents of a private letter he had written to a friend (which was found and picked up by the president from under his office door) were found to be offensive by the board of regents of Crowe's university. Crowe was dismissed. The CAUT appointed an investigative committee which found ". . . no doubt that Professor Crowe has been a victim of injustice, violative of academic freedom and tenure. . . . Rectification of the wrong . . . demands that the Board of Regents invite him to resume teaching duties. . . ." [37] After much haggling and with obvious reluc-

tance the board agreed to rehire Crowe. It was a victory for
the CAUT. The next year it developed a statement of principles similar to the 1940 AAUP statement and set of investigative procedures. Between 1960 and 1964 the standing committee dealt with thirty reported grievances, but only four
reached the stage of formal complaint. Between 1965 and
1970 there were, however, approximately 140 complaints, a
number of which led to formal investigation, and two of
which involved formal censure by the CAUT of the universities involved.[38]

The greatest problem faced by the AAUP and the CAUT
was that their investigations, findings, and recommendations
lacked legal authority. They had no means to enforce their
reports. Even the censure of the teacher's organization could
be, and was in many cases, ignored by the university concerned. Furthermore, some of the reports of investigation
lacked the authority of clarity and objectivity.[39] The investigation was an instrument of defense but not a completely effective one.

Nonetheless with the gradual acceptance of tenure for professors and the establishment of processes for the investigation of abuses of academic freedom and tenure, the professional associations had powerful tools with which to
influence and shape the attitude and policy of universities
toward acceptance of unorthodox views and dissident professors. The usefulness of these were lost only as professors began to disagree among themselves about what precisely academic freedom meant.

The Issues

One might expect that after a half century of debates and
trials the meaning of the term "academic freedom" would be
clear, the issues implicit in it well known, and its main tenets
accepted in theory and in practice. Such was not the case in
North America. It was not so partly because certain ambiguities were left unattended to and partly because new circumstances that arose after 1960 raised doubts about a few
principles previously considered settled.

The major questions involved were:

(1) Is the professor free to investigate, write, speak, teach in his or her area of scholarship on the campus "unfettered," without restraint or inhibition?

(2) Does the professor have the same freedom in his or her area of scholarship off the campus, that is, in the community and before the public?

(3) Is the professor free to speak in the classroom and on the campus on controversial issues not in his or her area of specialization and/or to take action on these?

(4) Is the professor free to write for, and speak to, the public on controversial issues not in his or her area of specialization and/or to take action in respect of these?

Freedom in teaching and research: In respect of the first two issues, the weight of opinion that evolved was clearly positive. The professor, as a professional person, must be free to pursue his or her studies, publish, and teach consistent with the best knowledge available. One of the classic statements of this principle was provided by President Lowell of Harvard in his report of 1916–17.

> Experience has proved, and probably no one would now deny, that knowledge can advance, or at least can advance most rapidly, only by means of an unfettered search for truth on the part of those who devote their lives to seeking it in their respective fields, and by complete freedom in imparting to their pupils the truth that they have found. This has become an axiom in higher education, in spite of the fact that a searcher may discover error instead of truth, and be misled, and mislead others, thereby. We believe that if light enough is let in, the real relations of things will soon be seen, and that they can be seen in no other way. . . .
>
> The teaching by the professor in his classroom on the subjects within the scope of his chair ought to be absolutely free. He must teach the truth as he has found it and sees it. This is the primary condition of academic freedom, and any violation of it endangers intellectual progress. . . .
>
> This brings us to the next subdivision of the inquiry, the freedom of the professor within his field of study, but outside

of his classroom. . . . Every professor must . . . be wholly unrestrained in publishing the results of his study in the field of his professorship. It is needless to add that for the dignity of his profession, for the maintenance of its privileges, as well as for his own reputation among his fellows, whatever he writes or says on his own subject should be uttered as a scholar, in a scholarly tone and form. This is a matter of decorum, not of discipline; to be remedied by a suggestion, not by a penalty. . . .[40]

Precise and acceptable as this statement was, it left unanswered some fundamental questions. Were the professors free to teach only their own conclusions, or should they be required to present to their students the findings of other scholars, even if such findings contradicted their own convictions? As we have seen (in Chapter 4), the professional associations—and practice as well—insisted that professors in their teaching must be neutral and objective, not proselytize their students, and not take unfair advantage of their superior learning in the classroom or before the public. The basis of scholarship was considered to be detachment and objectivity, and scholars, it came to be assumed, would practice their profession in this way in their research, their teaching, and their public appearances. In the 1960s this traditional assumption was severely challenged: objectivity was a myth, nonevaluative teaching was impossible, pure cognitive learning was nonsense. What was important was personal belief, conviction, and feeling.

Lowell's doctrine rested upon the values inherent in science and the scientific method. These implied that professors had no general claim to superior knowledge, "but must combine and organize skepticism and universality in their application of objectivity to their specific area of expertise, but with an understanding of the boundaries of their professional abilities." [41] In the early sixties questions arose about the validity of the empirical method and therefore about the restrictions it placed on the teacher in the classrooms. The new idea was frankly biased both in its selection of subject matter and in its approach to research and teaching.[42] It rejected the rigid discipline and code of science as it had evolved in the century past. This raised a new and profound question: Could university professors claim a freedom beyond that available to all citizens without being tied to some clear, rational, and responsible code such as that which traditionally prevailed among scholars and scientists?

In its first statement on academic freedom in 1915 the American Association of University Professors had said:

> So far as the university teacher's independence of thought and utterance is concerned—*though not in other regards*—the relationship of professor to trustees may be compared to that between judges of the Federal courts and the Executive who appoints them. University teachers should be understood to be, with respect to the conclusions reached and expressed by them, no more subject to the control of the trustees, than are judges subject to the control of the President, with respect to their decisions.[43]

This statement sought to press for great freedom for the professor, but it also implied major restraints, for judges were bound by a strict code of ethics that involved dedication to fairness and objectivity. The traditional posture of scholars was consistent with this view. They were disciplined intellectuals relying on cumulative knowledge in their pursuit of truth, humble in their awareness of the vastness of knowledge, and fair and careful in their assessments and assertions about the work of others. Approval for this kind of restrained freedom, in spite of many setbacks, gradually gained acceptance among trustees and to some degree among the public. But as we have seen, it was severely challenged by younger scholars in the late sixties who refused the restraints which the model of the judge required. In spite of the AAUP statement in 1940 that the teacher "should be careful not to introduce into his teaching controversial matter that has no relation to his subject," [44] many young professors were doing just that. The result was conflict of views which seemed to spill over into other issues and to create an unhealthy degree of disharmony on many campuses. The following extract from a *New York Times* report of a controversy at City College of New York is illustrative of the difficulties which emerged in the mid-1970s:

> An investigation of possible abuses of academic freedom in City College's long troubled history department has been begun.... Many of the professors have raised the issue of academic freedom, accusing each other of allowing the disputes to influence voting on promotion and tenure decisions.... The disputes have been so bitter that many professors are not on speaking terms and refer to each other as "Marxist" and "reactionaries." [45]

What was fundamental in these disputes were differences of view that only members of the academic profession could reconcile. If the traditional concept of academic freedom was not acceptable, what was to be substituted? No new responsible doctrine seemed to be emerging.

Another challenge to Lowell's definition of academic freedom on the campus came in the late sixties and early seventies when in Canada, England, and the United States certain speakers, espousing unpopular or controversial theories such as the role of genetic factors in influencing intelligence, were shouted down and prevented from speaking on campus by groups of students and faculty.[46] The opposition to the speakers was based on the assumption that "white supremacy and racial inferiority are no longer debatable issues—history teaches us that ideas have consequences, that the separation of thought from action is a device designed to protect bourgeois ideology while rendering its opposition ineffective,"[47] and that what would be said by these speakers would have an adverse effect on programs designed to eliminate inequalities in society.[48] The scholars who were prevented from speaking on many campuses were reputable professors from leading universities[49] and not inclined to political or racial bias. Nonetheless they were labeled "racists" and prevented from speaking. The issue, of course, was not the validity of their research; it was whether reputable scholars should have freedom to report the results of their research. There was a sufficient group on many campuses to deny them such freedom. This went to the heart of the traditional concept of academic freedom: "complete freedom in imparting to their pupils the truth that they have found." If such freedom was denied to those with unpopular views, it was again necessary to ask, What does academic freedom mean? The burden of opinion on campus was undoubtedly to allow all scholars to report on their research, but it was obvious that there was disagreement and conflict about this position.

Within the academic community there arose another related and direct challenge to the idea that knowledge can advance only by means of an unfettered search for truth in every field of knowledge. In the early seventies sober scholars were asking, "Are there areas of inquiry that should be placed off limits?" The question related to the work of physicists who laid the groundwork of the atomic bomb and who in the words of J. Robert Oppenheimer came to "know sin," to the work of geneticists in human engineering, to the work of anthropologists whose writings had frequently been used by governments to help subdue and control dissident groups.[50] The issue was dramatized at the University of California at Berkeley in 1973 when a new policy required researchers to consider procedures "that may place the reputation or status of a social group or institution in jeopardy" and suggested that the investigator "ask himself how the findings will appear to persons belonging to any identifiable group . . . studied and reported on."[51]

It was accepted in the tradition of scholarship that the responsibility of scholars did not go beyond investigation and the reporting of findings. Action in respect of these findings was the responsibility of others. Scholars should not be inhibited, even the medieval teachers said, because of fear that results of their research might be misused or found to be unpalatable to some. But with the dominance of research in every field of life, the moral responsibilities involved in producing new knowledge in some areas bothered many scholars. It was widely agreed that research that harmed human subjects or invaded the individual's privacy was unethical. But were there other limits? On this there was a wide range of opinion and certainly no consensus.

Freedom of speech on campus and in the community: In respect to the two other issues identified at the beginning of

214

this section, namely the freedom of the professor to speak on topics other than those on which he was a specialist in the classroom and in public, opinions also differed. President Lowell, in his well-known statement, argued that if a university restrains teachers from saying something of which it does not approve, "it thereby assumes responsibility for that which it permits them to say." He stated in part:

> The gravest questions, and the strongest feelings, arise from action by a professor beyond his chosen field and outside of his classroom. Here he speaks only as a citizen. By appointment to a professorship he acquires no rights that he did not possess before; but there is a real difference of opinion today on the question whether he loses any rights that he would otherwise enjoy. The argument in favor of a restraining power on the part of the governing boards of universities and colleges is based upon the fact that by extreme, or injudicious, remarks that shock public sentiment a professor can do great harm to the institution with which he is connected. That is true, and sometimes a professor thoughtlessly does an injury that is without justification. If he publishes an article on the futility and harmfulness of vaccination, and signs it as professor in a certain university he leads the public to believe that his views are those of an authority on the subject, approved by the institution and taught to its students. If he is really a professor of Greek, he is misleading the public and misrepresenting his university, which he would not do if he gave his title in full.[52]

The issue that arose here, however, was not the professor's right to freedom of speech as a citizen but whether academic freedom assured his right and thereby the support and protection of the university. What some members of the university community seemed to be saying was that while some citizens might be penalized for what they said or did, professors were protected from such penalty because of their position in the university. Academic freedom was interpreted to mean immunity from the kind of punishment to which the ordinary citizen was subjected. This carried the concept of freedom beyond that outlined by Lowell. It implied that academic freedom provided not only (1) freedom to teach and research unfettered and (2) freedom to speak on any topic as a citizen, but also (3) freedom from penalty in the exercise of either of the two freedoms above.

To this interpretation of academic freedom there was strong objection. Academic freedom, said Karl Jaspers, "does not mean the right to say what one pleases. . . . Practical objectives, educational bias, or political propaganda have no right to invoke academic freedom." [53] Why indeed should a professor have more freedom and protection to discuss a topic (about which he may know less) than the ordinary citizen?

> Faculty members cannot invoke their constitutional freedom of speech except as private citizens. They cannot expect the university with which they are professionally affiliated to come out in their support when they speak as private citizens. They are entitled to this protection only in matters relating to professional publication, but not in connection with casual political remarks, opinions, or newspaper articles. Academic freedom does not entitle them to special privilege over other citizens. . . . It does not entitle one to irresponsible pronouncements on public affairs. On the contrary, it obliges one not to cloak such casual pronouncements in a false air of authority, to be doubly careful about making them in the first place.[54]

Perhaps because of the difficulty professors had had in their universities in the United States when they spoke in public on controversial issues (as in the E. A. Ross case), there was insistence that academic freedom should provide just that assurance Jaspers said it could not have. A statement by the AAUP in 1972 was specific on this point: "When he [the professor] speaks or writes as a citizen he should be free from institutional censorship or discipline." [55] But to argue that the institutional position of professors

> . . . should not be affected by what they said as citizens was to urge immunity for them from the economic penalties that may repay unpopular utterances—the dwindling of clients, the boycott of subscribers, the loss of a job. Such a demand for immunity, exceeding anything provided by the constitutional safeguard of free speech, going even further than the "free-market" conceptions of the great philosophers of intellectual liberty, . . .[56]

The continued association of the need of the professor for support and protection in his scholarly activities with his desire for support and protection in his nonscholarly activities did much to cause confusion about precisely what academic freedom in the United States meant and "inadvertently delayed the specific assimilation of academic freedom into constitutional law." [57]

Logic seemed to suggest that the professor in activities other than his academic pursuits should not enjoy a privileged position.

> Specifically that which sets academic freedom apart as a distinct freedom is its vocational claim of special and limited accountability in respect to all academically related pursuits of the teacher-scholar; an accountability [related] solely to fiduciary standard of professional integrity.[58]

To argue otherwise, to claim that academic freedom involved a privileged position in nonscholarly activities, was not simply to cause confusion but to weaken the claim for what many considered the freedom that professional people could legitimately claim.[59]

Conclusion: By 1975 a new definition of academic freedom in respect of teaching and research was required. The university had worked gradually to have established the principles enumerated by President Lowell in 1915 and had by 1960 made considerable progress in establishing these. They had long ago been accepted in England, were now very largely the norm in Canada, and were a standard accepted in the best universities in the United States. Whatever attacks there were on these standards came from trustees, administration, or from those outside the universities. And while the courage and the skill of the academic staff varied considerably at different times and in the face of many crises, particularly in the United States, still it could be said that on the whole members of the academic staff were in agreement and united in opposition to any attack on these principles. But, as we have seen, new concepts, new practices, and new questions arose within this group that made reassessment essential. The attack on the established principles of academic freedom now were not by those outside but by those within the university.

The development of academic freedom had been quite different in England, Canada, and the United States, but by the 1960s there was fairly common agreement on its meaning and implications. And suddenly, in all three countries, the questions that arose about what had seemed to be established policy in respect of academic freedom were the same. In these three countries there were abuses of traditional views of academic freedom. The teaching of some scholars and the results of their research were not merely rejected—there was open opposition to them and a demand that they be repressed. Some topics of research were said to be potentially dangerous to society and should not therefore be subject to investigation. Research of all types should be examined for its consequences, and scholars should accept some responsibility for the use of their discoveries. All of these offended traditional doctrine.

Further, the "social contract" which permitted academic freedom but demanded a high level of responsible scholarship was consistently broken. Some professors were overtly doctrinaire in their teaching and sought deliberately to indoctrinate; some adopted the language of the student revolution, using obscenities and guerrilla tactics in the interest of their cause; some, embracing anarchistic behavior, rejected loyalty to the university, obedience to its regulations, or responsibility for its reputation.

Such abuses of academic freedom obviously could not be sustained. Either new definitions of what academic freedom was to mean were required, or the older traditions must be revitalized and made meaningful in the new situation. Above all there was required some consensus about the meaning and limits of academic freedom. The impression of a campus confused about its own purposes and codes, or of a community of anarchy, could only lead to the resolution of these issues by external authorities. The long battle for academic freedom by university teachers would, in this case, be lost by their inability to define directions and enforce discipline in a new era.

NOTES

1. Hofstadter and Metzger, 1955, pp. 403–404.

2. Ibid., p. 15.

3. Halsey and Trow, 1971, p. 117. Most observers of higher education confirm this impression. "In modern times an assumption has become accepted, at least in Britain, that it is the absolute right of universities to have complete freedom . . . and that the state should never in any way interfere" (Caine, 1969, p. 182).

4. Holland, 1972, p.2.

5. *Power of the People,* 1971, p. 6.

6. Cross, 1974, p. 7.

7. Carver, 1939, pp. 40–41.

8. C. McNaught, 1941, p. 333.

9. Hofstadter and Metzger, 1955, p. 426.

10. Ibid., p. 427.

11. Ibid., p. 439.

12. Ibid., p. 442.

13. Morison, 1965, p. 453.

14. Ibid., pp. 466–467.

15. Gardner, 1967, p. 329.

16. Ibid., p. 25.

17. Ibid., p. 137.

18. Ibid., p. 137.

19. Ibid., pp. 137–138.

20. Ibid., pp. 208–209.

21. Ibid., p. 209.

22. Ranzal, 1953, p. 13.

23. Pusey, 1954, pp. 335–345.

24. Ibid., p. 343.

25. Ibid., p. 341.

26. Ibid., p. 344.

27. There was in Canada the famous "Padlock law" in Quebec in the forties and the "War Measures Act" enacted by the federal government in the late sixties. Both were infringements on civil liberties and both were opposed by numerous university professors, but neither seemed to affect radically academic freedom in the university.

28. Lazarsfeld and Thielens, 1958, pp. 251–252.

29. "Dismissal at Stanford Is Endorsed," 1972, p. 5.

30. "Excerpts from Faculty Report on Militant Professor," 1972, p. 5.

31. Ibid., p. 5.

32. Hofstadter and Metzger, 1955, p. 481.

33. Ibid.

34. Ibid., pp. 487–488.

35. Ibid., p. 491.

36. Ibid., p. 493.

37. Harris, 1973, chap. 35, p. 55.

38. Ibid., chap. 35.

39. Hofstadter and Metzger, 1955, p. 494.

40. Quoted in Morison, 1965, pp. 454–455.

41. Lipset, 1970, p. 114.

42. The question of academic freedom and its meaning was the topic of heated debate among sociologists as well as among other scholars. See Becker, 1971, p. 13; Berger, 1971, pp. 1–5; and Riley, 1971, pp. 6–12.

43. Hofstadter and Metzger, 1955, p. 409.

44. Quoted in ibid., p. 488.

45. Maeroff, 1974, p. 34.

46. See Beloff, 1968, p. 204; Sanders, 1973, pp. 60–61; "Governing Council, Hastily Reconvened, Completed Thursday's Interrupted Business," 1974, p. 1.

47. Reinhold, 1973, sec. 4, p. 5.

48. Sanders, 1973, p. 70.

49. Shockley of Stanford, Herrnstein of Harvard, Banfield of Pennsylvania.

50. Reinhold, 1973, sec. 4, p. 5.

51. Ibid.

52. Quoted in Morison, 1965, p. 455.

53. Jaspers, 1965, pp. 142–143.

54. Ibid., pp. 142–143.

55. *AAUP Policy Documents and Reports,* 1971, p. 2.

56. Hofstadter and Metzger, 1955, p. 405.

57. Van Alstyne, 1972, p. 142.

58. Ibid., pp. 146–147.

59. Ibid., pp. 142–148.

chapter nine

●

THE STATE

By 1975 a central concern of North American universities was identical with that of their counterparts in Britain: how to retain independence in the face of pressures for increased state direction and control. The question of academic freedom was now as frequently defined in terms of institutional autonomy as of individual liberty.

The traditional concept of the university as a kind of monastic retreat, independent, supranational, endowed with rights belonging to no other institution, except perhaps the church, persisted up to the postwar period and almost throughout the revolutionary sixties.[1] The university was considered "a liberty" in the medieval sense, "an enclave, a corporate autonomy in society that derived its own freedom to act in proportion to the honor of its mission. . . ." [2] Indeed, to nourish this idea,

> . . . the university secreted a kind of ideal or mythology of itself as a temple of learning, far above the market place, distinct from the political world, both neutral as an institution and devoted to the normative function of evaluating human achievements.[3]

It needs hardly be said that the university seldom, if ever, achieved the degree of freedom its members cherished. It was always subject to the whim, the authority or the pressure, of monarchs, denominational groups, donors, or trustees, all of whom were influenced by their own prejudices and by public opinion. The university never had autonomy in an absolute sense. Nonetheless, there was a deep-rooted belief within the academic community that the university must be free and independent to be effective, and over the years there developed a considerable acceptance of this position by the societies under discussion here. By 1950 the university had a place of honor and respect in the community, withal an air of remoteness and a mystique which inhibited interference by any outside authorities.[4]

By 1970 it was widely recognized that such isolation or segregation was no longer feasible or realistic. The academic world was now grappling with the problem of what kinds of decisions properly belonged within the university and what kinds must be surrendered to public authority.

The reasons for this dramatic change were manifold. Within, growth and specialization had weakened the coherence of the university. The essential internal authority of the university was almost completely eroded in the 1960s. The frequent campus disruptions, the apparent lack of discipline, the obvious disagreements among faculty members, all affected prevailing views in society about the university. The mystique was torn away, the traditional respect diminished, and the idea of public control again emerged.

At the same time the university was being seen as an instrument of populist democracy: as an institution providing certain privileges which should be available to all. It was regarded, thus, as a means of fulfilling a specific political philosophy: the democratization of opportunity. The university was seen now also as an integral part of emerging state and national goals. The needs of society for specialized manpower and for practical research should, it was believed, be provided by the universities. These latter should be made to operate in a manner consistent with national aspirations. There seemed again to be in the air the cry of a newspaper some three centuries before: "Harvard College belongs to the people of Massachusetts and by the grace of God, the people . . . will yet have it and hold it. . . ."[5]

There were, of course, more immediate and pressing reasons for direct interest by governments in university affairs. Costs were escalating, planning was being carried out in each university with little regard to the plans of other universities or the needs of the state, and the claims of academic men to a special expertise and their institutions to special immunities were increasingly called into question.[6] Most important, of course, was the fact that the university was becoming almost wholly dependent upon the state for financial support. The state was now almost the sole benefactor of the university; it was in fact the "paymaster." It was inevitable that in this position the state would interest itself in efficiency and cost benefits. Coordination, direction, and control seemed to be required, certainly of finances, but perhaps of academic policy as well.

The conflict between the traditional isolated university and the public university responding to public demands was resolved by the emergence of systems of higher education in which universities were joined in an effort to eliminate waste, to coordinate planning, to share available public funds, and to develop common standards. Britain, Canada, and the United States each developed its own system for these purposes, and to a brief description of each we will now turn before examining some of the issues involved.

Britain

Among academic people, Britain in the modern period was considered to have the most effective and judicious system of appraising the financial needs of universities and of distributing grants to them. It achieved this reputation because of the manner in which judgments were made about, and the large degree of independence that was provided for, each university. It is instructive, therefore, to look carefully at the machinery developed in Britain and the gradual changes introduced there.

The basis of the British system was the University Grants Committee (UGC). It was conceived after World War I, but it was not until 1947 that it began to function as a major force in higher education in Britain. It is this recent period that is of interest to us here. Three factors about its operation need to be examined: the composition of the committee, the relation of the committee to government, the relation of the committee to universities.

There were twenty-one members of the University Grants Committee: a full-time chairman (a former academic), two part-time vice-chairmen, thirteen members who were teaching in universities but served on the committee on approximately a one-fifth-time basis, two members from other fields of education who served on a similar basis, and three members from industry.[7] While the members served the committee in a personal capacity and not as representatives of any special interest, the very heavy academic influence was obvious.

The responsibility of the committee was to "collect, examine, and make available information relating to university education throughout the United Kingdom," [8] and "to assist in consultation with the universities and other bodies concerned, the preparation and execution of such plans for the development of the universities . . . to ensure that they are fully adequate to national needs." [9] The most important link with government was the recommendation made every five years by the committee regarding the total financial needs of the universities. The government might provide for this total request or modify it somewhat, but it was not to concern itself with the grants to any individual university. It had authority only in respect of the total amount; it had little information about details of the budget of any university and no authority in respect of individual grants.[10]

On the basis of consultation with the universities the committee provided three kinds of grants to universities: (1) single block grants to be used at the individual university's discretion, (2) capital grants to individual projects, subject to review by the Minister of Works as to economy and suitability, and (3) earmarked grants for educational work, some recommended by individual universities and many recommended by government departments in the interests of the national welfare.[11] For purposes of the operating budget the UGC and the government worked on the basis of a five-year period. Universities were asked to calculate in detail their needs for each of the five years about eighteen months before the end of the existing five-year period; the UGC then reviewed these estimates in light of submissions of other universities and recommended to the government a total sum for all universities in each of the five years following. The total provided by the government was then allocated by the committee. Each university was given a block grant:

> When the letter goes from the UGC to the individual universities there is no financial detail and no headings, there is simply a straight total sum for each of the next five years. The original submission from the university was detailed, the allocation to the university is a block grant, with no detail at all. This is an essential and cardinal element in the whole system. It means that inside the total sum the university is free to deploy the money as it chooses. . . . This freedom, within the budgetary total, is as nearly complete as any freedom in this world can be, and it is genuinely appreciated by the universities. In a word, the UGC does not run the universities: it tries to provide them with the resources to run themselves.[12]

Capital grants and grants for special projects were based on rather different procedures. There were earmarked grants for particular buildings or educational projects, for particular periods; these were more closely supervised by a government agency.

Working independently but in close contact with the UGC was the vice-chancellors committee, the members of which were the vice-chancellors of all British universities. This committee itself worked on questions of university needs and national policy for higher education. There were many personal friendships and associations which kept the two committees in communication with each other on an informal as well as a formal basis, and there was unquestionably a very strong influence by the vice-chancellors on policies adopted by the UGC.

The advantages of these procedures to the universities were obvious. They were not required to make their case to government or even to a lay group: they discussed their needs with a committee, most of whose members were practicing academics. Parliament had little authority or control over universities; it merely provided the total fund which the University Grants Committee allocated. Further, once the UGC made its five-year grant, each university was free to use this money as it saw fit. The university, in this system, was assured not only of a sympathetic hearing in respect of its needs, but a very large degree of independence in its operations. Little wonder the British model was admired by academics everywhere!

This state of euphoria was not to continue. Grants for universities increased from £4.3 million in 1945–46 to £211 million in 1966–67. Both the rate of increase and the size of the grants were alarming to government. Two developments ensued.

Under pressure from government[13] the UGC began to take a firm hand in the direction of universities in its jurisdiction. It argued for different specialties in different universities, for coordination of planning, for the creation of something approximating a master plan.[14] In an attempt to make this more palatable to the universities the committee warned that "most academics [should] prefer the judgment of their peers and colleagues to instruction from a government department." [15] That the days of *laissez faire* were over, however, was increasingly evident and not more so than in the committee's memorandum of guidance to universities as the latter prepared their budgets for the years 1967 to 1972. The letter stated:

> . . . that the major increases in enrollment must be in the number of students in the arts rather than the sciences, that the number of postgraduate students for which the committee had provided was considerably smaller than the universities had wished, that postgraduate studies should be shifted from the more traditional courses to those which are more vocational and shorter in duration, that the universities should cooperate much more closely with industry, and that there should be much greater collaboration among the universities and between the universities and other sectors of higher education. The committee recently announced that not more than 35 per cent of the members of the academic staff could hold appointments at the level of senior lecturer and above.[16]

The second development that was to shatter the "old boy network" for arranging university affairs was the recommendation, subsequently adopted, by a committee of Parliament that the Comptroller and Auditor General should have access to the books and records of the University Grants Committee and to those of each university.[17] The universities had been the only organization receiving public funds which had not been subject to scrutiny by the Comptroller and Auditor General, who reported to Parliament on matters of financial administration and control. In effect, the recommendation was to terminate the privileged position of the universities and to bring them into the public domain. It was, naturally perhaps, resisted by the universities, and their arguments for resisting are both revealing and important.

The Committee of Vice-Chancellors and Principals was particularly fearful of the results of the proposed change. It argued that university accounts were already professionally audited, that the UGC had acted responsibly and effectively, and that "the fundamental accountability of the university to Parliament is best rendered through the interpretative mechanism of the UGC." [18] The proposal of the Comptroller and Auditor General to check "that value for money was obtained" was fraught with danger, said the vice-chancellors, for there are many instances where "economy and value could not be assessed except in relation to the whole academic picture—an assessment which requires expert knowledge of university work." The vice-chancellors committee was upset also by the prospect of examining variations between universities in expenditures for similar purposes.

> This approach implies that activities with similar purposes ought to incur similar costs . . . an implication dangerous to universities . . . even if it were successfully accomplished, the application of a mainly statistical and accounting approach could lead straight to the suppression of diversity and independence in academic development.[19]

The Association of University Teachers was concerned, as was the vice-chancellors committee, that the proposal was merely a first step or a means or a "cover-up" by which government could place a restraining and controlling hand on the universities:

Many academics remain unconvinced that the ultimate intention of accountability is not a massive increase in Government control. The memorandum of the Comptroller and Auditor General does not dispel that fear. We note that he would wish to examine the methods adopted by the University Grants Committee to assess the universities' requirements and to determine the subsequent allocation to them of recurrent grants. This can have little point unless there is the possibility that he will then be able not only to propose changes in the methods but to enforce them, when he cannot bring to the task that experience of university needs and priorities which guides the University Grants Committee. Given that a university is *sui generis* in not being simply a teaching institution but also a research institution and that these two functions are inextricably tangled, the external formulation of norms is a difficult enough task even when done by a body like the University Grants Committee with vast university experience: we suspect that it is an impossible one for the Comptroller and Auditor General without his interfering, or seeming to interfere, with academic priorities and freedoms of the universities and their academic staffs.[20]

This change and the resistance to it is highly significant. The arguments of the academics reveal all the traditional fears of interference in the kind of insulated community academic people had tried to create for themselves. Yet, in Britain where there was great respect for academic tradition and university independence, when all the arguments were carefully and respectfully heard, the parliamentary committee came down against the universities. This committee reported:

Your Committee therefore reach the conclusion that if the C. & A.G. were given access to the books and records of the UGC and the universities no such harm would or need result as would justify Parliament in continuing to exempt from its normal requirements this large and growing expenditure of money from Votes. If, as is claimed, the financial systems of the UGC and universities are sound and effective in practice, they have nothing to fear from examination by the C. & A.G. On the contrary, the reassurance afforded to Parliament should bring considerable advantage. On the other hand, if weaknesses exist, it is only right that they should be identified and remedied. Your Committee are of the opinion that it should be possible to devise conventions which would prevent any harm to the proper autonomy of the UGC and the universities and to take steps to set at rest any fears that examination by the C. & A.G. would prove a threat, or could develop into a threat, to proper academic freedom.[21]

The essence of all this was that while an attempt would be made to respect university tradition, changes would be made. There was to be a delicate readjustment which would involve loss of autonomy by the individual universities. The British, of course, are skillful in avoiding apocalyptic change, and no rapid or radical alteration would likely result. What had occurred up to 1975 was a gradual accommodation by all parties to a new set of circumstances.[22] This was the requirement that the universities be responsible and responsive to Parliament and to the people. Quietly but nonetheless effectively, there had been a shift in the locus of decision making in respect to universities in England.

Canada

Education in Canada was a matter for provincial jurisdiction, but in the modern era it was the federal government that gave the first impetus to university growth. A number of forces converged in 1950 to make this feasible: the federal grants to returning veterans of World War II, which helped to increase university enrollments; the report of a royal commission on the national development in the arts, letters, and science (the Massey commission); and the growing interest in research by many federal government departments.[23]

The federal government in 1951 accepted the following recommendations of the Massey commission:

(a) that in addition to the help already being given for research and other purposes the Federal Government make annual contributions to support the work of the universities on the basis of the population of each of the provinces of Canada;

(b) that these contributions be made after consultation with the government and the universities of each province, to be

231

distributed to each university proportionately to the student enrollment;

(c) that these contributions be sufficient to ensure that the work of the universities of Canada may be carried on in accordance with the needs of the nation;

(d) that all members of the National Conference of Canadian Universities be eligible for the federal grants mentioned above.[24]

These grants, modest in the beginning (based on a 50 cents per capita formula and totaling $7 million in 1951), were doubled in 1956 and increased gradually thereafter until, in 1966–67, the grants reached an average of $5 per capita and amounted to $100 million.[25] These grants were given to the NCCU which, in turn, paid them directly to the eligible universities. There was strong objection, particularly by the government of Quebec, to this action as an infringement on provincial rights; and in 1967, the federal government altered its procedure by making grants for universities directly to the provinces (on the basis of 50 percent of university operating costs), each of which in turn made grants to universities in its province. Federal government assistance was thus provided indirectly to the universities and more directly through funds it provided to the Canada Council and the National Research Council. But after 1967, the effective granting agency for operating funds for the Canadian university was the government of the province in which it was located.

The provincial means of distributing funds varied in the ten provinces, but all except the smallest moved toward the British model of providing a buffer committee between the government and the university. Provincial systems evolved, much like the British form, but on a very much smaller scale. The largest and most sophisticated system emerged in Ontario, and this, by the early seventies, was the model toward which other provincial systems seemed to be moving.

The development of the Ontario system may be divided into approximately three phases. In the first, from about 1960 to 1965, there was appointed by the government an advisory Committee on University Affairs (CUA), composed of businessmen and senior civil servants charged primarily with the responsibility of advising the government on the size of the grant each university in the province should have for both capital and operating expenses. At the same time the Committee of Presidents (COP) was formed, much like the vice-chancellors committee in Britain, to study, coordinate, and plan the development of higher education in the province. The relation between these two committees was close, with the university affairs committee depending a good deal on the presidents' committee for guidance and direction on larger matters of pol'cy but reserving for itself the right to determine what sums should be recommended to the government for each university. It was a highly informal, somewhat politically oriented system, in which cooperation between universities seldom overcame the determination of each university to get as much money, and obtain as many favors, as it could for its own operation.

There were three important developments in the second stage, from 1965 to 1970. In 1966 there was organized a separate Ministry of University Affairs under the jurisdiction of a very able political leader (who later became premier of the province) sympathetic to the cause of higher education. The existing Committee on University Affairs was considerably strengthened; a full-time chairman (a former academic) was appointed; a number of academics were added to the committee; and while it was not given any executive authority, it moved with the support of the minister decisively to give form and direction to a system of higher education for Ontario. The Committee of Presidents moved apace, establishing a permanent secretariat, expanding its representation from universities, and organizing more than twenty standing committees to deal with policy matters in crucial areas of the system. On the whole there was considerable satisfaction with these arrangements, primarily because the system was expanding, money was adequate to the needs, and the three central agencies worked closely together. Most of the major policy decisions of the government during these years had previously been worked out carefully by the CUA and the COP and reviewed with ministry officials. There was, however, an obvious trend toward centralized planning: the old days of individual political bargaining were past. A formula system for direct grants from government to each university, on the basis of the number and distribution of students in that university, was established; this system alleviated to some extent the competition by individual universities for special favors from the government or from the Committee on University Affairs. While thus an increasing number of policy decisions was made by these central bodies, the universities were relatively happy, for they had adequate funds, were consulted by the CUA and government in respect of major policy decisions, and within the parameters of this system had a good deal of autonomy.

The third phase of development, from 1970 to 1975, led to a situation not unlike that in England and in the United States but with its own peculiar distinction. The Committee of Presidents became in 1971 the Council of Ontario Universities, expanded its secretariat to twenty-five full-time people, its budget to approximately one million dollars, and its structure to include forty-three separate committees.[26] It was, relative to the situation, a large and effective effort in voluntary cooperation, and its achievements were considerable in respect of reviewing and legitimizing many fields of graduate and professional work in individual universities, cooperative library services, computer operations, a central research office, etc. The government's Committee on University Affairs was renamed the Council of University Affairs in 1974 and reorganized with eleven members from many occupations and geographic areas (a "democratic committee"); but it was not given the executive authority some had wished. Still, these councils worked closely together and continued to support a number of joint committees on finance, instructional development, and graduate work.

It was in the government—in the Ministry of University Affairs—that the most significant developments took place, however. This Ministry, which had a modest staff of approximately one hundred people in 1971, was expanded, after assimilating responsibility for the colleges of applied arts and technology and various cultural activities, to well over a

234

thousand staff members in 1972.* Relative to the other two provincial agencies in higher education, it was a huge, well-financed, and powerful machine. It was soon to assert its position. The days of consultation and cooperation may not have ceased, but a series of unilateral decisions made by the government—particularly one to raise substantially the fees for graduate students—made it abundantly clear that it was going to act directly and decisively in areas in which it considered action essential.27 Subsequent actions by the government that required radically tightened, if not deficit, budgets in most universities only confirmed the determination of the ministry to exert firm fiscal control over the publicly supported universities. There were indications also that it was impatient with the pace and nature of change in individual universities and with the academic ethos supported by the two provincial councils. Such was the tone of the admonition given to the universities in late 1974. The premier of Ontario and the provincial minister of university affairs, "each reported independently—in the view of the Government, productivity must increase radically, unnecessary duplication must be eliminated, and the basic style of university life must be transformed." 28 If more blunt direction had ever been given to Ontario universities, it has not been recorded.

Thus, "the case history" of Ontario, indicative of trends in other provinces, points to the development of a system based on voluntary cooperation which proved to be too slow and/or too indecisive for a government faced with multiple fiscal and social problems; the growth of a huge government bureaucracy related to higher education; and a clear and obvious movement by government to take charge—to direct and to shape the system of higher education in the province.

United States

There is such a vast array of institutions of postsecondary education in the United States and such a variety of arrangements for their guidance and control by governments that it

*And its name was changed to the Ministry of Colleges and Universities.

is not possible to point to any single model as typical of the whole. A few generalizations relative to the development of systems of higher education may, however, be illuminating.

All systems of higher education that emerged in the United States were state systems.* As in Canada, education was a matter of state jurisdiction; although the federal government, as we will see, influenced the development of universities by its practice of conditional research grants, the actual funding and control of public universities was a state responsibility. Statewide systems of higher education tended to develop in states where (1) there were multiple public institutions of higher education; (2) these multiple institutions competed with one another for students, research, grants, educational programs, for faculty, and for prestige; and (3) these institutions were dependent on the state government for the major part of their budget.[29]

Where these conditions prevailed, there developed coordinating bodies: in some cases boards of trustees or regents of the multiple-campus state universities (as in New York or California); in other cases state boards or planning councils to coordinate and guide practice in a wide variety of relatively independent campuses (as in Illinois or Ohio). In almost all cases the boards were composed of laymen—in only a very few situations were political or academic officers members.

In the United States the effort has been made to avoid either choice by the presence of laymen who are appointed by public officials but who, once appointed, are protected from governmental interference by their terms of office. They are also protected by the very concept of trusteeship, which by definition makes the trustees both bridge and buffer between the university and government.[30]

By 1966, forty-one states had such coordinating organizations, all with the object of rationalizing the facilities and ser-

*In both Canada and the United States, military education was a federal responsibility.

vices of all the institutions of postsecondary education in the state.[31]

The trend, in the postwar period, was away from voluntary coordinating bodies (such as the Council of State University Presidents in Michigan) to statutory boards. These boards took two forms: (1) with advisory powers only and (2) with varying degrees of authority over such matters as educational programs, budgets, admission standards, and tuition.[32] In both situations the effort was to bring about economies through planning and coordination, to the end that the system as a whole would be efficient and effective in serving the educational needs of the state. Many observers believed that to be effective a coordinating agency had to have considerable authority (the Board of Higher Education in Illinois and the Ohio Board of Regents) to resist legislative pressures on the one hand and, on the other, to require a degree of coordination from public universities in the state.[33] But there was no clear trend in this direction; indeed, as we shall see, there was an increasing disposition for the governments to keep a good deal of control in their own hands.

California developed perhaps the finest and most widely copied plan of higher education on a state basis: a three-tier system with strict differentiation of function. In this system, (1) the universities were the guardians of research and of training associated with high-prestige occupations (medical, law, academic); (2) the state colleges prepared students for more advanced academic work and trained students for occupations such as teaching; (3) the junior colleges prepared students for further academic work and trained them for more vocational occupations.[34] This was part of a long-term plan for postsecondary education in California, which, as it was implemented, probably served a higher percentage of the population at various levels and in various skills more successfully than in any other jurisdiction in the world.

The management of the state systems of higher education in the United States depended primarily on two techniques: a master plan and a plan of budget procedures.[35] Details of master plans varied from state to state, but generally speaking they established goals for a five- or ten-year period, fixed relations between different kinds of institutions (e.g., junior colleges and universities, as in California), and created a design or profile for each individual institution.

> . . . these plans can and often do set the mission of various segments of public higher education in the state. They can limit institutions to undergraduate education and reserve graduate education for a special class of institution, or they can designate the function of some institutions as specifically teacher education and limit others to offering only the first 2 years of instruction. In cases where master plans exist, institutions are accountable to the broad purposes outlined in the plan.[36]

Budget procedures also varied widely, only a few, however, relying on a formula for grants such as existed in some of the Canadian provinces. A method (followed in the State University of New York) that approximated early British practice was for the board of trustees to present a single budget for all its campuses and activities and to defend this single budget before a legislative committee of the state government. Once the money was granted by the legislature, "each campus thereafter has its own portion which it administers with a very high degree of independence." [37]

But all public universities were not so fortunate. A study of state-university relations in 1959 had said, "Public officials who may be ill-equipped to make educational decisions are moved into a position where they govern higher education without bearing any visible responsibility for its success or failure." [38] This complaint arose because of the practice of "line-budgeting," in which each item of a detailed budget could be approved, modified, or disallowed by a government bureaucrat or legislative committee. To give an example of this practice, the 1965 budget of the University of California had $100,000 cut from the university press, $600,000 from teaching assistants, and $600,000 from the provisions for out-of-state graduate students. If the university had been asked to reduce its budget by the total of these amounts ($1,300,000), it could have rearranged its priorities in light of this reduction and its current needs. But what happened, in effect, was the determination of educational policy by the state legislature.[39] And a well-informed student of trends in higher education, in reviewing this problem, said, "I feel certain that state agencies have strengthened their detailed fiscal control, even over public institutions that presumably possess constitutional autonomy." [40] The development of such a trend would inevitably mean the decline of the independence of the university.

There were, of course, in the United States—as there was not in Canada or Britain—hundreds of private colleges and universities which sought to raise funds from a wide variety of sources, to retain their independence, and to keep apart from state systems. But as costs soared, these universities found it increasingly difficult not to seek at least a degree of public support. Almost all such support carried some requirements or insisted upon some standards which hitherto would have been a matter for internal discussion and decision. Increasingly, governments attached conditions to any contribution made to a university. The large grants from the (federal) Department of Health, Education, and Welfare, for example, required the recipient university, by 1970, to conform to the formal civil rights code of the federal government. A major grant to Columbia University was held up in 1971 because the university was unable to file an acceptable plan for providing equal employment opportunities,[41] and other universities were under similar pressure to conform to government regulations. The federal government was in this year providing one-fourth of all the funds by public institutions of higher education[42] and even more—a third—of the current income of private universities.[43] It seemed inevitable that such large grants would, as in the case of Columbia, involve a more active interest in the institutions to which it made grants.

The situation in the United States was by 1975 much the same as in Canada and England. The composition and terms of reference of buffer boards might be somewhat different, but the heavy hand of government was apparent, not merely in regulating expenditures but in drawing the parameters of future university development. Even the private universities were being affected, for few of these were completely independent financially. University autonomy was greatly reduced in the third quarter of the century, and further restrictions seemed possible. A firm grasp of the relevant issues seemed essential.

Issues

By 1975 there were few people who doubted that the heavy financial involvement of governments in universities required that the former interest itself in the affairs of the latter, at least to the extent that it could assure taxpayers that their money was being well and wisely spent. But could this be done without conflict with the long and cherished belief and tradition that the university functioned best when it was free of external controls? The universities' "efficiency is a function of their academic freedom and initiative," said the British vice-chancellors,[44] a sentiment with which most academics would agree. Could the state's need to require universities to be accountable and the public demand for access and flexibility be reconciled with the university's desire for independence?

Of the two forces, the state's demand was more insistent and more powerful. The resistance of academic people in Canada, England, and the United States to government intervention had been brushed aside—politely in some cases and brusquely in others, but the effect was the same: the state was to have authority to act in respect of the universities for which it provided large grants from public funds.

Given this premise, the universities were required to develop a strategy that would accommodate the demands of the state with the least possible effects on the university's autonomy. Two possible lines of defense were a strong supportive "buffer committee" and a clear statement by the universities of areas of university life in which the state had a legitimate interest and areas in which autonomy must be preserved.

The buffer boards or committees had in Canada, England, and the United States different composition and different terms of reference. This did not seem to alter the dominant drives of the day—for expansion in the sixties and for restriction in the seventies, for greater accessibility, for more coordination, for more extensive planning of university systems. In all three countries the trends were the same; it could not be said that the University Grants Committee was more effective than the board of the State University of New York or the Council of University Affairs in Ontario. Each might have some advantage in some detail, but all seemed to be responding in somewhat similar manner to the state's demand for coordination and the public's demand for a more open and flexible program in the university.

Nonetheless, it seemed possible in 1975, when the major expansion of university was complete and more settled conditions prevailed, for the evolution of stable systems in which the buffer committees or boards could play a major role. From the viewpoint of the universities, it was important that these committees be (1) influential, (2) understanding of university traditions, and (3) given considerable executive authority. All these conditions the University Grants Committee met, but in the early seventies it seemed to lose some of its influence, perhaps because of the heavy representation of academic members on the committee. To government officials, the UGC must have appeared to be, in the face of crucial issues, a biased committee which favored the universities as opposed to the interest of the state. A balanced committee in terms of the three criteria suggested above was not easy to come by. One or more of the requirements were frequently missing. In this case the university had to be as resourceful as the medieval university, finding new strategies and tactics for new situations. A statement by a Canadian group is instructive, for while it recognized government authority, it sought to keep the issues in the public domain, where the university could fight them if necessary:

> The Government must have authority to act in respect of the university system for which it provides finance. We hope that this authority will be used with great restraint; that it will be exercised primarily after consultation with, and normally after agreement by, the universities. We hope also that the Government will create, support, and use a Commission on

University Affairs such as we have recommended. *In addition we consider it essential that the advice of such a Commission to Government on major policy matters should be made public as should the Government's response.*[45] [Italics added]

The most urgent question was that of the areas in which the universities considered the government had the right, and the areas in which they considered it did not have the right, to influence or direct university policy. At stake here was the fundamental question of institutional freedom: university autonomy.

The Carnegie Commission sought in 1971 to come to grips with this issue. It emphasized that academic freedom required the absolute right of universities to appoint and promote faculty members and administrators, to determine courses of instruction and course content, to award individual degrees, to select and conduct research projects, to publish and otherwise disseminate research results, and of course, to enjoy freedom of inquiry, speech, assembly, and other constitutional rights.[46] Similarly the Robbins report stressed the rights of universities in respect of appointments, curricula and standards, admission of students, and the determination of the balance of teaching and research within the university. These were considered basic. The selection of research projects and the freedom to publish or of speech were assumed in Britain.[47] In Canada, England, and the United States there was wide agreement about the essential freedoms the universities must have.

It was in respect of the rights of the state that differences and difficulties arose. The Carnegie report, for example, suggested that state authority was appropriate in the following eleven areas:

(1) Numbers of places available in state institutions and in specific programs where there are clear manpower needs;

(2) Number and location of new campuses;

(3) Minimum and maximum size of institutions by type;

(4) General admissions policy;

(5) General level of institutional budgets including construction budgets;

(6) General level of salaries;

(7) Accounting principles;

(8) General functions of institutions;

(9) Major new endeavors;

(10) Effective use of resources;

(11) Continued effective operation of the institutions within the general law.[48]

On such matters the Robbins report was far more cautious, and its reservations were suggestive of the difficulty encountered in defining the separation of powers of state and university. Robbins differed from the Carnegie report by assigning to the university the right to select its own students and to determine its own size. While recognizing the possible conflict between a university's desire to remain small and the state need for expansion, Robbins came down on the side of the university. In such a conflict, "if when all the reasons for change have been explained, the institution still prefers not to cooperate it is better that it be allowed to follow its own path."[49]

But, while sympathetic to a very considerable degree with the rights of the university, Robbins saw the inevitability of some outside controls:

Public policy does not necessarily involve the development of all institutions of higher education at an equal pace. There must be selection. There must be the judicious fostering of some more than others. . . . To decide all such problems there must be a body with power both to allocate and also to deny. And, in so far as the development of the policies of individual institutions is influenced and conditioned by such decisions, the necessary restrictions on complete liberty are readily apparent. It is limitations of this sort, with all their administrative implications, that we have in mind, when, in emphasising the claims of academic freedom, we stipulate that they must be consistent with the maintenance of coherence throughout the system as a whole.[50]

Ten years after this report appeared, this discussion with its fine distinctions seemed academic. There was evidence that the state was determined to mold the university system into an instrument for the achievement of national goals and that the limitations on university autonomy would be far greater than Robbins envisaged.[51] In 1975 the Carnegie statement seemed the more realistic document. The task of the university was to find the means of influencing decisions of the government on the eleven items on which the state was conceded to have authority and to retain essential university freedoms.

There were in the early seventies, particularly in the United States, examples of "exploring legislation" designed to test the feasibility of various kinds of state controls in higher education. It was reported in 1970 that in twenty-nine of fifty states legislation was passed in respect of campus unrest and antidisturbance regulations, and that many legislatures were showing interest in fixing faculty teaching loads.[52] The president of Ohio State University said in an address in 1973:

Around the country, right now, there is pressure in one or more states for the following:

(1) Standardized course offerings for "general education" in the first two years.

(2) A standard calendar for all state universities.

(3) Round-the-clock (7 A.M. to midnight) operation on a 12-months-a-year basis.

(4) Legislatively mandated teaching loads of nine hours at the graduate level, 12 hours at the undergraduate level.

(5) A single computer system, a single library system for a state.

244

(6) A job-classification system locking every professor and employee in an appropriate niche.

(7) Space-utilization and building-construction standards that treat all universities as if they were alike in all respects.[53]

These were probably extreme cases and not likely to represent the trend. But what was clearly apparent was that less power and less influence on university policy resided on the campus. Academic freedom—in terms of institutional autonomy—was not merely restricted but threatened with a reduction ad absurdum.

Two further issues require brief mention here. In the face of what seemed to be irresistible pressure toward statewide planning of higher education, the question of the nature of the planning process arose. Many of the "master plans" popular in all three countries tended to lock in all universities in a rather rigid system. Was it possible to provide more flexibility? Martin Trow identified two distinct planning processes. One he called "prescriptive planning," which "aims to spell out in detail the size and shape of the system of higher education over the next several decades—what will be taught, to whom, to how many, and in what kind of institutions, at what expense," [54] and the second "systems planning," which has as its aim "the evolution of a system of higher education marked by diversity and flexibility." [55] The forces for prescriptive planning, he suggested, were everywhere dominant, even though they were incompetent to deal with unforeseen developments and inconsistent with any substantial degree of university autonomy.

In many countries the struggle to contain diversity takes the form of an effort to maintain tight controls over standards, costs, functions, forms . . . all in the service of the traditional values of higher education. . . . Diversity is seen not only as a threat to the power of the state over a major claimant on public resources: as a threat to orderly governmental and bureaucratic process; as a challenge to the norms of equity and equality; diversity is also seen as academic anarchy, and a threat to the traditional values of higher education itself. . . . *Everywhere one sees the distaste of central governmental agencies for the messiness and unpredictability of genuine and*

evolving diversity, and their continued efforts to bring their sys-
tems back under control and along desired lines of devel-
opment.[56] [Italics added]

The movement in the early 1970s was clearly toward prescriptive planning. The University of Toronto, which for a
quarter of a century had been the leading university in Canada, with the largest and most prestigious library, faculty,
and graduate school, requested special consideration in 1969
for its position and additional funds to retain its status as "a
national institution." This request was quickly and briskly rejected by the provincial Committee on University Affairs,
whose view was that all universities should be treated in the
same way.[57] Bureaucracy cannot readily tolerate exceptions
to the rule. Indeed the essence of bureaucracy is the rule and
strict adherence to it. As universities came to be locked into a
statewide plan, they all came increasingly under the influence of the state bureaucracy and therefore under strong
pressure to standardize in all aspects of their work.

Secondly, these changes raised the fundamental question
of the validity of the claim that universities could function
effectively only if they had a large degree of freedom. If in
1950 universities had been asked if it would be possible to
operate with the controls in effect in 1975, most would probably have predicted disaster for the university. And yet the
controls have been introduced with apparently little loss to
the effectiveness of the university. Indeed there have been
gains: the elimination of wasteful duplication; the introduction of useful standards for admission, teaching responsibilities, and expenditures; the sharing of scarce resources;
the relating of programs to public need. Was the need for autonomy simply a myth perpetuated by professional academics who wanted to be left alone to go their own way as they
wished?

Even those most devoted to university autonomy could not
deny that external interference had on occasion stimulated
and revived the university at times when it required revitalization. The constant criticism of the university in the seventeenth and eighteenth centuries, the royal commission on

Oxford and Cambridge in 1850, the contribution of lay people on university boards in the United States and Canada, the frequent studies of universities in North America, the student revolt in the 1960s—all these had stimulated and sometimes shocked the university into much-needed reform. The university, like all institutions, tended to rely too heavily on tradition. The counterforce—the revolutionary force—had most often come from outside the inner councils of university.

But if there is sense in the admonition that "revolution without tradition is blind," there requires some consideration of those aspects of university life which seem essential to its good health. It is not simply a myth to suggest that scholarly and creative work require leisure and freedom. Nor is it a myth that professional academic people are the best equipped to appraise the quality of work and to establish standards in their fields of specialization. Nor is it a myth that competition among universities gave each a vitality they might not otherwise have. Nor is it a myth that campus autonomy facilitated diversity and innovation. There is much to support the usefulness of these practices. The key to the future may well lie in the possibility of modifying the powerful drive of the state to plan, coordinate, and standardize sufficiently to permit some university traditions to continue.

NOTES

1. See Jaspers, 1965, p. 19.

2. Nisbet, 1971a, p. 61.

3. Hoffman, 1970, p. 186.

4. Indeed it could be said with some assurance that "the higher the prestige of a given university in the academic world, the more probable total segregation was" (Nisbet, 1971a, p. 56).

5. Morison, 1965, p. 288.

6. Trow, 1973, p. 19.

7. "University Grants Committee," 1967, sec. 2.

8. Ibid., sec. 1.

9. Ibid.

10. Wolfenden, 1972, p. 136.

11. Kneller, 1955, pp. 50–60.

12. Wolfenden, 1972, p. 138.

13. McConnell, 1971, p. 114.

14. Wolfenden, 1972, p. 139–140.

15. Ibid., p. 139.

16. McConnell, 1971, p. 114.

17. "Parliament and Control of University Expenditure," 1967, sec. 29.

18. Ibid., app. 8, sec. 19.

19. Ibid., app. 8, sec. 15; see also app. 8, secs. 13–14.

20. Ibid., app. 9, sec. 6.

21. Ibid., sec. 29.

22. Perkins, 1972, p. 282.

23. Bissell, 1972, pp. 182–183. "The provision since 1952 of annual grants to universities, and in the support of research and scholarship through such agencies as the National Research Council; and it could have been added that support for research and scholarship was also provided by other research councils—Defense Research Board (1947), and Canada Council (1957), Medical Research Council (1960), and by more than a dozen government departments, Agriculture, and Health and Welfare for example" (Harris, 1973, chap. 35, p. 40).

24. Harris, 1973, chap. 35, p. 5.

25. "Federal Grants to Canadian Universities," 1975.

26. Hansen, 1974, pp. 1–6.

27. Council of Ontario Universities, 1971–72, pp. 4–7.

28. Macdonald, 1975, p. 1.

29. Millett, 1972, p. 45.

30. Perkins, 1972, p. 283.

31. McConnell, 1966.

32. Ibid., p. 83.

33. Ibid.

34. Smelser, 1972, p. 25.

35. Millett, 1972, p. 46.

36. Mortimer, 1972, p. 17.

37. Gould, 1972, p. 18.

38. *The Efficiency of Freedom*, 1959, p. 12.

39. McConnell, 1966, p. 79.

40. Ibid., p. 78.

41. Mortimer, 1972, p. 14.

42. Kerr, 1970*a*, p. 112.

43. McConnell, 1966, p. 91.

44. "Parliament and Control of University Expenditure," app. 8, sec. 7.

45. "Ontario and Its Universities," 1973–74, p. 518.

46. Mortimer, 1972, p. 24.

47. Britain, Committee on Higher Education, 1963, pp. 230–235.

48. Mortimer, 1972, p. 24.

49. Britain, Committee on Higher Education, 1963, p. 232.

50. Ibid., p. 234, para. 722.

51. "Education: A Framework for Expansion," 1972, sec. 106.

52. Mortimer, 1972, p. 17.

53. Enarson, 1973, p. 16.

54. Trow, 1973, p. 70.

55. Ibid., p. 71.

56. Ibid., pp. 73–74.

57. Ross, 1972, pp. 242–258.

part four

THE
FUTURE

chapter ten

✸

THE UNIVERSITY
AND THE FUTURE

A famous Russian countess, asked what she did during the Bolshevik revolution of 1917, replied, "I survived!" [1] This was indeed no small accomplishment for a titled lady at that time.

The university has survived! In spite of all the misfortunes of man and the calamities of mankind, the university has continued for over eight hundred years. It could have done so only if it served some fundamental human and social need. This it has done (providing for man's insatiable desire to know and for society's need for knowledge and skilled manpower), albeit not always consistently or effectively. At times the university was the slave of the state, at others the servant of the church, and on occasion seemingly the victim of anarchy. But the steady, pulsating passion of the university was for knowledge. the accumulation, preservation, development, and transmission of knowledge. However deviant it was at times and however numerous the heresies committed in its history, the university always returned to this function. And when it did this, in a manner that served both individual and social needs, it not only survived, it flourished.

Perhaps more significant than its mere survival has been its persistence of form and identity. The university was still recognizable in 1975 as a derivative of the medieval university, not only in the West, but everywhere in the world. Scholars are disposed to emphasize the changes, the devia-

253

tions, the digressions in history and in the development of an institution. But what is remarkable about the university is how much of its form and character has remained the same over many centuries and in many different cultures.

In the university there have always been students, professors, administrators; a division of function—subjects, faculties, colleges, institutes; programs of study involving lectures, courses, assignments, and examinations; a structure of government in which masters had considerable control over academic affairs; a framework of rules and regulations which involved evaluation by masters of those to be certified for graduation, appointment, or promotion; rituals with masters in colorful gowns at convocation and commencement; collections of books and scientific equipment; a campus with buildings which often attempted to symbolize in physical terms the idea of community; an ethos in which leisure and learning were joined in a way that was unique in society.

This combination of people, forms, procedures, and purposes constitutes the continuum in the university since the eleventh century. The persistence of certain patterns of organization and work, of belief and behavior, of form and structure should make us sensitive to the fundamental strength and the conservative nature of the university, and reluctant to conclude that its age-old traditions will not be able to accommodate or assimilate the radical thrust of any new era.

It cannot be assumed from this that the university was inflexible or static. The lesson to be gleaned from its development is that it was able to make numerous significant changes within a continuing form and structure. The radical pressures of the modern period seem far more likely to lead to a profound alteration of character. Yet the changes of the past were seen, at the time, to be equally dramatic. Consider, for example, just a few of the major changes in the hundred years before 1950.

Perhaps the most significant of these was the shift from scholasticism to science. This was the turn from dogma, formalism, and revealed truth to the search for knowledge through the systematic study and observation of natural phenomena, which began in the university early in the nineteenth century but was not completed for many decades thereafter. The change was of far greater importance than the introduction of the first "science subjects," chemistry, physics, and biology. It created a different intellectual climate in the university. The values of science—objectivity, neutrality, humility, skepticism, system—became the values of the academic enterprise. The scholar, whether in philosophy, psychology, or physics, became committed to the same values. Dogma and indoctrination were unacceptable. Further, the introduction of science did a good deal to broaden and loosen the curriculum, facilitating the beginning of the elective system, creating new subjects, providing leads for other subjects (especially the social sciences) to find a legitimate place in the university.

Another example of change prior to 1950 was the gradual movement to select the constituency of the university on the basis of merit. There could be no question that the earlier universities were predominantly class institutions, in which children from wealthy families occupied most of the available places. But as the importance of the university as a gateway to the professions and to higher social status was recognized, and as the movement for equal opportunity grew in popularity, universities began to create admission standards that favored the intellectually able student. Thus the "meritocratic society"—a society in which the rewards went to the most talented and accomplished.[2] This movement strengthened the university, made it a more serious and a more productive enterprise, without altering its form or purpose.

There were other significant alterations in program and policy within the university between the two world wars. Vocational and utilitarian programs, with a long and controversial history in the university, now multiplied in number and attracted increasing numbers of students. The accelerated growth of these programs permitted the university to serve new social needs, to become a more visible, and for many, a more valuable, institution in society.

These are but illustrative of continuing change in the ethos and character of the university. Undoubtedly they provided traumatic experiences for many and were not consummated

without conflict and pain. But what is of the greatest significance is that all were contained within the prevailing structure and concept of the mission of the university. The institution was sufficiently flexible to adapt new ideas and practices
without altering its fundamental character. Indeed, many of
these changes were responsible for the dynamic development
and growth in status of the university, which by the early
postwar period reached a height it had not enjoyed since medieval days. The striving for excellence, the search for new
knowledge, the products of both the vocational and nonvocational parts of the university were consistent with the popular mood and the needs of society. The university adapted
to these needs and was still a strong, viable organization in
1950 with deep, recognizable, traditional roots.

More fundamental changes were beginning to take form,
but in spite of these there was little to shake the image of the
university as the locus for knowledge and advancement in
society or to suggest it was other than a unified and civilized
community pursuing aims useful to the individual and valuable to society.

Changes from 1950 to 1975

The changes in the third quarter of this century were profound—or seemed to be. The great prestige of the university
in the fifties and early sixties disappeared under the impact
of new social forces. Great waves of uncertainty resulted
from a loss of direction from within the university and from
fresh skepticism about higher education in society. But
twenty-five years is a short time in the life of an institution as
old as the university, and one could not with certainty desig-
nate any alterations in policy or procedure during this brief
span as permanent. A sudden change in the social climate or
in the ethos of the university might well alter what seemed to
be in 1975 an irreversible drift to a new type of institution.

Nonetheless, the new developments appeared of more serious consequence and of wider impact than those in the century past. The latter, as indicated, were all contained within
the existing norms and structure of the traditional university.

Changes in the period under consideration threatened to alter these in a manner which precluded a return to tradition and seemed to require new forms, orientation, and purpose. The forces of revolution appeared to be sufficiently powerful to force a major change in tradition.

In the quarter century considered here we see four developments that had potentiality for permanence. These were (1) the acceptance of the populist philosophy in the university, (2) the alteration of the hierarchical structure of the university, (3) the disintegration of the normative order of the university, and (4) the changed status of the university in society. While some of these had roots in the past, they came abruptly on the scene in the late sixties and acquired what seemed to be a commanding position in the 1970s. If these movements matured, a quite new kind of institution would emerge in the future.

Populist philosophy: In Western societies there had been for centuries a slow but gradual movement to extend what were rather loosely called "citizenship rights" universally across the population.[3] The pace of this movement was not only greatly increased in the postwar period but its meaning expanded to the extent that reasonable men were arguing that inequalities created by birth and natural endowment were undeserved and that such inequalities should be compensated for.[4] The university was elitist, whether it chose its students by social class or by merit, and as such was under sharp attack by the forces of egalitarianism that grew in strength and influence in the sixties and seventies. But the populist movement went further than this, for it involved elements of anti-intellectualism which depreciated the cognitive tradition of the university.

The response of the university was to acquiesce to this pressure, and almost everywhere there could be seen a loosening of access and curriculum requirements, an effort to accommodate a much larger constituency, and an attempt to adjust study programs to meet the abilities and the time schedules of various types of students. Even in Britain, the most tradition-bound in this respect, one could see a response to these forces. In 1972 the Secretary for Education and Science presented to Parliament a statement which referred to work of his ministry as:

> . . . a broadly organized effort to enable all members of society, with their widely differing aspirations and capacities, *once they have left school behind to learn where, when, and what they want in the way that best suits them.* So far as resources allow the Government wishes to see advances made across the whole of this broad front.[5] [Italics added]

A number of universities in the United States that adopted a policy of "open admissions," the Open University in England, and some part-time and evening colleges in Canada provided, in effect, admission to university to all who wished to study for a degree almost regardless of ability or past achievement. The tide of egalitarianism was strong and promised to eradicate undergraduate admission standards of any kind.

The effect on curriculum was equally dramatic, for a strong current developed to equate certain experiences, particularly work experience, with academic courses. Major commissions in both the United States and Canada recommended such recognition for work experience.[6] One study reported:

> In 1972, two thirds of American colleges and universities recognised projects and work done off campus as part of the qualifications for a degree. Fourteen per cent of the teachers asserted that work experiences are as good educationally as academic courses, and 9 per cent grant credit for projects even when they are not supervised by teachers. At a third of the institutions, "independent study" or work done outside the college or university could make up as much as a quarter of the requirements for a degree. More astonishingly, 28 per cent of these institutions permit undergraduates to teach other undergraduates. Three fourths now permit students to define their own courses of study and arrange their major subjects as they wish; they also allow them to initiate new courses.[7]

The "loosening" in academic life was evident also in more

flexible standards of grading, for the pressure seemed to be not simply for equal opportunity but for equal results; "if some persons are to be better off, the lesser advantaged are also to be better off . . . if one gains so must the others." [8] There was some evidence that high failure rates were not acceptable.[9] And when both students and finances were in short supply in the early seventies, there seemed to be little disposition to fail students.

The populist movement affected other parts of the university as well, particularly the whole structure of government. The result, as we have indicated earlier, was student representation on many committees and councils, "open meetings," and the emergence of a much more politically oriented campus.

The cumulative effect of egalitarian pressures was to create a rather different ethos. It could be seen

> . . . in the derogation of the IQ and the denunciation of theories espousing a genetic basis of intelligence; the demand for "open admission" to universities on the part of minority groups in the large urban centers; the pressure for increased numbers of blacks, women, and specific miniority groups such as Puerto Ricans and Chicanos in the faculties of universities, by quotas if necessary; and the attack on "credentials" and even schooling itself as the determinant of a man's position in the society. A post-industrial society reshapes the class structure of society by creating new technical elites. The populist reaction, which has begun in the 1970's, raises the demand for greater "equality" as a defense against being excluded from that society.[10]

It is interesting to note that while the populist revolt led to a vast expansion of university enrollments, this did not necessarily increase social equality,[11] for those who responded to "openness" and more flexible requirements tended not to be the disadvantaged people. "To rely on pure demand is to build on huge middle class bias" [12] was the conclusion of one observer, which contained the suggestion that active recruiting of minority groups was essential if the equality that was being sought was to be achieved. Nor could the egalitarian movement claim, in spite of its strength and impact, that all universities had lost or would lose their elitist posture or their academic emphasis. By 1975 universities were in a "steady state," neither growing nor declining very much in enrollment, while junior and technical colleges seemed to be continuing to grow.[13] And the impact of the movement varied by country, state, and university. It could not be claimed that populism or mass intake had everywhere been paralleled by a change from nonvocational to vocational education,[14] nor that all traditional standards and practices were altered. Nonetheless the egalitarian movement had affected all systems of higher education to some extent. Some changes, such as those in governance, flexibility in admission standards, and in curriculum, seemed almost irreversible. Some degree of erosion of tradition was obvious, but only the future could determine how much further this would continue and how fundamentally it would alter the university.

Hierarchical structure: The three major groups in the university whose role was altered after 1950 were the students, the professors, and the administrators.

The traditional role of the student in the university was that of a child-learner. By 1970 this fixed and established role had changed. The student was now an adult at age eighteen and legally free to determine where and how he or she would live. In many universities students were members of one or more of the senior governing bodies, and in some this position was established by university statute or by state law. In a few universities they had "parity"—that is, equal representation with professors on important university councils or committees. The role of student changed in other respects—as numbers grew, university attendance became less a privilege than a right; fewer students lived on campus; more worked part time; and the university became a less-absorbing enterprise than for students in previous decades. Further, as the state became almost the sole source of funds for the university, students were conscious that the taxes they or their parents paid were being used to support the university. Many students now regarded their role as that of consumers or purchasers of a packaged good with the right to demand good service and a good product. Their new role was more properly defined as similar to that of a member of a cooperative grocery store; they were now "member-consumers" with rights both to have a say in policy and to demand quality and service at reasonable prices. The traditional role of child-learner which had existed for centuries was abolished almost completely in the course of a decade.

The model of the monastery defined the traditional relation of the professor to the university. The latter was the object of deep loyalty to which the teacher devoted long hours, often for an extremely small stipend. We have already noted (in Chapter 4) the gradual change in this role—increasing interest in research, publishing, consulting, conferencing, to the point where it could be said of professors in 1970:

> The university as an institution had become for them nothing more than a provider of resources and services; . . . everything apart from getting on with their own intellectual tasks was disregarded.[15]

For many professors the university became merely a base from which to operate. Among many competing roles, his or her role as teacher, or as parent-guide, or as department head was not of first importance; he or she was no longer deeply committed to the university as an institution; his or her interests and involvements were widespread; and his or her own career was only partially determined by assignments within the university. The professor's role in the university was similar to that of an employee in any secular consumer-oriented enterprise, in which there is relatively small commitment to the institution or its customers. The "significant others" for the professor were those in his or her own specialized field, often outside his own university; his professional obligations were worldwide. In the university his contacts with those in other specialties were largely for the purpose of protecting or improving their common lot, thus the interest in faculty associations and later in trade unions.

In 1950 the role of the head of the university was quite different in Canada, England, and the United States. The

English vice-chancellor was usually a person of academic prestige, appointed for a limited term, with little authority and a very small administrative staff. In Canada presidents were chosen more for their administrative experience and skills than for their prestige as academics (although they were most often university teachers): their appointments were for an indefinite term; and they had considerable authority in administrative matters, a modest administrative staff, and a good deal of influence in academic affairs. In the United States the university president, appointed and supported by a lay board, was often a man or woman of prestige in the community, was expected to "lead the university," often to raise funds, to continue in office indefinitely or as long as he was successful. The American president tended to have a large administrative staff and to have considerable authority even in academic affairs. By 1975 these differences tended to disappear and the role of the head in all universities to become much the same. As universities became larger, more complex, and as the influence of the state increased and that of laymen decreased, all developed administrative staffs—a university bureaucracy—directly responsible to the president or vice-chancellor. But as new forms of governance and participatory democracy spread within the university, the head had less authority and was called upon to reconcile differences, avoid confrontations, seek agreements, act as mediator among various groups and factions in the university. He or she thus became a kind of manager-politician: a manager of a large administrative operation; a politician in assisting in the evolution of policy. The university head was now almost everywhere appointed for a term of office—five to seven years—and whatever authority he or she exercised was often subject to challenge on the campus.

Clark Kerr suggested that the head must in these circumstances be much more the political leader:

> . . . his conduct will be less in the committee room and more in the open. He will appeal more to mass groups and less to representatives . . . he will be more visible, more accessible, more of a public personality. Thus he will be more like the mayor of a big city walking in the streets, meeting the people,

wrestling in public with the great issues of the day and less the executive with his experts working in comparative silence with other elites.[16]

In every organization there is some order of rank and status—a hierarchical order. In the university of 1950 this was fairly clear. The university head was "first among equals" among his or her academic colleagues; the senior professors were not far behind and of equal rank in the determination of academic policy, and students were wards, subject to the arbitrary authority of the first two in respect of their academic work and their behavior. By 1975 this hierarchical order had collapsed. Many of the lines separating individuals and groups by rank and status were now blurred; for example, a student might have lower status than the professor in the classroom, but he or she might sit as an equal to this same professor on some important university policy committee. But even this distinction was not firm, as some younger professors preferred equal status with students in the classroom.

What emerged were three groups—students, administrators, professors—distinct and separate from each other. The three groups were required to work together on university committees, and the ethos of the day was that they treat each other as equals and with respect. But occasional confrontations made it obvious that this was an uneasy arrangement, that each group sought to protect and further its own interests, and that underlying all was a continuing struggle for ascendency.

The breakdown of the hierarchical order meant a major change in the university, and the lack of new status arrangements led only to confusion. The stability of the old order was gone. The relation of student, professor, and administrator that had existed for centuries may have been obsolete in 1950, but it had provided a structure that people understood and accepted. One knew one's place. The new era involved new relationships, but in 1975 precisely what these were was not clear. Until a new order was established, there would inevitably be tension and conflict.

Disintegration of the normative order: Throughout the centuries the university developed its own normative order.[17] It was, of course, modified and altered at different times and in varying circumstances, but there was a cumulative experience which led most university people, prior to 1950, to believe that there was broad and general agreement on fundamental issues such as the purpose of the university, the nature of scholarship, the value of the life of the mind, the "cognitive orientation" of the university, the underlying respect for colleagues, the resolution of conflict by debate and discussion, the importance of the humanistic tradition, the need for loyalty to the university, the responsibility of the teacher for as great a degree of objectivity as possible in one's teaching.

There were, as has been pointed out, sharp differences of opinion regarding the major direction of the university in the United States in the latter part of the nineteenth century; there was a spate of books on the aims of education in Britain between the two world wars; there was mild discussion at national conferences of universities in Canada about graduate work and the quality of the undergraduate program after 1920. But all these debates and discussions were within a framework that assumed agreement on fundamental issues. Some may have felt that the university was not living up to its potential, was not performing as well as it might, was not placing emphasis on the proper subjects, but there were no voices proclaiming the universities to be evil or elitist or irrelevant. Disagreements were low-key and not likely to threaten "the cake of custom" which lay heavy on the university.

What was involved was a distinctive way of life—a humane, liberal, and aristocratic civility in which a degree of eccentricity and nonconformity was tolerated, scholarship honored, and the world's cultural heritage revered.[18] It was a civilized, leisurely life-style in which academic seminars, committees, and social parties might stir sharp debate but not hostility or confrontation. The whole of the enterprise was largely separated from society with its problems and tensions. The university was a genteel community apart from the ugliness of the larger world. This was the idealized campus.

In many situations all of this was a veneer which covered petty jealousies, bitter struggles for power, and insensitivity to social need.[19] But the image and the assumptions which underlay it persisted, and after 1950 older professors often spoke nostalgically about the past when "all professors were gentlemen." However unrealistic was this picture of campus life, its overt disintegration began in many universities long before 1950. Increasing size, specialization, and functions had already begun to challenge university norms. But it was the revolt of the sixties that fully exposed this deviation and that shattered completely the image of a community of loyal scholars united by common goals and agreed-upon standards of behavior.

The breakdown of the normative order was not restricted to goals or to any single part of campus life. It permeated every aspect of the university. The divisions and differences were of a new order: the nature of scholarship, with the "new scholars" disputing in varying ways the liberal tradition, the ethos of science, and the relevance of the empirical method that had been dominant in the university for over a century; the separateness of the university, with many insisting that the institution must be active in dealing with social injustice; the neutrality of the scholar faced with the challenge that "there is something obscene about the scientist who claims he is not responsible for the uses to which his science is put";[20] the cognitive core of the university confronted by the argument that feelings and sentiment were of equal import; the mutual respect among colleagues no longer recognized by some professors who dealt overtly with one another with hostility and attempts at censorship; the civility of campus life disrupted by demonstrations, obscenities, violence; the traditional curriculum opposed by a system of nontraditional studies geared to the needs of the student, which "de-emphasizes time, space, and even course requirements";[21] loyalty to the institution eroded by those serving their profession or some higher cause; the posture of the scholar obliged "to present a broad range of knowledge with all its uncertainties and ambiguities" challenged by the political activist "expected to be an advocate of a particular point of view." [22] The list of conflicting ideas and behavior patterns could be extended almost indefinitely: in total they signified not simply the disintegration of the old order but the difficulty of bringing some degree of cohesion to the campus of the future.

The complexity of the situation was highlighted by the violence which appeared on some campuses in the sixties. Traditional norms opposed such violence (although some professors supported some violent demonstrations), but traditional norms also opposed any intrusion in campus affairs by external authorities (although some professors approved such action). The result was an inability to act clearly and decisively, a lack of strong support for the administration however it acted, and a general impression of irreconcilable differences that made for chaos.

Many observers spoke sadly but realistically of the obvious lack of confidence and consensus in the university:

> . . . the old assumptions regarding the shared unspoken values of academic men, cutting across disciplinary lines, can no longer be sustained—and where these shared values are no longer shared whether because of political students or dissident faculty, the old forms of university government by discussion and consensus begin to break down.[23]

Whatever may be said of a well-understood and accepted normative order—be it ancient or modern—it provides a common focus for the resolution of issues and conflict: "It is only through what might be called the eyeglasses of the norms we live by that we perceive and interact with the factual order." [24] Without these "eyeglasses" consensus is difficult to achieve. It was clear in the universities that since people saw the issues with different perspectives, in different contexts, from different value-positions, there was, in 1975, little agreement about many questions, particularly those we have detailed in earlier chapters: goals, governance, academic freedom, and the state.

Because he was close to universities in both England and North America, it is worth quoting Shils on the cracks in the consensus about belief and practice in the university:

> . . . Just as radical reformers have demanded that all meet-
> ings of academic governing bodies be open to all, so there are
> now senior and junior academics who see nothing wrong with
> transmitting to the public press documents which have been
> prepared in confidence for free discussion within the univer-
> sity or institute. The purloining of documents and correspon-
> dence, and their unauthorised transmission to the press, is
> now no longer uncommon, and it has occurred even in Great
> Britain which had until recently been immune from this sort
> of activity.[25]

The disintegration of the long-established normative order
in the 1950–1975 period represented another fundamental
change in the university. Without it people were at a loss, not
only in respect of beliefs and values, but to know how to go
about rebuilding a new order. There were no common "eyeglasses." Some thought of traditional methods of debate and
discussion; others relied on conflict and confrontation to further their aims.

Essential elements in the cement that had kept the university together were an established hierarchy and a well-understood normative order. These are fundamental aspects of
structure in any organization, but particularly to one like the
church or the university in which beliefs and values are the
wells from which the organization draws its nourishment.
Both beliefs and values were rocked by the turbulence of the
sixties, leaving the university disorganized and seemingly unable to cope with the many pressing demands made upon it.
If the price of autonomy was to be consensus and stable organization within, the university in 1975 seemed unable to
meet the cost.

Decline in status: There have been many peaks and valleys
in the status of the university. One of the peaks was the early
days of the medieval university; a valley was the long period
between 1500 and 1850. A point of high prestige was undoubtedly the years immediately following the last world
war; a depression, as far as public sentiment about higher
education was concerned, occurred in the 1970s.

Some of the reasons for the decline of public confidence in the university are not difficult to identify. The frequent campus disruptions; the lack of authority in university affairs; the attack of scholar by scholar; the dissatisfaction of students, resulting in an unusual number of dropouts; the emphasis on nonvocational subjects when many students seemed to want "training for a job"—all combined to raise questions about the course and direction, if not about the absolute value, of the university. The regular exposure of campus problems to public scrutiny by the news media served only to accentuate these difficulties.

Public confidence was not increased by a prolonged debate that arose in the early seventies about the value of education—more precisely about the worthwhileness of spending large amounts of public money on education. The locus of the debate was the United States, and its focus related to issues internal to that country, but the questions and doubts raised were relevant in both England and Canada. In capsule form, some researchers were saying that (1) the quality of schools attended by black children and those attended by white children in the United States was more nearly equal than anyone supposed; (2) the gap between the achievement of black and white children got wider, not narrower, over twelve years at school; and (3) therefore there was no reason to suppose that increasing the flow of resources into the schools would affect the outcome in terms of achievement, let alone eliminate inequality.[26] To this was added the "controversy of the genes," largely centered around an original essay by psychologist Arthur Jensen, in which he argued that genes were mainly responsible for the average fifteen-point IQ difference found between American blacks and whites. Others went on to point out the advantages held by those with genes which produced high IQ and high achievement (which was rewarded in the school system) and which therefore produced greater inequality in society.[27] In other words, schools merely rewarded the able and did little in themselves either to remove inequality or to change the ability or status of their pupils. And similarly, to the question "What does the university really do for its students?" research could answer only that collegiate environments change students as a lens gathers light—simply focusing and sharpening what was there to begin with—and that conversions from one attitude or interest or level of capacity to another were rare in higher education.[28] The discussions which centered around these findings and these views were prolonged, heated, and often at a sophisticated level of dispute, but the total effect was to raise in the public mind a question that had not seemed relevant for many decades: How valuable is formal education? The seeds of doubt about the high priority given to education as a means of solving many personal and social problems were firmly sown.

That the status of the university declined rapidly during this period there could be little doubt. A prominent Canadian, a former newspaper publisher, in a nationwide address in 1973 called for greater government control of universities ("the idea of an inviolable campus is absurd") and suggested that universities were no longer in the forefront of intellectual thought but merely the physical milieu where classes took place.[29] This view was not without some support in Canada. In the United States ". . . the best poll taken on confidence in higher education showed that in 1966 about 61 per cent of the American people would express a great deal of confidence in higher education; last year [1972] it was down to 33 per cent." [30] And while budget restrictions were operative everywhere, financial cutbacks in England seemed sufficiently severe to suggest that the former priority of the university in government budget allotments had dropped sharply. A typical vice-chancellor's report in 1974 said that as a consequence of reductions in government grants, "departments cannot for the time being recruit additional or replacement academic staff unless their staff/student ratio is worse than 1:13.8, *a figure which would have been unimaginable only a few years ago*" (italics added).[31]

The university, as suggested, had had its good days and its bad days. It had survived the difficult times and perhaps would do so again. But there were some new elements in the situation which held potentiality for changing its orientation and position in the future. Because of its dependence on public funds, the university was now, more than ever before, in competition with other demands for public services—health, welfare, transportation, environmental needs, etc. The university was now in the public domain and its support subject to shifts in social values and public demand. Further, the university had lost to a considerable degree its monopolistic position in higher education; its budget was now often considered along with other institutes of postsecondary education: community, technical, and art colleges. It was now in competition with these institutions for educational grants and under pressure to justify its much higher per-student costs. It was possible to rationalize the cost of research, sabbatical leaves, and "long vacations" only to a society sympathetic to the pursuits of higher learning. When such understanding and support was absent, investment in lower-cost institutes seemed the greater value.

Of critical consideration was the power of the state to exercise authority over the university program. This authority was exercised to varying degrees and in divergent ways in the many different jurisdictions. Sometimes it depended upon such a variable as the personality of a senior civil servant or even a junior bureaucrat. What was important was the locus of power, power which would undoubtedly be used if there was strong public sentiment in respect of the university's position vis-à-vis (1) other general demands on the public purse, (2) the needs of other educational institutions, or (3) programs or functions which the public would regard as being properly located in the university.

The change in status in the university might be a temporary state in the seventies. But it put the university on notice that any decline in the esteem in which it was held by the public could quickly and decisively affect its well-being. The power and the authority were in other hands.

Conclusion: The difficulty in evaluating the above changes is that of judging how deeply they penetrated the traditional life of the university. On the surface the arguments supporting fundamental change were compelling. The old values were threatened, the old structure altered, the old methods of dialogue challenged. The quiet civility of the campus of the past seemed almost to have disappeared completely. What appeared to be emerging was a new form of organization of many interests, functions, and groups loosely bound together in a modified democratic form of government, seeking to serve the interests of its members but subject at any moment to be required by external authorities to change plans, policy, or direction.

What was central, of course, was (1) the degree of commitment to the preservation, transmission, and development of knowledge at a level beyond that in schools and community colleges and (2) the right of scholars to judge their peers, evaluate their students, appraise the quality of academic programs. There could be many superficial changes in organization that would have little effect on the core of the university. But if the mission and the means of fulfilling this mission were altered, then, indeed, a new and different institution would evolve.

There was evidence that these fundamentals were under duress. The overt disrespect of tradition and the past, the demand for vocationalism and relevance, the easing of admission standards, the increased flexibility of the curriculum, the demand for "more teaching and less research," the role of students in the evaluation of teachers and courses, and the general "loosening" of academic discipline and standards all seemed to be directed at the heart of the university—the elimination of all the traditional ideas and standards.

But to reach this easy conclusion is to ignore the strength of the academic tradition, which remained largely unaffected in many institutions and in the lives of many scholars. Oxford and Cambridge were not separated from this tradition, nor were many of the best graduate schools in Canada and the United States. Thousands of dedicated scholars in these three countries continued as scholars had for centuries before them—pursuing with ceaseless diligence their special studies and passing on their knowledge and wisdom to their most able students.

Further, to assume "state control" was to assume the absence of any internal veto by the university. It could not be taken as fact that because of differences and dissension within the university there was not still sufficient vitality and resilience to resist some external pressures. Such resistance might vary by university, by state, or by national system. But as Archer[32] has pointed out, the variables involved in society-university linkages are multiple and complex, and one could not readily assume the dominance of society or that uniform patterns of higher education would emerge everywhere.

Thus in 1975 one could posit a picture of the university changed in many significant ways and on the verge of radical transformation. But one would also have to recognize the breadth and depth of traditional forces still very much alive in the university. The precise outcome of the interaction of the traditional and revolutionary pressures in the university was a matter for the future—to which we now turn.

The Future

Predictions about the future, however profuse and profound they may be, are seldom accurate. There were in the early seventies many new schools of "futurists": some who tended to "eternalize the present"; some who assumed that tendencies and movements of the present would spread and accelerate; and some who predicted social change in areas where refined statistical measures and complex computer-based technology were applicable. But all these futurists and others failed to establish a firm, comprehensive, and scientifically based method of describing the future of society and its institutions.[33]

The reason, of course, is that there are always new developments that elude the forecaster: new techniques and technologies in industry, large changes in the values of various sections of society, major alterations in the balance of power in the state or nation, new types of leaders in various fields who emerge unheralded to lead new movements or to revitalize old institutions. There have always been, and probably will always be, unforeseen developments that adversely affect the accuracy of forecasts of the future.[34] And who was to say in 1975 what configuration of developments would emerge to produce what developments in an institution as complex as the university?

Our approach to the future form and character of the university is therefore tentative. It will suggest that, barring major developments such as "war, famine, or plague," the shape of the university will depend on (1) the capacity of the university to come to grips with and to resolve internally some of the problems it will face in the final decades of the twentieth century and (2) the attitude of society to the university and the value it will place on higher education.

The university: The central problems within the university in the future will be those of defining its role in society and finding a structure of government that will permit it to function effectively. Without the resolution of these issues the university will drift aimlessly, moving only by coercion or popular demand.

"Governments which lose wars are governments that have undertaken to do more than they can." [35] This self-evident truth could readily be applied to the university in the postwar period, and by 1975 it was becoming obvious to many within the university. "Colleges and universities should not attempt to provide all things for all men" [36] seemed to be heard more frequently on campus. And financial restrictions in the seventies required a much closer look at priorities. Further, the spread of other kinds of postsecondary education permitted the university to be more restrictive in its programs. It seemed, then, that in the future the university would be less expansive, more conservative in defining its functions, and more clearly focused on tasks in higher education that it was better equipped, in terms of tradition and resources, to carry out than any other institution in society. On many peripheral matters it would have to be flexible and meet the demands society would make on it. There would be more opportunity for the disadvantaged but talented student to attend university, more flexibility in respect of time and place in studying for a degree, and many new and innovative undergraduate programs.[37] Indeed, the whole of the undergraduate program could well become more of an "explorative experience" in which students would have an opportunity to try several different programs of study before determining one that had special attraction for them.[38] But all these changes could take place without altering the structure of the university or changing its mission.

The permissiveness which had permeated and grown in the elementary schools had undoubtedly penetrated the universities in the sixties. It was clear that in terms of personal behavior such permissiveness would continue in the university. *In loco parentis* was dead. A new campus life-style would emerge. A great decline in "student services" was probable in the immediate future. On the other hand there were indications in the late seventies that there was a growing reaction to loose, unsupervised, and low-standard academic work. Society did not want ill-prepared doctors, lawyers, or professionals of any kind. Shoddy and indifferent workmanship hardly added to the university's reputation. In the seventies there were indications, particularly among numerous prestigious scholars, that the future would see a stiffening of standards and a demand for a higher level of performance by students, particularly those moving into graduate and professional education. The traditional purpose of the university to preserve, develop, and transmit knowledge, seemed about to be reasserted. It would not continue to be diverted for the sake of a "relevance" that, however popular for the moment, held little promise of disciplined study in depth and breadth. A condition of a successful future for the university was clarity of aims and functions in an increasingly complex society. After years of turbulence in the sixties and seventies there seemed to be among academic people a desire and a determination to make this a reality.[39]

While it is possible to be reasonably certain about the above, it must be said that a very great deal depends on how the conflict regarding the nature of scholarship is resolved. There are now numerous types of "new scholars" who oppose the liberal-scientific ethos of the traditional university. One or more of the "new schools" may represent the wave of the future. Perhaps the days of the dominance of science are past. But what is crucial is the manner in which the issue is settled. If a bitter public engagement ensues, if universities or departments become possessed by one or another school of thought, if intolerance or censorship of colleagues with differing views becomes acceptable, then of course, the university must face a dubious future. But there are signs that this will not happen. There seems to be a growing recognition even among the most radical dissenters that "nobody's right of dissent is safe if any one person or group can suppress ideas of which they disapprove." [40] The intolerance of the sixties and early seventies appears to be on the wane, and the possibility exists that the debate on the nature of scholarship will, in the future, be carried on in an atmosphere of civility. The scholasticism-science issue continued for many decades; the present issue may well require similar time for resolution. What is important is that it be carried on within a campus framework of freedom and tolerance for diverse views. There are, we believe, justifiable grounds for optimism that this will be the case.

Thus it appears possible for the university to begin to build, on the foundations of the past, a future that will permit expression of new ideas and programs that would have been considered inappropriate in the early postwar period. The forces of revolution will not be silenced, but it seems likely they will be contained within an intellectual environment with strong traditional overtones.

What seems less possible is the achievement of a stable governing structure. The hierarchical arrangements that emerged in the postwar period did not appear to be subject to early change. Students were adults—indeed were being joined by many older adults in the classroom—and they would have their say about the character of the university. Professors were professionals—perhaps members of unions—and infrequently devoted to the university. The presidents and vice-chancellors were less powerful and often anonymous figures on the campus and in the community.[41] The issue was complicated by the size of the university and the variety of functions it performed. The common solution of government by representation of "all estates" meant more committee work and usually that by the politically and non-research-oriented students and professors.[42] The absence of a central authority ("the hole in the center") was obvious.

> In a well-functioning periphery, there is loyalty to the university, not just to disciplines or departments. The creation of the loose consensus which reinforces the ethos of the university and its derivative virtues is the function of such an institutional centre.[43]

There was not such a center in the university in 1975, and there appeared no immediate hope that one would emerge.

This is undoubtedly a major issue for the university of the future. For, lacking a strong center, ideological debates will spill over into every area of university life, including management. If power blocs of different ideological schools became active in electing members to central councils, these councils would become political arenas in which the welfare of the university as a whole would be of less import than victory for a particular group. The future will require a strong, resourceful center to which members of the community can give loyal support in both good days and bad.

Society and the university: In the future the public attitude to the university may well be decisive. As already suggested, by 1975 the university was no longer insulated from society. Its deliberations and activities were not only in the public domain, but it depended so largely on public monies that it could not be insensitive to popular moods and pressures.

In Britain and in Canada all universities were in effect "public universities," receiving from 60 to 90 percent of their income from the public treasury. In the United States there were still many private colleges, but enrollment data for several decades indicated an increasing proportion of students attending public universities relative to those in private universities, with a ratio in 1975 of about 3 to 1.[44] Many of the smaller, less well-endowed private universities and colleges were, in the seventies, in great financial difficulty, and of the others most depended to a considerable degree on grants from state or federal governments. Without support from governments, there was little hope for the university's future. The nature of the relationship of the university to society was therefore critical in all these countries.[45]

The broad trends of society's relation to the university were clear. There was (1) a decline in the prestige of the university relative to other institutions in society, (2) considerable pressure for egalitarianism in all aspects of life including higher education, (3) a greater degree of centralization in government and the development of systems of higher education in which uniformity was valued, and (4) pressure from the economic system for greater vocationalism in all phases of education. The development of these trends in the future would inevitably bring the university under more rigid state control, reduce diversity, lower academic standards, and make humanistic and research traditions less important elements in the life of the university.

There could be no assurance, however, that such trends would continue in the direction indicated. Indeed, if trends in public education were to be relied upon, it could be seen that there were periods of high centralization often followed by a movement to decentralization,[46] and that public attitudes to education were frequently subject to rapid change. Such could also be the case in respect of the university.

There was undoubtedly still considerable latent support for strong, independent, and traditionally oriented universities. At a very minimum, universities would be supported if only to provide a place of learning for large numbers of interested youth. No modern industrial society could keep all its citizens between the ages of sixteen and sixty-five engaged in useful and valid employment.[47] In the United States alone there were in 1970 nearly fifteen million youths in the eighteen to twenty-one age group.[48] It was unlikely that society in the future would tolerate high unemployment rates for this group. And while the university was expensive, it was, in reality, less costly than many other possible alternatives to traditional employment.[49] The university would be seen then, in the future, as one of many useful institutions to which youth could profitably turn before facing the employment market. It was an argument for the maintenance of healthy institutions of higher education that few politicians would ignore.

But there would be other, more noble reasons for support of the university. Society's need for sophisticated and technical knowledge was increasing, and the university was likely to be the major institution producing both this knowledge in its many varied forms and the trained people who could use the knowledge in other institutions, such as government and industry. It seemed inevitable as society became more complex, more dependent on a technology the basis of which was pure research, and as many new problems emerged that required knowledgeable people (oceanographers, ecologists, Asian scholars, communication experts, etc.) that the university would be called upon more frequently and more insistently for help. There would be other kinds of teaching and research institutions but none likely to be as comprehensive or with as wide a perspective as the university. The great resources of the university in "knowledge" will be a powerful weapon to oppose those who would control or degrade it.[50]

Further, of course, there was no evidence to suggest that man's age-old curiosity and desire for knowledge had decreased. Indeed, the contrary was probably true, as people of all ages turned to the university for courses, many in esoteric fields which had no relation to "vocationalism." The "insatiable desire to know" had provided a solid base of support for the university in all societies in the past. It is difficult to conceive of it not doing so in the future.

In spite of the egalitarian trend of the seventies, there was also some recognition of the crucial importance of the contribution that could be made to society only by its most talented members.

> All civilised countries depend upon a thin clear stream of excellence to provide new ideas, new techniques, and the statesmanlike treatment of complex social and political problems. Without the renewal of this excellence, a nation can drop to mediocrity in a generation. The renewal of excellence is expensive: the highly gifted student needs informal instruction, intimate contact with other first-class minds, opportunities to learn the discipline of dissent from men who have

278

themselves changed patterns of thought; in a word (if it is one which has become a five-letter word of reproach) this sort of student needs to be treated as *elite*.[51]

The traditional university devoted to scholarship and excellence had, therefore, many assets in modern society. The dominance of populism and the state in educational policy was related not only to shifts in popular mood but also to weaknesses within the university. Even if there were no shifts in public attitude, the university's position could be improved if it could present its case from a strong unified base. Indeed, one could postulate a theory that the greater the internal coherence and strength of the university, the greater its independence and autonomy.

If the university is to regain its former poise and status, it must find the means of achieving a broad consensus and an effective governing structure within the organization. This will depend on restoring faith in the university as an institution and a sense of trust in one's colleagues who are joined in this enterprise. The problems of the university of the future are similar to those of government, as defined by Walter Lippmann some years ago.

What is it that has shaken the nerves of so many? . . . It is the doubt whether there exists among the people that trust in each other which is the first condition of intelligent leadership. That is the root of the matter. The particular projects which we debate so angrily are not so important, the fate of the nation does not hang upon any of them. But upon the power of the people to remain united for purposes which they respect, upon their capacity to have faith in themselves and in their objectives, much depends. It is not the facts of the crisis which we have to fear. They can be endured and dealt with. It is demoralization alone that is dangerous.[52]

NOTES

1. A similar remark has been attributed to many famous persons, notably both to Talleyrand and to Abbé Sieyès in relation to the French Revolution.

2. Young, 1958.

3. Ford, 1973, p. 52.

4. Rawls, 1971, p. 100.

5. "Education: A Framework for Expansion," 1972, sec. 106.

6. *Report on Higher Education,* 1971; "The Learning Society," 1973.

7. Riesman and Grant, 1973, p. 315.

8. Bell, 1973, p. 442.

9. Trow, 1973, p. 13.

10. Bell, 1973, p. 410.

11. Ford, 1973, p. 53.

12. Ibid.

13. Touraine, 1974, p. 103.

14. Archer, 1972, p. 18.

15. Shils, 1970, pp. 1–7.

16. Kerr, 1970*b*, pp. 161–162.

17. The normative order we take to be the cumulation of experience, solutions of recurrent problems, regulations and rules supported by authority, and interpretations of goals and values that arise, take root, and come to be the ideas and practices that are dominant in the life of an institution and to which members of the institution conform (Williams, 1968, pp. 204–208).

18. Aaron, 1971, pp. 14–15.

19. See, for example, Snow, 1959.

20. Berger, 1971, p. 5.

21. Watkins, 1974, p. 5.

22. Lipset, 1970, pp. 106–107.

23. Trow, 1970, p. 30.

24. Nisbet, 1970, p. 229.

25. Shils, 1973*b*, p. 288. Riesman and Grant, for example, state: "Agreement is lacking not only about what, if anything, should be required parts of the curriculum, but about where

the curriculum ends and the world begins: some of the reform-
ers insist that 'experience' of life and work be counted towards
a degree" (Riesman and Grant, 1973, p. 315).

26. Hodgson, 1973, p. 42.

27. For an excellent discussion of these issues, see Bell, 1973,
pp. 408–455; for a more popular summary, see a *Time* essay:
"What the Schools Cannot Do," 1973, pp. 56-60.

28. Hodgkinson, 1972, p. 9. Fritz Machlup has said: "The
greater earning capacity of college graduates compared with
high school graduates, is no doubt, to a large extent the result
of superior native intelligence and greater ambition; it would
be quite wrong to attribute all of the incremental earnings to
the investment in college education" (Machlup, 1970, p. 40).

29. Dilschneider, 1973, p. B14.

30. Moynihan, 1973, p. 11.

31. *Vice-Chancellor's Report for the Year 1973-74*, p. 2.

32. Archer, 1972, pp. 1-35.

33. Wrong, 1974, pp. 26-31.

34. See Trow, 1973, p. 48; Wrong, 1974, pp. 26-31; Heilbroner, 1973.

35. Shils, 1972*a*, p. 10.

36. Keniston, 1970, p. 66.

37. Examples are programs in occupation and professional development, personal and social development, humanistic and
liberal development. See Touraine, 1974, pp. 264-265.

38. See, for example, Wolff, 1969.

39. Panel on Alternate Approaches to Graduate Education,
1973. See also Nisbet, 1970; Ulam, 1972; Minogue, 1973; and
Belshaw, 1974.

40. K. McNaught, 1974, p. 7.

41. Scnias, 1975, p. 1.

42. Lipset, 1970, pp. 116-117.

43. Shils, 1973*a*, p. 27.

44. In the critical area of graduate studies, for example, 74 percent of the students were in public universities in 1975 compared to 26 percent in private universities. Comparable figures
for 1929-30 were 43 percent and 57 percent (*A Fact Book on
Higher Education*, 1973, p. 73:35)

45. Pifer, 1971, p. 5.

46. Ravitch, 1974.

47. Jerome, 1972, pp. 202-203.

48. Pifer, 1971, p. 13.

49. "While the average annual real cost of having a student in college at the undergraduate level, including educational and general costs and board and lodging, is not more than $4,000 (perhaps $6,000 if foregone earnings are included), the cost of having the same person serve as a recruit in military service is $7,500, as a Peace Corps volunteer nearly $10,000, and as a VISTA volunteer, $7,800. It should also be remembered that of the total annual expenditure on higher education only half comes from public tax sources, whereas in military and other national service programs, the *entire* burden falls on the tax-payer" (Pifer, 1971, p. 14).

50. Bullock, 1975, p. 17.

51. Ashby, 1971, pp. 101-102.

52. Reston, 1974, p. 7.

REFERENCES

Aaron, B. *Some Painful Realities.* Los Angeles: UCLA Institute of Labor and Industrial Relations, 1971.

AAUP Bulletin, Boston, December 1915, p. 35.

AAUP Policy Documents and Reports, 2, Washington, D.C., 1971.

AAUP "Statement on Professional Ethics," *AAUP Bulletin,* **52** (1): 57–58, 1966.

Annan, Lord Nöel, "Putting Back the Clock." *Times Higher Education Supplement,* Nov. 17, 1972, p. III.

Archer, M. S. (ed.) *Students, University and Society: A Comparative Sociological Review.* London: Heinemann, 1972, Introduction, pp. 1–35.

Armytage, W. H. G. *Civic Universities.* London: Benn, 1955.

Arnold, M. *Higher Schools and Universities in Germany.* London: Macmillan, 1868.

Arrowsmith, W. "The Future of Teaching." In A. Eurich (ed.), *Campus 1980.* New York: Delacorte, 1968, pp. 116–133.

Ashby, Sir Eric. *Patterns of Universities in Non-European Societies.* London: DSASA, 1961.

_____. *Masters and Scholars.* London: Oxford University Press, 1970.

_____. *Any Person, Any Study: An Essay on Higher Education in the United States.* New York: McGraw-Hill, 1971.

Bayley, J. "Dr. Leavis's Unwinking Eye." *Listener,* July 20, 1972, pp. 86–87.

Becker, H. S. "Reply to Riley's 'Partisanship and Objectivity.'" *American Sociologist,* **6:** 13, 1971.

Bell, D. "By Whose Right?" In H. L. Hodgkinson and L. R. Meeth (eds.), *Power and Authority.* San Francisco: Jossey-Bass, 1971, pp. 153–172.

_____. *The Coming of Post-Industrial Society: A Venture in Social Forecasting.* New York: Basic Books, 1973.

Beloff, M. *The Plateglass Universities.* London: Martin Secker & Warburg Limited, 1968.

Belshaw, C. S. *Towers Besieged: The Dilemma of the Creative University.* Toronto: McClelland and Stewart, 1974.

• REFERENCES •

Ben-David, J. "The Universities and the Growth of Science in Germany and the United States." *Minerva,* **7:** 1–35, 1968–69.

————. *American Higher Education: Directions Old and New.* New York: McGraw-Hill, 1972.

———— and A. Zloczower, "Universities and Academic Systems in Modern Societies." *European Journal of Sociology,* **3:** 45–84, 1962.

Berger, P. L. "Sociology and Freedom." *American Sociologist,* **6:** 1–5 1971.

Berton, P. *The Last Spike.* Toronto: McClelland and Stewart, 1971.

Bigelow, C. C. "Report of the President 1972–73." *CAUT* (Canadian Association of University Teachers) *Bulletin,* **22**(1): 18–21, September 1973.

Bill, E. S. W. "Review of University Reforms in Nineteenth Century Oxford." *Sunday Times,* Apr. 1, 1973, p. 39.

Bissell, C. T. "Canada." In J. A. Perkins (ed.), *Higher Education: From Autonomy to Systems.* New York: International Council for Educational Development, 1972, pp. 175–184.

Blishen, B. R., F. E. Jones, K. D. Naegele, and J. Porter (eds.). *Canadian Society: Sociological Perspectives.* Toronto: Macmillan, 1968.

Blumer, H. Preface to *Professionalization,* by H. M. Vollmer and D. L. Mills (eds.). Englewood Cliffs, N. J.: Prentice-Hall, 1966, p. xi.

Bressler, M. "The Liberal Synthesis in American Higher Education." *Annals of the American Academy of Political and Social Science,* **404:** 183–193, 1972.

Britain, Committee on Higher Education. "Higher Education." *Report of the Committee Appointed by the Prime Minister under the Chairmanship of Lord Robbins, 1961–63.* London: HMSO, 1963.

Bullock, A. "Why Universities Are Not a Luxury." *Times Higher Education Supplement,* Feb. 14, 1975, p. 17.

Bundy, M. "Were Those the Days?" *Daedalus,* **99**(3): 531–567, 1970.

Caine, Sir Sydney. *British Universities: Purpose and Prospects.* Toronto: University of Toronto Press, 1969.

Califano, J. A., Jr. *The Student Revolution: A Global Confrontation.* New York: Norton, 1970.

Campbell, D. "After the Counterculture, What?" *Chronicle of Higher Education,* Oct. 16, 1972, p. 12.

Carver, H. "Premier Hepburn and the Professors." *Canadian Forum,* **19:** 40–41, 1939.

• REFERENCES •

"Characteristics of 42,345 College Teachers." *Chronicle of Higher Education,* Aug. 27, 1973, p. 4.

Clark, B. R., and M. Trow. "The Organizational Context." In T. M. Newcomb and E. K. Wilson (eds.), *College Peer Groups.* Chicago: Aldine, 1966, pp. 17–69.

Clark, S. D. "The American Take-over of Canadian Sociology: Myth or Reality?" *University Affairs,* Ottawa, September 1974, pp. 16–18.

Corson, J. R. *The Governance of Colleges and Universities.* New York: McGraw-Hill, 1960. Rev. ed., 1975.

Council of Ontario Universities. *Stimulus and Response.* Sixth Annual Review, 1971–72.

Cross, M. S. Introduction to *The Decline and Fall of a Good Idea.* Cooperative Commonwealth Federation—New Democratic Party (CCF–NDP) Manifestoes, 1932–1969. Toronto: New Hogtown Press, 1974.

Crouch, C. "Britain." In M. S. Archer (ed.), *Students, University and Society: A Comparative Sociological Review.* London: Heinemann, 1972, pp. 196–211.

Dexter, F. B. *Sketch of the History of Yale University.* New York: Henry Holt and Company, 1887.

Dilschneider, D. "Call Police If Needed, Universities Are Told." *Toronto Star,* Nov. 1, 1973, p. B14.

"Dismissal at Stanford Is Endorsed." *Chronicle of Higher Education,* Jan. 17, 1972, p. 5.

Duryea, E. D. "Evolution of University Organization." In J. A. Perkins (ed.), *The University as an Organization.* New York: McGraw-Hill, 1973, pp. 15–37.

"Education: A Framework for Expansion." *Report presented to Parliament by the Secretary of State for Education and Science.* London, December 1972, sec. 106.

The Efficiency of Freedom. Committee on Government and Higher Education. Baltimore: Johns Hopkins, 1959.

Enarson, H. L. "University or Knowledge Factory?" *Chronicle of Higher Education,* June 18, 1973, p. 16.

Encyclopaedia Britannica. "Universities," 1967, vol. 22, pp. 862–879.

Etzioni, A. *A Comparative Analysis of Complex Organizations.* New York: Free Press, 1961.

"Excerpts from Faculty Report on Militant Professor." *Chronicle of Higher Education,* Jan. 17, 1972, p. 5.

A Fact Book on Higher Education. Washington, D.C.: American Council on Education, 1973.

"Faculty-Student Views on Colleges." *School and Society,* **99:** 262–264, 1971.

Fashing, J., and S. E. Deutsch. *Academics in Retreat.* Albuquerque: University of New Mexico Press, 1971.

"Federal Grants to Canadian Universities." Memo prepared by D. McCormack Smyth, Toronto: York University, Jan 27, 1975.

Flacks, R. "The Liberated Generation: An Explanation of the Roots of Social Protest." *Journal of Social Issues,* **23**(3): 52–75, 1967.

Fleming, W. G. "Aptitude and Achievement Scores Related to Immediate Educational and Occupational Choices of Ontario Grade 13 Students." Report No. 3. Department of Educational Research, College of Education, University of Toronto, 1958*a*.

————. "Ontario Grade 13 Students: Their Aptitude, Achievement, and Immediate Destination." Atkinson Study of Utilization of Student Resources, Report No. 4. Department of Educational Research, College of Education, University of Toronto, 1958*b*.

Flexner, A. *Universities: American, English, German.* Rev. ed. London: Oxford University Press, 1968.

Ford, B. "Conclusions and Reflections." *Universities Quarterly,* **28:** 50–58, 1973.

Friedenberg, E. Z. "The University Community in an Open Society." *Daedalus,* **99**(1): 56–74, 1970.

Fulton, J. *Memoirs of Frederick A. P. Barnard.* New York: Macmillan, 1896.

"A Future of Choices, a Choice of Futures." *Report of the Commission on Educational Planning.* Alberta: Queen's Printer, 1972.

Garbarino, J. W. "Faculty Unionism: From Theory to Practice." *Industrial Relations,* **10:** 1–17. 1971.

————. "Precarious Professors: New Patterns of Representation." *Industrial Relations,* **11:** 1–20, 1972.

Gardner, D. P. *The California Oath Controversy.* Berkeley: University of California Press, 1967.

Gay, P. *The Enlightenment: An Appreciation.* New York: Knopf, 1967.

George, D. U. "Collective Bargaining: The Management Rights Issue." *University Affairs* (Ottawa), November 1974, p. 8.

• REFERENCES •

Goodman, P. "The New Reformation." *New York Times Magazine,* Sept. 14, 1969, p. 33.

Gould, S. B. "New York: The State University." In J. A. Perkins (ed.), *Higher Education: From Autonomy to Systems.* New York: International Council for Educational Development, 1972, pp. 15-21.

"Governing Council, Hastily Reconvened, Completed Thursday's Interrupted Business." *U of T Bulletin,* Apr. 1, 1974, p. 1.

Grant-Robertson, Sir Charles. *The British Universities.* London: Benn, 1930.

Green, V. H. H. *The Universities.* Middlesex, England: Penguin Books Ltd., 1969.

Gross, E. "Universities as Organizations: A Research Approach." *American Sociological Review,* **33:** 518-544, 1968.

Gross, N. "Organizational Lag in American Universities." *Harvard Educational Review,* **33**(1): 58-73, 1963.

Gusfield, J. "Beyond Berkeley." In H. S. Becker (ed.), *Campus Power Struggle.* Chicago: Aldine, 1970, pp. 15-26.

Halsey, A. H. "British Universities." *European Journal of Sociology,* **3:** 85-101, 1962.

_____. "Ancient Grip on New Universities." *Times Higher Education Supplement,* July 5, 1974, p. 5.

_____ and M. A. Trow, *The British Academics.* Cambridge, Mass.: Harvard, 1971.

Hansen, B. L. "The Balance between Economic Efficiency and Political Rationality: A Description of Planning for Ontario Universities." Paper presented to Ontario Council of Universities at Laval University, Quebec, 1974, rev. Jan. 8, 1975.

Harris, R. "A History of Higher Education in Canada." Draft, 1973. Forthcoming, University of Toronto Press, 1976.

Hart, J. M. *German Universities: A Narrative of Personal Experience.* New York: Putnam, 1874.

Haskins, C. H. *The Renaissance of the Twelfth Century.* Cleveland: World Publishing, 1957.

Heilbroner, R. L. *An Enquiry into the Human Prospect.* New York: Norton, 1973.

Herklots, H. G. G. *The New Universities, An External Examination.* London: Benn, 1928.

287

Higher Education for American Democracy: A Report of the President's Commission on Higher Education. New York: Harper, 1947, vol. 1.

Hill, C. "The Radical Critics of Oxford and Cambridge in the 1650's." In John W. Baldwin and Richard A. Goldthwaite (eds.), *Universities in Politics.* Baltimore: Johns Hopkins, 1972, pp. 107–132.

Hodgkinson, H. L. "Does a College's Unique 'Environment' Really Do Anything for Its Students?" *Chronicle of Higher Education,* Oct. 16, 1972, p. 9.

Hodgson, G. "Do Schools Make a Difference?" *Atlantic,* **23:** 35–46, 1973.

Hoffman, S. "Participation in Perspective?" *Daedalus,* **99**(1): 177–221, 1970.

Hofstadter, R., and W. P. Metzger. *The Development of Academic Freedom in the United States.* New York: Columbia, 1955.

Holland, J. "Professor Griffith Says Attacks on Academic Freedom Are Endemic." *Times Higher Education Supplement,* Nov. 17, 1972, p. 2.

Hyde, J. K. "Commune, University, and Society in Early Medieval Bologna." In John W. Baldwin and Richard A. Goldthwaite (eds.), *Universities in Politics.* Baltimore: Johns Hopkins, 1972, pp. 17–46.

Jaspers, K. *The Idea of the University.* London: Peter Owen Ltd., 1965.

Jencks, C., and D. Riesman. *The Academic Revolution.* New York: Doubleday, 1968.

Jerome, J. "Radical Premises in Collegiate Reform." *Annals of the American Academy of Political and Social Science,* **404:** 194–206, 1972.

Joughin, L. *Academic Freedom and Tenure.* Madison: University of Wisconsin Press, 1967.

Keniston, K. "What's Bugging the Students?" In D. C. Nichols (ed.), *Perspectives on Campus Tensions.* Washington, D.C.: American Council on Education, 1970, pp. 47–67.

Kerr, C. *The Uses of the University.* Cambridge, Mass.: Harvard University Press, 1963.

————. "Governance and Functions." *Daedalus,* **99**(1): 108–121, 1970*a*.

————. "Presidential Discontent." In D. C. Nichols (ed.), *Perspectives on Campus Tensions.* Washington, D.C.: American Council on Education, 1970*b*, pp. 137–162.

Kneller, G. F. *Higher Learning in Britain.* Berkeley: University of California Press, 1955.

Knott, P. D. *Student Activism.* Dubuque, Iowa: Wm. C. Brown Company, 1971.

Kuhn, A., and A. Poole. "Working-Class Students Going up to University." *Times Higher Education Supplement,* Dec. 8, 1972, p. 13.

Ladd, D. R. "Achieving Change in Educational Policy in American Colleges and Universities." *Annals of the American Academy of Political and Social Science,* **404:** 207–216, 1972.

Ladd, E. C., Jr., and S. M. Lipset. *Professors, Unions, and American Higher Education.* Berkeley: Carnegie Commission on Higher Education, 1973.

Lazarsfeld, P. F., and W. Thielens, Jr. *The Academic Mind.* Glencoe, Ill.: Free Press, 1958.

"The Learning Society." *Report of the Commission on Post-secondary Education in Ontario.* Toronto: Ministry of Government Services, 1973.

Letter of Beard to Butler, Minutes of the Trustees, vol. 38. New York: Columbia University, Oct. 8, 1917.

"Let the Professors Work Harder." *Toronto Star,* Nov. 21, 1974, p. B4.

Lipset, S. M. "The Politics of Academia." In D. C. Nichols (ed.), *Perspectives on Campus Tensions.* Washington, D.C.: American Council on Education, 1970, pp. 85–118.

Lyte, H. C. M. *A History of the University of Oxford from the Earliest Times to the Year 1530.* London: Macmillan, 1886.

MacArthur, B. "Blue-Ribbon British Panel Calls for Radical Reforms." *Chronicle of Higher Education,* Oct. 16, 1972, p. 5. (1972*a*)

————. "Britons Ask the Basic Question: Why the Modern University?" *Chronicle of Higher Education,* Nov. 6, 1972, p. 6. (1972*b*)

————. "Students Resolve to Break Down Professor Power." *Times Higher Education Supplement,* Dec. 1, 1972, p. 6. (1972*c*)

————. "In Britain: Fewer Students." *Chronicle of Higher Education,* Oct. 15, 1974, p. 3.

McConnell, T. R. "Governments and the University: A Comparative Analysis." In W. M. Cooper, W. G. Davis, A. M. Parent, and T. R. McConnell, *Governments and the University.* Toronto: Macmillan, 1966, pp. 69–92.

————. "Faculty Government." In H. L. Hodgkinson and L. R. Meeth (eds.), *Power and Authority.* San Francisco: Jossey-Bass, 1971, pp. 98–125.

Macdonald, H. I. "State of the Budget." *York Gazette,* Jan. 29, 1975, p. 1.

Machlup, F. *Education and Economic Growth.* Lincoln: University of Nebraska Press, 1970.

Mackintosh, W. A. "These Seventy-Five Years: Presidential Address." In E. G. D. Murray (ed.), *Our Debt to the Future.* Toronto: University of Toronto Press, 1958, pp. 12–22.

McGrath, E. J. *Should Students Share the Power?* Philadelphia: Temple University Press, 1970.

McNaught, C. "Democracy and Our Universities." *Canadian Forum,* **20:** 333, 1941.

McNaught, K. "A Challenge to U of T: Right of Dissent in Peril, Says Teacher." *Toronto Star,* July 18, 1974, p. 7.

McNeill, W. H. *World History.* London: Oxford University Press, 1971.

Maeroff, G. I. "Inquiry Started at City College." *New York Times,* June 23, 1974, p. 34.

Mallet, C. E. *History of the University of Oxford.* New York: Longmans, 1924, vol. 1.

Mayhew, L. B. "American Higher Education Now and in the Future." *Annals,* **404:** 44–57, 1972.

Merton, R. K. *Social Theory and Social Structure.* Glencoe, Ill.: Free Press, 1957.

Millett, J. D. *Financing Higher Education in the United States.* New York: Columbia, 1952.

—————. "The Management of State Systems of Higher Education." In J. A. Perkins (ed.), *Higher Education: From Autonomy to Systems.* New York: International Council for Educational Development, 1972, pp. 43–51.

Minogue, K. R. *The Concept of the University.* Berkeley: University of California Press, 1973.

Moberly, Sir Walter. *The Crisis in the University.* London: SCM Press, 1949.

Morison, S. E. *Harvard in the Seventeenth Century.* Cambridge, Mass.: Harvard, 1936, vol. 1.

—————. *Three Centuries of Harvard, 1636–1936.* Cambridge, Mass.: Harvard, 1965.

Mortimer, K. P. *Accountability in Higher Education.* Washington, D.C.: American Association for Higher Education, 1972.

Moynihan, D. P. "Peace: Some Thoughts on the 1960's and 1970's." *Public Interest,* **32:** 11, 1973.

Mullinger, J. B. *The University of Cambridge.* Cambridge: University Press, 1884, vols. 1, 2.

• REFERENCES •

"The Murray Report and Recommendations." *Times Higher Education Supplement,* Nov. 11, 1972, pp. i–iii.

Newman, C. "The Best Years of My Life and Other Lies." *MacLean's,* January 1972, pp. 32.

Newman, J. H. *The Idea of a University.* New York: Doubleday, 1959. Image Books edition.

"The 'New' Scholars: A Special Report." *Chronicle of Higher Education,* Oct. 23, 1973, pp. 9–10.

Nisbet, R. *The Social Bond: An Introduction to the Study of Society.* New York: Knopf, 1970.

————. *The Degradation of the Academic Dogma.* New York: Basic Books, 1971*a.*

————. "The Future of the University." *Commentary,* February 1971, pp. 62–71. (1971*b*)

"Ontario and Its Universities." York/University of Toronto Higher Education Seminar, 1973–74. *Minerva.* **12**(4), 515–521, 1974.

"Oxford Discussions on Higher Education." *Minerva,* **10**(2): 295–318, 1972.

Panel on Alternate Approaches to Graduate Education. *Scholarship for Society.* Princeton, N.J.: Educational Testing Service, 1973.

"Parity on Governing Council Voted Down." *University Affairs* (Ottawa), December 1974, p. 16.

"Parliament and Control of University Expenditure." *Special Report from the Committee of Public Accounts.* London: The House of Commons, Jan. 20, 1967.

Parr, J. G. "Text of a Speech Presented to the Ontario Universities' Council on Admissions." *York Gazette,* Dec. 14, 1974, pp. 41–42.

Parsons, T., and G. M. Platt. *The American University.* Cambridge, Mass.: Harvard, 1973.

Perkins, J. A. "The Future of Coordination." In J. A. Perkins (ed.), *Higher Education: From Autonomy to Systems.* New York: International Council for Educational Development, 1972, pp. 279–286.

Pierson, G. W. *Yale: The University College, 1921–1937.* New Haven, Conn.: Yale, 1955.

Pifer, A. "The Report of the President." *Annual Report of the Carnegie Corporation of New York.* New York, 1971.

Powell, R. S., Jr. "Student Power and Educational Goals." In H. L. Hodgkinson and L. R. Meeth (eds.), *Power and Authority.* San Francisco: Jossey-Bass, 1971, pp. 65–84.

291

Power of the People: Fifty Years of Pictorial Highlights of the Communist Party of Canada 1921–1971. Toronto: Progress Books, 1971.

Pusey, N. M. "Freedom, Loyalty and the American University." *Association of American Colleges Bulletin,* **40**: 335–345, 1954.

Ranzal, E. "McCarthy Charges 'Mess' at Harvard." *New York Times,* Nov. 6, 1953, p. 13.

Rashdall, H. *The Universities of Europe in the Middle Ages.* F. M. Porvicke and A. B. Ender (eds.). London: Oxford University Press, 1936, vols. 1, 2, 3.

———. "Student Life in the Middle Ages." In C. G. Katope and P. G. Zolbrod (eds.), *Beyond Berkeley.* New York: Harper & Row, 1966, pp. 276–283.

Ravitch, D. *The Great School Wars 1805–1973.* New York: Basic Books, 1974.

Rawls, J. *A Theory of Justice.* Cambridge, Mass.: The Belknap Press, Harvard University Press, 1971.

Reed, T. *The Blue and White.* Toronto: University of Toronto Press, 1944.

Reinhold, R. "A Limit on Scholarship." *New York Times,* Dec. 3, 1973, sec. 4, p. 5.

Rejai, P., and R. Stupak. "The Kiss of Death for Faculty Power." *Chronicle of Higher Education,* Oct. 10, 1972, p. 8.

"Report of the General Secretary," *AAUP Bulletin,* **59**(2): June 1973.

Report of the Royal Commission on the University of Toronto, Toronto: L. K. Cameron, Printer to the King's Most Excellent Majesty, 1906.

Report on Higher Education. Report of Special Task Force on Higher Education. Washington, D.C.: Department of Health, Education, and Welfare, 1971.

Reston, J. "U.S. Congress on Trial in Fateful Decision." *Globe and Mail.* Toronto, July 30, 1974, p. 7.

Riesman, D., and G. Grant. "Evangelism, Egalitarianism, and Educational Reform." *Minerva,* **11**(3): 296–317, 1973.

Riley, G. "Partisanship and Objectivity in the Social Sciences." *American Sociologist,* **6**: 6–12, 1971.

Robbins, Lord C. B. *Autobiography of an Economist.* London: Macmillan, 1971.

Ross, M. G. "New-Style Youth: Tolerant, Probing, Turned In." *Toronto Telegram,* Apr. 14, 1971, p. 17.

• REFERENCES •

_____. "The Dilution of Academic Power in Canada." *Minerva*, **10**(2): 242–258, 1972.

Rubinoff, L. (ed.). *Tradition and Revolution.* Toronto: Macmillan, 1971.

Sanders, I. T. "The University as a Community." In J. A. Perkins (ed.), *The University as an Organization.* New York: McGraw-Hill, 1973, pp. 57–78.

Savio, M. "The Berkeley Student Rebellion of 1964." In C. G. Katope and P. G. Zolbrod (eds.), *Beyond Berkeley.* New York: Harper & Row, 1966, pp. 83–88.

Schick, E. B. "Campus Ferment and Tranquility, 1970–71." *School and Society*, **100**: 93–95, 1972.

Scott, W. R. "Professionals in Bureaucracies: Areas of Conflict." In H. M. Vollmer and D. L. Mills (eds.), *Professionalization.* Englewood Cliffs, N.J.: Prentice-Hall, 1966, pp. 265–275.

Semas, P. W. "The Perilous Presidencies." *Chronicle of Higher Education*, Feb. 3, 1975, p. 1.

Sexton, P. C. Review of *The American University*, by Talcott Parsons and Gerald M. Platt. *Contemporary Sociology*, **3**(4): 298, 1974.

Sheffield, E. F. "Canadian University and College Enrollment, Projected to 1965. *Proceedings; National Conference of Canadian Universities*, Ottawa, 1955, pp. 39–46.

Shils, E. "The Hole in the Centre: University Government in the United States." *Minerva*, **8**(1): 1–7, 1970.

_____. "Intellectuals and the Center of Society." *The University of Chicago Magazine*, July/August 1972a, pp. 3–13.

_____. *The Intellectuals and the Powers and Other Essays*, Chicago: University of Chicago Press, 1972b.

_____. "The American Private University." *Minerva*, **11**(1): 6–29, 1973a.

_____. "Trojan Horses." *Minerva*, **11**(3): 285–289, 1973b.

Smelser, N. J. "California—Three Layers and Coordination." In J. A. Perkins (ed.), *Higher Education: From Autonomy to Systems.* New York: International Council for Educational Development, 1972, pp. 23–34.

Smyth, D. McCormack. "Structures for University Government to the Beginning of the 20th Century." Doctoral dissertation, University of Toronto, 1972.

Snow, C. P. *The Masters.* New York: Macmillan, 1959.

• REFERENCES •

Sparrow, J. *Mark Pattison and the Idea of a University.* Cambridge: Cambridge University Press, 1967.

Stevenson, A. E. *What I Think.* New York: Harper, 1956. Excerpt from "The Educated Citizen," Address at the Senior Class Banquet, Princeton University, Mar. 22, 1954.

Storr, R. J. *Harper's University: The Beginnings.* Chicago: University of Chicago Press, 1966.

Sutherland, G. "Is There an Optimum Size for a University?" *Minerva,* **11**(1): 53–78, 1973.

Thompson, D. F. "Democracy and the Governing of the University." *Annals,* **404:** 157–169, 1972.

Touraine, A. *The Academic System in American Society.* New York: McGraw-Hill, 1974.

Trevelyan, G. M. *British History in the Nineteenth Century.* New York: Longmans, 1923.

Trow, M. "Conceptions of the University: The Case of Berkeley." *American Behavioral Scientist,* **11**(5): 14–21, 1968.

———. "Reflections on the Transition from Mass to Universal Higher Education." *Daedalus,* **99**(1): 1–42, 1970.

———. "Problems in the Transition from Elite to Mass Higher Education." Paper prepared for an OECD conference on mass higher education, June 1973.

Truscot, B. *Redbrick University.* London: Faber, 1943.

Ulam, A. *The Fall of the American University.* New York: The Library Press, 1972.

Ulich, R. *Education in Western Culture.* New York: Harcourt, Brace & World, 1965.

"University Grants Committee: Composition and Procedures." Memorandum by the University Grants Committee in *Special Report from the Committee of Public Accounts.* London: House of Commons, Jan. 20, 1967, app.

U of T Monthly. U of T Archives, Toronto, Robarts Library.

"Urban University Professors Happiest Workers in U.S." *Chronicle of Higher Education,* Jan. 15, 1973, p. 6.

Van Alstyne, W. W. "The Specific Theory of Academic Freedom and the General Issue of Civil Liberties." *Annals of the American Academy of Political and Social Science,* **404:** 140–156, 1972.

Veblen, T. *The Higher Learning in America.* New York: Sentry Press, 1965.

• REFERENCES •

Verger, J. "The University of Paris at the End of the Hundred Years' War." In John W. Baldwin and Richard A. Goldthwaite (eds.), *Universities in Politics*. Baltimore: Johns Hopkins, 1972, pp. 47–78.

Veysey, L. R. *The Emergence of the American University*. Chicago: University of Chicago Press, 1965.

Vice-Chancellor's Report for the Year 1973–74. University of York, England, 1974.

Watkins, B. T. "Goodbye, Tradition." *Chronicle of Higher Education*, Oct. 21, 1974, p. 5.

Watt, D. C. "More Oligarchic Stodge: The Murray Report Has Failed to Grant Academic Self-Government." *Times Higher Education Supplement*, Mar. 7, 1973, p. 14.

"What the Schools Cannot Do." *Time*, Apr. 16, 1973, pp. 56–60.

"Where College Faculties Have Chosen or Rejected Collective Bargaining Agents." *Chronicle of Higher Education*, June 10, 1974, p. 24.

Wilensky, H. L. "The Professionalization of Everyone." *American Journal of Sociology*, **70:** 137–158, 1964.

Williams, R. M. "Norms." *International Encyclopedia of the Social Sciences*. New York: Macmillan and Free Press, 1968, pp. 204–208, vol. 11.

Wilson, W. "What Is a College For?" *Scribner's Magazine*, **46:** 574, 1909.

Wolfenden, Sir John F. "Great Britain." In J. A. Perkins (ed.), *Higher Education: From Autonomy to Systems*. New York: International Council for Educational Development, 1972, pp. 133–141.

Wolff, R. P. *Ideal of the University*. Boston: Beacon Press, 1969.

Woodring, P. "Who Makes University Policy?" In C. G. Katope and P. G. Zolbrod (eds.), *Beyond Berkeley*. New York: Harper & Row, 1966, pp. 147–151.

Wrong, D. H. "On Thinking About the Future." *American Sociologist*, **9:** 26–31, 1974.

Yankelovich, D. "The New Naturalism." *Saturday Review*, Apr. 1, 1972, p. 35.

Young, M. *The Rise of the Meritocracy, 1870–2033: The New Elite of Our Social Revolution*. New York: Random House, 1958.

Zangwill, O. L. Preface to *The Idea of the University*, by K. Jaspers. London: Peter Owen Limited, 1965, pp. 9–14.

INDEX

NOTE: The letter *n.* following a page number indicates that entry is cited (in Notes at end of chapter) under superscript number on that page.